AMERICAN JESUITS

THE MACMILLAN COMPANY
NEW YORK · BOSTON · CHICAGO · DALLAS
ATLANTA · SAN FRANCISCO

MACMILLAN & CO., LIMITED
LONDON · BOMBAY · CALCUTTA
MELBOURNE

THE MACMILLAN COMPANY
OF CANADA, LIMITED
TORONTO

AMERICAN JESUITS

BY

JAMES J. WALSH
M.D., Ph.D., Sc.D., K.M., K.C.St.G.

AUTHOR OF

"The Thirteenth Greatest of Centuries," "Psychotherapy,"
"The Century of Columbus," "The Church and
Healing," "The Popes and Science," etc.

NEW YORK
THE MACMILLAN COMPANY
1934

Nihil Obstat

ARTHUR J. SCANLAN, S. T. D.

Censor Librorum.

Imprimatur

✠ PATRICK CARDINAL HAYES

Archbishop, New York.

New York, September 29, 1934.

SET UP BY BROWN BROTHERS LINOTYPERS
PRINTED IN THE UNITED STATES OF AMERICA
BY THE FERRIS PRINTING COMPANY

TO

THE AMERICAN JESUITS

*after sixty years
of friendship*

PREFACE

THERE are at the present time, three hundred years after their landing in Maryland in 1634, approximately 5,000 Jesuits in this country out of the nearly 25,000 in the world. The Order is growing rapidly. Its members take vows of poverty, chastity and obedience, which cut them off from many of the satisfactions of life that men hold most dear. Their mode of life is strict in the sense that they are intensively occupied with the work assigned to them though their spirits are blithe enough. In spite of the cult of comfort and personal satisfaction which has grown to be so prominent a feature of life in the twentieth century the number of applicants who ask for admission among the Jesuits is constantly growing.

Young college men of sixteen to twenty, usually those who have been among the most talented students and the best liked in their classes at Jesuit schools, who know the Jesuits very well after years of close association, ask to be allowed to become candidates for admission to the Order. After a noviceship or period of trial for two years, they are received into the Order. A series of additional houses for novices have been opened in various parts of the United States during the twentieth century and they are practically all crowded to capacity. The surprise to those who are brought at all intimately in touch with these young men is the happiness they manifest during their noviceship. Their parents are sometimes inclined almost to resent the cheerful contentedness their sons enjoy in spite of the fact that they are away from home during the years when family affection is most strong, but fathers and mothers are soon won over to proper appreciation of their boys' satisfaction with this new mode of life which would seem at first glance to be such a trial.

At the present time there are some 60,000 students in attendance at the Jesuit institutions of learning, their high schools, colleges and universities in this country. The numbers have increased rapidly during this twentieth century, so that unless some very serious setback in American educational life should take place it would seem as though there would probably be 100,000 students in the Jesuit schools of this country before 1950. Their students are drawn particularly from the sons of men who have themselves been educated by the Jesuits. Thoroughly satisfied with the education which they received, they want their sons to have the advantage of similar training of mind and heart and soul, for Jesuit education does not stop at cultivation of the intelligence but tries to train the whole man.

Ignatius Loyola prayed that his Little Company of Jesus should have persecution as its badge, as it had been the badge of their Lord and Master. His prayer was heard. Probably no set of men have been so much misunderstood as the Jesuits. The supreme surprise with regard to them is to find how many books have been written about them and how few of the writers have ever known a Jesuit personally. That is the principal reason for the writing of this book. I am myself a graduate of a Jesuit college (Fordham) and I have known Jesuits intimately for some sixty years. I have been in rather close personal touch with them in nine countries. I was for six years a member of the Order, but left it for definite health reasons with deep regret. That experience enabled me to know the Jesuits ever so much more thoroughly than would otherwise have been possible.

In this country we should judge the Jesuits by their lives and work among our own people. Jesuits all over the world are the same. They live under the same Constitutions and Rule and are under the same General at Rome. What they accomplished as missionaries among the Indians in the colonial times and in more recent years as educators and missionaries, as war and prison and almshouse chaplains, reveals their character. What they have done in education represents an extremely important chapter in the history of education in this country. This constitutes the material by which to estimate the significance of the Order, not only in this country but all over the world. They are Americans like ourselves, deeply interested in their nation and what it stands for in world affairs, anxious to be good citizens, ready to do their patriotic duty in times of crisis no matter what the cost.

In every phase of life on this continent Jesuits have done deeds of daring for the benefit of others. Their rapid growth in recent years when young Americans are crowding their novitiates, demonstrates the appeal they have to the enthusiastic minds of youth who know them well. These young men are anxious to have a part with this group, whose history is so full of heroism, and whose future is so replete with promise of opportunity for the development of the best possibilities of human nature.

Reverend Dr. Peter Guilday, professor of American Church History at the Catholic University, was kind enough to read the proofs of this volume and to make many valuable suggestions.

CONTENTS

AMERICAN JESUITS

INTRODUCTION

THE Society of Jesus, commonly called the Jesuits, was founded by Ignatius Loyola and six of his student friends at the University of Paris. He was the son of a Spanish noble family, born about the time of Columbus's discovery of America, and became a page at court in the time of Ferdinand and Isabella. As a young man he entered the army and this seemed his destined career. He fought with distinction against the French at the siege of Pampeluna (1521) when he was about thirty years of age and was so badly wounded that he had a halt in his gait ever after. His convalescence was prolonged because he insisted on having his leg rebroken at the cost of awful torture in those pre-anesthetic days to prevent visible deformity. With time on his hands he asked for some of the Spanish romances of chivalry, but as they were not available he read the life of Christ. He was so deeply impressed by his reading that he resolved henceforth to live a spiritual life and make existence have a meaning in terms of eternity. He spent several years at spiritual exercises as a solitary and realized that if he were to accomplish anything in life he must have an education.

He took his place on the benches beside schoolboy beginners to learn Latin, and at the age of thirty-seven (1528) entered the University of Paris. He was a charity student and spent his vacation wandering through various parts of France, Spain and the Netherlands, collecting alms which supported him during the academic year. He gathered around him at the university a group of six students who had learned to love and thoroughly respect him for his sincerity and earnest way of life and they resolved to form a company bound together by vows of poverty and chastity. They were all of them serious students most of them with ambition for a university career, but Ignatius aroused

I

a new spirit in them. None of Ignatius's companions was young, only one was a priest, five were Masters of Art, that is licensed by the degree of M. A. to teach some branch or branches at the university.

They were not carried away by youthful enthusiasm, but were mature men to whom reason appealed more than anything else. A favorite expression of Ignatius, and one which affected his companions deeply, was, "What shall it profit a man if he gain the whole world and lose his own soul?" This expression, frequently repeated at appropriate times, had won over to almost filial friendship with Ignatius the brilliant young teacher at the University of Paris, Francis Xavier, who was destined to do almost incredible work as a missionary in the East and to stamp his personality on missionary enterprise for all time.

Ignatius and his companions took vows of poverty and chastity in a little chapel on Montmartre in Paris, August 15, 1534. After further years of intimate association and study at the university, they set out together on a pilgrimage to the Holy Land in the hope of converting the Mohammedans there, or if that proved impossible, of finding inspiration for a life of prayer and devotion in the land blest by the footprints of the Lord. They traveled on foot and it took several months to reach Venice. They subsisted on alms on the way, lodging in hospitals where they repaid the hospitality accorded them by service to the patients. Ignatius had had experience of hospital lodging in his alms-collecting journeys before this and for many years after the foundation of his "Little Company of Jesus," as with his military propensities he liked to call it, all novices among the Jesuits were required to spend a month in a hospital as a trial of character for the exercise of charity under difficult circumstances. One reason for this seems to have been that experience of this sort fitted the young Jesuits to meet many of the emergencies of missionary life and enabled them to have some idea as to what they should do when they themselves or others were ill and a physician was not available.

Their journey to Venice was disturbed by serious storms and they were often thoroughly drenched. It would seem as though they must have suffered severely in health from exposure as well as from the insufficient food taken rather irregularly, which was all they had. Some of them fell ill from time to time as might have been expected from the calls upon their strength by travel and austerity, and after the torrents of rain in Lorraine they went through snowstorms in Burgundy for it was an exceptionally severe winter. When they arrived in Venice a journal kept by one of them tells that "we went with hearts full of joy to lodge in the hospital—four in the hospital of St. John and St. Paul where Ignatius had secured quarters and three at the Incurables."

They found that owing to war between Venice and the Turks it would be impossible for them to embark for Jerusalem. They then turned their course toward Rome. The journey was quite as severely tried by the weather but such was their joy of spirit that they took no harm and one of them was even cured during the forced marches of an affection of the feet from which he suffered. They were heartily welcomed by the pope. He gave permission for those among them who were not yet priests to be ordained. The pope had them discuss theological propositions in his presence and frankly told them that he was highly edified to see so much learning joined with so much humility.

Pope Paul III, one of the great popes of the Renaissance, was convinced that already there were too many religious orders and that the multiplication of them led to serious abuses. On being presented with a summary of the proposed Rule of Ignatius and his companions, he exclaimed, "The finger of God is here." He gave them every encouragement to go on with their good work and granted permission for the drawing up of Constitutions. Up to this time they had been bound together by their vows of chastity and poverty, but after this they took the third vow of obedience. Ignatius in spite of his humility that would have refused the position was chosen superior.

He was commissioned to draw up the Constitutions for the Order and did so in prayer and patience, spending some fifteen years at the task. He consulted the older members of the community freely. They tested his regulations in various houses and

Ignatius definitely settled the wording and the significance of his Constitutions only after many experiences. These Constitutions as drawn up by Ignatius and adopted by the first Congregation of the Society, that is the formal assemblage of delegates from all the various houses (1558) have never been changed. The text of the Constitutions now in force agrees accurately with the Constitutions as they are preserved in Ignatius's own handwriting in the original copy containing his various manuscript corrections.

In spite of the almost universal declaration on the part of writers on the subject, when Ignatius Loyola and his companions began their work as Jesuits there was no special purpose to oppose Protestantism. As Father Pollen, S.J., points out in his article on the Society of Jesus in the Catholic Encyclopedia: "The Society was not founded with the avowed intention of opposing Protestantism. Neither the papal letters of approbation nor the constitutions of the order mention this as the object of the new foundation. When Ignatius began to devote himself to the service of the Church he had probably not heard even the names of the Protestant reformers. His early plan was rather the conversion of the Mohammedans, an idea which a few decades after the final triumph of the Christians over the Moors in Spain (Granada, the capital of the Moorish kingdom in Spain fell in 1492) must have strongly appealed to the chivalrous Spaniard."

When that outlet for his zeal for conversions was closed by the Turco-Venetian war, so far as Ignatius himself was concerned he would have been quite willing to give himself and his companions entirely to the teaching of catechism to children and the giving of instruction to the poor and ignorant. The pope found other work for them to do and it was not long before they were attracting wide attention because of their religious zeal and success.

Within twenty years after their foundation the Jesuits multiplied so rapidly that at the time of St. Ignatius's death (1556) there were twelve provinces of the Society of Jesus, that is twelve definite geographic territories ruled over by provincials, each with a hundred or more subjects under him. Italy, Sicily, Portugal, Aragon, Castile, Andalusia, upper Germany, lower Germany and France were the European provinces, but besides, there was a province in India which included Japan, a province in Brazil with missions almost directly under the equator, and finally a province in Ethiopia in Africa under almost similar conditions. Already there were well above a thousand members of the new Order and the drift toward the Jesuits of young men of all ranks and social conditions, above all those possessed of brilliant talents but still more of determined character and strong personality, had only just begun. By the end of the century, less than sixty years after their approval by the pope, the new Order counted its numbers by the thousands.

The Council of Trent was in session not long after the foundation of the new Order and the Jesuits were so prominent in its proceedings that the name of the Society of Jesus came to be known favorably all over Europe. Jesuit theologians were the leaders of thought in that Council which shaped Catholic thinking so profoundly. Their modest presentation of their opinions, combined with the thoroughness of their treatment of the many difficult problems that had to be solved by the Council and expressed in definite formulas, gave the Jesuits a prestige that made many of the cities of Europe desire a Jesuit foundation.

The Jesuits continued to increase in numbers until shortly after the middle of the eighteenth century when there were nearly 25,000 of them in the world. Altogether they had some 728 colleges, some of which counted their students by the thousand. As early as 1584, the Golden Jubilee of their foundation, the Roman college, the central institution of the Jesuits, had over 2,100 students. Throughout the seventeenth century the number of the students at the College of Louis le Grand in Paris was between 2,000 and 3,000. In the second half of the seventeenth century Rouen had nearly 2,000, Amiens about 1,500. In Rennes there were 2,500 in attendance and in Toulouse some 2,000. Nor was it only in the Latin countries that the attendance was so high. Munich in Bavaria had over 1,000; Münster had over 1,300, Utrecht in Holland over 1,000, and Antwerp and Brussels in the Netherlands had each some 600 students. Altogether there were some 200,000 students in the Jesuit schools and colleges in Europe. The average attendance was not lower in each of their schools than 300 and there were over 700 schools.

They had colleges all over the world, in Mexico, in the important cities of South America, in Canada, in the Philippines, in Portuguese India, and their missions scattered everywhere could be looked upon as schools although mainly elementary schools. As to how well their work was done in these mission schools old and modern we have the testimony of Senator Vest of Missouri who in a speech before the United States Senate [1] said that in his inspection of the Indian schools undertaken at the request of the Senate, "I did not see in all my journey a single school that was doing any educational work worthy of the name unless it was under the control of the Jesuits." He confessed, "No man ever went among these Indians with more intense prejudice against the Jesuits than I had when I left the city of Washington." He declared that they were really civilizing and educating the Indians.

It is interesting then to note the names of the members of the Order who are held up to the Jesuits themselves for special reverence and emulation. In a single word they are those who have been proclaimed saints by the Church because they exhibited heroic virtue during their lives. They include Ignatius Loyola, the founder, and Francis Xavier, the great missionary of the Order, who in a few strenuous years brought many thousands of Orientals into the Church. Then follows St. Francis Borgia so intimately related to the reigning house in Spain that on the death of the queen he was appointed to accompany her body in the funeral cortege. In the performance of that duty he was required to see the coffin opened before it was lowered into the grave so as formally to recognize the body. The vision of the corrupting flesh that had been so beautiful as a woman a few days before led him to see the meaning of life through the lens of death. He devoted himself thenceforth to making life have a meaning in terms of another existence than this. He was elected the third General of the Society, a post for which his experi-

[1] "Congressional Record," April 7, 1900.

ence in the diplomatic world of his time gave him special capacity.

He is followed by a roll of Jesuit saints, each one different from the other, each one exhibiting some special trait or characteristic, each of them the subject of special veneration on the part of his brother Jesuits. There is Stanislaus Kostka, a member of the high nobility of Poland, who at the age of sixteen made the long journey to Rome on foot to become a Jesuit, only to die as a novice. Then there is Aloysius Gonzaga, a prince of the Italian noble house of that name, who resigned his position as head of the house in favor of his brother and found happiness and peace of heart as a Jesuit. Both of these were destined to live short lives as Jesuits, but their names are forever famous because of their faithfulness to their vocation and their exemplification of the rules of conduct becoming a Jesuit, the outward sign of their inward grace. A third name, that of a youth of very different character, was to be added to this group of young saints,—John Berchmans. He was the son of very humble parents and his distinction was that he followed the rules laid down for scholastics or students before ordination among the Jesuits so exactly that it was said that if the rule book were lost it could be rewritten from observation of his conduct. His canonization some two hundred years after his death was practically a declaration that to observe the Jesuit rules perfectly requires sainthood.

After a duke and two princes comes St. Alphonsus Rodriguez, who was just a lay brother doing the humble duties of the house as a domestic servant, but doing them so well that he was sanctified by them. As a result Rodriguez has been looked up to as a model religious. The influence that he exerted was felt deeply by Father Peter Claver, the next of these Jesuit saints, who declared that he owed more to Brother Rodriguez than to any one else. Father Claver devoted himself for forty years to the care of the Negro slaves from Africa who were landed in large numbers at Cartagena in South America. These Negroes had been torn from their homes, crowded beneath the decks of vessels in the most noisome conditions, cruelly maltreated, suffering deeply from the heat and only too often from the contagious diseases which spread so rapidly among them in their crowded quarters aboard ship. No wonder they believed the white men were all their enemies and it was dangerous for the whites to approach them. When the slave ships landed at Cartagena, Father Claver had friends among the dock hands tell him of their coming and hurried down with substantial food for the poor starved Negroes and with medicines and bandages to treat the ills of these much abused human beings.

But there are many other Jesuit saints, as for instance, St. John Francis Regis, famous for what he accomplished by missions among the country peoples in France. He desired ardently to go to Canada for missionary work among the Indians where there was the greatest risk of death preceded by awful torture as he knew from the "Jesuit Relations," the letters from the missionaries. When his superior decided that his missionary work should be done in France he devoted himself so successfully to missions among the poor that within a very short time after his death at the early age of forty-three he was venerated as a saint and pilgrims from all over France came in crowds to his tomb. The Curé d'Ars, himself proclaimed a saint a few years ago, to whose feet came 20,000 pilgrims a year in the generation before ours, attributed whatever he was able to accomplish in his lifetime to the example of St. John Francis Regis.

Then there was St. Francis de Hieronymo who preached to the poor in the slums and the poverty-stricken environs of Naples, whose influence was so widely and deeply felt, that often there were from 10,000 to 15,000 present at the monthly general Communion. The people proclaimed him a saint and in due course his formal canonization took place and he came to be held up as a model for his brother Jesuits in their work as missionaries.

These are the sort of men, forgetful of self, thoughtful of others, ready to make sacrifices of all kinds, working long years in fecund obscurity, avoiding publicity, who are held up to the imitation and emulation of the Jesuits. In their earlier years in the Order the reading of the lives of the saints is a daily duty and they are recommended above all to read the lives of the Jesuit saints and as far as possible to imitate them. As the years go on most of the Jesuits come to have the lives of the Jesuit saints, particularly, so deeply engraved upon their minds that they readily find material for examples for themselves and others in their work. The young Jesuits are not encouraged to become great scholars nor distinguished scientists, though if they prove to have talents in the intellectual order they are given opportunity to develop their special knowledge so as to be able to teach others properly. From their earliest years in the Order they are incited to follow their rules just as closely as possible and to remember that what has been accomplished by these saintly Jesuits who preceded them can be achieved in our time if men are only willing to give themselves unselfishly to the performance of duty as that is made clear to them.

About the middle of the eighteenth century when the influence of the Jesuits had reached a climax of achievement in all its purposes, the Order fell a victim to the intrigues of politicians, was banished from Portugal and Spain, and in 1773 was suppressed by the pope. The leading Protestant historians—Ranke, the German historian of the popes; Sismondi, the Italian; Schoell, the Frenchman; J. V. Mueller, another German, as well as others, declared that the suppression was brought about not because of any fault of the Jesuits but because of the tyranny of ministers of state. The movement against them began with Pombal the minister of state in Portugal and spread to Spain and France. The spirit that brought about the catastrophe of the French Revolution was already in the air and the Jesuits were looked upon as the most dangerous and formidable opponents of revolutionary designs. The ministers of the Bourbon kings, heedless of the serious dangers ahead of them, insisted with the pope that he must suppress the Jesuits. Pope Clement XIV yielded at last to the insistence of the ministers and in 1773, "in order to preserve the peace of the Church," suppressed the Society. His brief, says Schoell, the Protestant historian, "condemns neither the doctrines nor the morals of the Jesuits. The complaints of the governments against the Order are the only motives alleged for its suppression."

In two countries in Europe, Russia and Prussia, the reigning monarchs refused to allow the publication of the brief of Clement XIV suppressing the Society of Jesus. Curiously enough to the names of both of them, Frederick II of Prussia and Catherine II of Russia, the title Great has been attached by historians. Both of these rulers were persuaded that the Jesuits were excellent teachers and that so far from alienating their subjects from their monarchs by their teaching they inculcated patriotism. These rulers were quite convinced that Jesuit scholarship made them leaders in many chosen fields of learning and that there was nothing to which they applied themselves in which they had not proved eminently successful. They looked upon them as the most broad-minded teachers in Europe.

As a matter of fact, just at the time of the suppression a series of Jesuits throughout Europe were doing excellent work in the physical sciences and were looked up to as among the most important representatives of the science of the day. Lalande, the distinguished French astronomer, in his "Bibliographie Astronomique" enumerates no less than forty-five Jesuit astronomers and altogether eighty-nine Jesuit astronomical publications from 1750 to 1773, the year of the suppression. They were in charge of literally more than a score of observatories and Lalande says that "after the deplorable catastrophe to the Society most of the observatories shared the fate of the Order."

The immovable attitude of the Russian and Prussian rulers as to the suppression of the Jesuits in their dominions kept the Order alive and provided a seed for the future rebirth of the Society. This came in 1814 when Pope Pius VII by a bull revoked the brief of Pope Clement XIV and reestablished the Society. Many old men who had been members of the Society in their earlier years and whose hearts had been well-nigh broken when the suppression tore from them their happy way of life were glad to have the chance to take up their membership once more. The French Revolution had come and gone and demonstrated how sadly destructive of all that is good and beautiful even a cultured people may become as the result of the elimination of religion from their lives.

The countries of Europe that had known them before were

glad to welcome the Jesuits once more. During the century and a quarter elapsed since then the Jesuits have grown rapidly all over the world. They are almost as numerous now as they were at the time of the suppression. They are teaching all over the world at the present day—they have some 60,000 students in the schools here in the United States—and they have missions of all kinds among the pagans on all the continents.

They represent, as they did before the suppression, the very forefront of leadership among conservative Catholics. This is recognized very thoroughly by the radicals of our time, that is by those who are opposed to Christianity and particularly to that old-fashioned form of it, Catholicity. The Jesuits still are what they were called long ago, the right arm of the Church. It is easy to understand, then, that they meet with determined opposition from radical governments in many places. This is particularly true in Catholic countries when for a time radical politicians gain a foothold and almost as their first act want to send the Jesuits into exile *and above all to confiscate their property*. They continue to be as they were and as their founder prayed for them to be, the target of anti-Christian forces. In France, Italy and Spain this has been illustrated and above all in the Latin American countries. They expect such treatment and go on with their work in spite of it. The Master was treated with contumely and they expect no better treatment than He received. They continue to be the beloved friends of those who know them best and among their intimates have been some of the finest characters of recent history, as is very clear from certain of the chapters of this book.

It would be perfectly possible to collect a sheaf of the finest compliments that have been paid to the Jesuits at various times and above all on occasions when for political reasons they were the subject of persecution. Francis Bacon a century after the foundation of the Jesuits proclaimed them great teachers and expressed regret that being what they were they were not on his side. Oscar Browning in his article in the "Encyclopædia Britannica" on "Education" says of them: "For nearly three centuries they were the best schoolmasters in Europe; they revolutionized instruction as completely as Frederick the Great modern warfare." England in recent years has been the country which above all others has held the Jesuits in high regard, as if making up for the time when the name of Jesuit was a byword and to be a Jesuit was by that very fact to be declared a traitor to one's country not only with life forfeited but with death of the most harrowing description outlined by statute.

But Germany, the other great Protestant country of Europe, has had a number of distinguished scholars who have paid high compliments to the Jesuits. Frederick Paulsen, for instance, for many years the professor of philosophy at the University of Berlin, in his "History of Higher Education" describes the striking success which the Jesuits achieved in education in the sixteenth century and discusses the reason for this success. He asks, "What was the secret source of the power of these men? Was it that they were men filled with 'wickedness' as Raumer has said of them, or was it that they were more cunning and hypocritical, more unscrupulous than the rest?"

Replying to his own question Professor Paulsen says "No" very emphatically to both inquiries and adds: "There is in the activity of the Order something of the quiet yet irresistible manner of working which we find in the forces of nature. Certainty and superiority characterize every movement. . . . The system of the Society of Jesus from its fundamental principles to the minutest details of discipline is admirably fitted and adapted to its ends. The greatest possible intellectuality and scholarly power in the individual is preserved without derangement of the organization which has made the Order such a power in education at all times."

If the number of distinguished men who have been the product of this system may be taken as a fair criterion of the merits of Jesuit education, then their methods of teaching must be held in high admiration. The Jesuit pupils were many of them among the most prominent men in Europe during the sixteenth, seventeenth and eighteenth century. There were poets like Calderon, Tasso, Corneille, Molière, Fontanelle, Goldoni; prose writers like Cervantes, for he seems to have counted himself among the pupils of the Fathers; orators like Bossuet and Bourdaloue; philosophers like Descartes, Muratori, Justus Lipsius, De Vico, Montesquieu, Malesherbes; scientists like Galileo and Buffon; statesmen like Richelieu and Ferdinand; commanders of armies like Tilly, Wallenstein and Condé; church dignitaries whose names are forever famous like the gentle soul-winning St. Francis de Sales, and the scholarly Pope Benedict XIV who has been called the most learned of the popes.

Of some of their distinguished pupils the Jesuits have not been particularly proud. Voltaire was one of these. He was the intimate associate of men who stopped at almost nothing in their effort to eradicate Christianity at the end of the eighteenth century. Voltaire had his redeeming feature. He refused to calumniate the Jesuits. He said very emphatically, "I will not stoop to the meanness of defaming the Jesuits. The best years of my life were spent in their schools and while with them I never listened to any teaching but what was good nor ever witnessed any conduct but what was exemplary." [2]

The restored Society of Jesus, the Jesuits of our own time, has furnished abundant evidence in the past hundred years, that the Jesuits still possess the precious secret of bringing out the intellectual powers of students, and, as in the olden time, have made the vast majority of their students devoted admirers of their masters. Almost in our generation Pope Leo XIII, greatest of nineteenth-century popes and one of the great popes of all time, the problem solver of the modern world, whose magnificent papal documents are still quoted as representing the best solutions of our social difficulties, was a pupil of the Jesuits. So too was that distinguished astronomer, Father Secchi, and that

---

[2] When Voltaire came to die he sent for Father Gaultier, S.J., whom he had known for many years and said to him: "If you like, we'll get the little affair over with." He then made his Confession and received Holy Communion. In his last will Voltaire said that he wished to die in the Catholic Church in which he had been born, trusting that God in His mercy would forgive him. The Jesuits have had many other experiences in reconciling to the Church on their deathbed men who devoted many years of their lives to intolerant opposition to the Church and their Order. In France particularly opportunities of that kind have been the source of great consolation to the Jesuits in the midst of the tribulations that politics have brought to them.

scholarly bibliophile whom we shall return to later, Father Ehrle, the librarian of the Vatican Library.

By their rules the Jesuits are not allowed to accept ecclesiastical dignity except by the special command of the pope. In spite of this on a number of occasions, finding the assistance of Jesuits in the work of the Congregations (special committees of Cardinals) in Rome indispensable, the popes have raised some of the Jesuits to the rank of Cardinal. Among these Jesuit Cardinals are some of the most learned men of their times. The Jesuits point with pride to such distinguished scholars as Cardinals Bellarmine, Franzelin, de Lugo, Angelo Mai, Mazzella, Odescalchi, Pallavicino, Pazmany, Tarquini, Toledo and Tolemei. These men were specialists in some branch of knowledge that gave them high prestige throughout the world and made their selection as Cardinals a tribute to the ecclesiastical authorities of their time.

There were men like Cardinal Robert Bellarmine, only recently canonized, whose name was a household word in the universities of his day, and whose apologetic writings drew down on his devoted head literally many hundreds of printed volumes at a time when there was not so much amenity in controversy as there is now. He was the most written-about man of his time. These are only the pick of a large group of Jesuits who were raised to the cardinalate. Typical among them in our own day were Cardinal Billot and Cardinal Ehrle, so well known to the scholars of the world. During all the forty years while he was librarian of the Vatican Library, Father Ehrle was the constant resource and unfailing support of research workers in the library and was himself looked up to as one of the most distinguished scholars of his day. The greatest consolation of his long life was to be able to look back and rejoice over the fact that he had been a member of the Society of Jesus and died as one.

There have been many tributes to the success of the Jesuits in education in the modern time. The "London Times" when M. Ferry, the Minister of Education in France, was seeking for excuses for suppression of the Jesuit schools, said in a leading article:

"We should have liked to see a frank admission on the part of prominent members of the Left (in the French Parliament) of the real causes of the success of the ecclesiastical schools. It is no use putting it down to wiles and artifices of any kind. . . . The simple truth seems to be that the schools of the Jesuits and other religious bodies are better in many respects than their competitors. They satisfy parents of boys more than the lycées. The traditional teaching skill of the Jesuits is not extinct. It is their habit to pay attention to the moral as well as the intellectual training of the lads committed to their care."

The best testimony to the profound scholarship and the indefatigable intellectual industry of the Jesuits is to be found in Sommervogel's "Bibliothèque de la Compagnie de Jesus" (Library of the Society of Jesus) (1890-1901). This presents as far as possible a bibliography of the books written and published by Jesuits. This work has an honored place on the reference shelves of all the great libraries of the world. It consists of nine large octavo volumes, though the bibliographic notes are condensed meticulously, and comprises altogether the bibliography of some 13,000 different Jesuit writers down to the beginning of the twentieth century. Some of these writers are the authors of huge folios and not a few of them are represented by a long series of large volumes. Almost needless to say, once a man has published a book he very seldom stops there, but as a rule goes on to publish others. Undoubtedly many books written by Jesuits have not seen the light because Jesuit standards of self-criticism are high and permission to publish is given only if there is assurance in the mind of the censor appointed for that purpose that the book is worthy of the spiritual and scientific prestige of the Order.

A great many books have been written by Jesuits in the twentieth century so that Sommervogel's list must have very notable additions made to it. There are probably more than 15,000 writers for whom place must be made in a bibliography that would be complete to date. It would not be too much to say that Jesuit writers have on the average written five books each. Very probably nearly 100,000 different works, perhaps more, have been published by the Jesuits. Sommervogel's list of books does not include a great many minor works which would ordinarily find their way into a bibliography.

Besides his *Bibliothèque,* Sommervogel has compiled a "Dictionnaire des ouvrages anonymes et pseudonymes publiés par les religieux de la Compagnie de Jesus" (Dictionary of Anonymous and Pseudonymous Works Published by the Religious of the Society of Jesus). This adds many hundreds of works to the number of those published under the names of members of the Order.

Father Carayon, S.J. published in London, 1864, a "Bibliographie Historique de la Compagnie de Jesus." This contains the works that have been written about the Jesuits, not only those that praise but also those that blame, those that were written by enthusiastic friends and by bitterly intolerant enemies of the Society. Altogether this bibliography contains 4,370 titles. At the present time seventy years later this number would be well above 5,000 probably above 6,000. The work of the Jesuits from the days of their foundation to our own time has always attracted the attention of a great many serious-minded scholars, whether that attention was favorable or unfavorable. There is probably no mere human institution that has been the subject of so much comment on the part of educated men as the Society of Jesus. While their friends have been supremely enthusiastic in their praise, the surprise is to find how often those who were entirely out of sympathy with their work because of religious differences of opinion felt themselves compelled to pay high tribute to their merits.

What the Jesuits are proudest of is the fact that more than thirty of their members have been canonized by the Church, that is proclaimed, after exhaustive examination of their careers, to have lived lives of heroic virtue, thoughtful of others, forgetful of themselves, intent on doing good, and after solemn judicature granted the appellation saint. More than a hundred members of the Society are among the Blessed, the official ecclesiastical title preliminary to sainthood conferred by the solemn judgment of the Church. Then there is a large group of Jesuits to whom the title Venerable has been accorded by the Church as a proclamation that they practised virtue to an heroic degree and that their writings contain nothing contrary to Catholic faith. These constitute in the minds of Jesuits the representatives of their Order in the fullest sense of that term. Besides these who have been picked out for the Church's honors there have been thousands of others who have lived sanctified lives in humble obscurity, accomplishing marvels of good for those with whom they were brought in contact. The American Jesuits serve to illustrate this trait very strikingly. Some four hundred years of history demonstrate that the character of the Order has remained what it was made by the constitution drawn up by Ignatius, *Ad Majorem Dei Gloriam.*

CHAPTER I

OUR FIRST JESUITS—FATHER KINO, MISSIONER, EXPLORER, RANCHMAN

THE Jesuits, that is members of the Society of Jesus, came into what is now the United States not long after the middle of the sixteenth century. Since then they have almost continuously been in some part of that territory down to the present time. The Order came into existence in 1534 but until the approval of their rule by the Pope in 1540 and the election of Ignatius Loyola, their founder, as first General, attracted almost no attention. The brilliant distinction achieved by many of the colleges which they founded in Spain and Italy particularly but also in many other parts of Europe and the attention which the astounding missionary work of St. Francis Xavier in the East attracted, very soon led to a rapid increase in the number of members of the Order. Their growth in Spain was phenomenal and within seven years the Spanish province established in 1547 was divided into three so as to facilitate administration.

It is not surprising, then, that as early as 1568 fourteen Jesuits were sent from Spain to Florida as missionaries to the Indians. King Philip II of Spain was very much interested in the Jesuits and he had high hopes that they would be able to convert the Indians in America and make of them good Christian citizens of New Spain as most of the American continent was called at that time.

These Jesuits at once devoted themselves to the spread of knowledge of religion and to the training in civilization of the Indians. Brother Domingo, S.J., translated the Catholic catechism containing all the necessary truths for faith into the native Guale tongue which was spoken in what is now Georgia and neighboring territory. His colleague, Brother Baez, S.J., compiled a grammar of the Indian language. These were the first textbooks of any kind written in the United States (1570). Father Segura was the superior of the mission in Florida and soon realized that missionary work among these Seminoles would prove an extremely difficult, if not almost imposible, task. They were wild and savage, treacherous to the last degree, occupied with hunting and fishing and fighting, but not interested in anything else. Before long Father Segura had to confess failure for the mission under him so far as the Indians on the coasts of Georgia and South Carolina were concerned.

He did not give up, however, but transferred his efforts to the shores of Chesapeake Bay where with six other Jesuits he founded a mission at Axacana. The site of this Indian town is rather hard to locate but consensus of opinion places it somewhere in Virginia on the Rappahannock. Professor Bolton in "The Spanish Borderlands" of "The Chronicles of America Series" (New Haven, Yale University Press, 1921) tells the sad story of their missionary labors. It was not a long tale. Within a few months after their arrival the fickle Indians turned against them and slew Father Segura and his entire band of Jesuits in 1571. There were Spanish Jesuit martyrs, then, in Virginia over three hundred and fifty years ago.

After this sad experience the Jesuits abandoned Florida for Mexico finding there a much more favorable missionary field. There the natives were more civilized and more to be depended on and above all the political sovereignty established by the Spaniards assured reasonable safety for the missionaries and their work. Bolton notes that the Jesuits on the Pacific slope, that is in territories that now belong to the United States, made important contributions to civilization. They created a series of missions among the Indians which added greatly to the happiness of the natives and brought about their thorough conversion to Christianity. The Jesuits, like their Franciscan successors in the next century, succeeded in making their converted Indians like work and that, when one considers the sort of Indians they were dealing with, represents almost a miracle of achievement.

One Jesuit particularly who worked in the Southwest of the United States has come into striking prominence during the past dozen years. To know even a little of what he accomplished makes it easy to understand his posthumous fame three centuries later. This hero of the Pacific slope in the conversion and civilization of the Indians was Father Kino, S.J. The story of his life told largely by himself properly controlled from other sources has been a revelation to historians. His achievements are almost legendary in the prowess they display and except that the account of them, very definitely documented, has been the subject of careful study by one of the most distinguished historians of that region, they would seem almost impossible.

We owe to Professor Bolton of the University of California and his untiring research as well as his persistent devotion to the work, the details of the life of this great Jesuit hero of the Southwest. In the Foreword to his precious little volume, "The Padre on Horseback," which is a sketch of the life of Father Kino, Professor Bolton says:

"Famed among his contemporaries and eulogized by his successors, he nevertheless gradually dropped from view. Then one day his autobiography was discovered in a dusty archive (be it said by Professor Bolton himself after a heartbreaking search in which anyone with less pertinacity would surely have failed). The precious manuscript lost for a century and a half revealed an astounding personage."

The more one learns about Father Kino the easier it is to appreciate that Bolton's use of the adjective "astounding" is thoroughly justified. He says of him for instance: "Southwestern cowboys stand aghast and almost skeptical at his well-authenticated feats in the saddle. Geographers spread his fame as explorer and cartographer. Italy hails him as a noble, if nearly forgotten, son. Germany is proud to have been the inimitable Jesuit's schoolmaster. Spain points to him as one of the most puissant builders of her colonial empire. Mexico cherishes his memory as a conspicuous pioneer in the vast and historic west coast. California lauds him as the inspirer of Salvatierra, her first successful colonizer. Arizona reveres him as her most pro-

digious and exemplary pioneer." Professor Bolton has gathered
and worked up an abundance of historical material that amply
justifies this highly laudatory description of the great Jesuit
missionary.

Eusebio Francisco Kino, S.J. was born in Segno, a little village
not far from the city of Trent. This territory has changed hands
so far as government is concerned several times since then but it
is well known as the seat of the great Council of the Church
that was held there just about a hundred years before Kino's
birth. He was baptised August 10, 1645. His family spelled the
name Chino but when he came to America he wrote his name
Kino. Spaniards sometimes wrote it Quino. There was an excellent reason for the change. In Spain Chino with a soft ch is the
word for Chinaman. In Mexico it was the name applied to certain people of mixed blood considered of low caste. In its German form the name would have invited ridicule almost inevitably
especially among students.

Kino made his studies in the Universities of Freiburg and
Ingolstadt and his favorite subject was mathematics. He was
instructor of mathematics at Ingolstadt when in 1676 the Duke
of Bavaria and his father, the Elector, came on a visit to the
city. They engaged in a discussion with the young Jesuit teacher
and were so deeply impressed by his ability that they made him
an offer of a professorship in the University of Ingolstadt. They
were deeply intent on making that university the equal at least
of the other German universities in teaching talent. Such an
offer would ordinarily be expected to settle a young man's career
for a lifetime but Kino had suffered from a very severe illness
when he was eighteen and when he had sunk so low that his
life was actually in the balance and was despaired of by the
physicians he made a vow that if he recovered he would enter
the Society of Jesus and would offer himself for missionary work.
He became a Jesuit when he was twenty. In honor of the great
Jesuit missionary, St. Francis Xavier, he took the additional name
of Francis.

His superiors waited to see his character develop before sending him on the missions. In 1678 when he was thirty-three years

of age and just ordained he and a score of companions sailed from Genoa for Cadiz where they were to take passage for the West Indies. The band of devoted Jesuits who had set out from Genoa together were destined to scatter to the ends of the earth. "Their travels over the face of the globe take rank with the wanderings of Ulysses" (Bolton). Eight were sent to New Granada, ten came to Mexico and some went to the Orient. "Fathers Borango, Tilpe, Strobach, de Angelis and Cuculinus, went to work among the heathen of the Marianas Islands, Mancker and Klein went to the Philippines, and Gerstl to China, Ratkay worked in Sonora, Neuman in Neuva Vizcaya, Kino in California, Sonora and Arizona. Of the four who went to the Marianas Islands three—Borango, Strobach and de Angelis— won the martyr's crown." This was the way the Jesuits were dispersed over the world in that precious century after the death of their Holy Father Ignatius and his most faithful follower St. Francis Xavier.

Kino had distinguished himself in mathematics but he was no mere mathematical genius but one of the most talented students in his college. The same thing might be said of his missionary companions. Ordinarily it might be presumed that as these men were going to be missionaries among the ignorant, benighted savages, the men chosen for such work would be taken from the less brilliant of the Jesuits reserving the particularly intelligent ones for the educational and missionary work at home in Europe where they would be properly appreciated. What actually occurred, however, was almost exactly the opposite of this. The missionary priests were very unusual men as a rule. For instance, St. Francis Xavier had been one of the most brilliant young teachers at the University of Paris when Ignatius changed worldly ambition to religious zeal by the words: "What doth it profit a man to gain the whole world and lose his own soul?" Many of the missionaries were among the most talented of their fellow students in the colleges where they were educated. Nearly always they were men who were looked upon as outstanding scholars, yet distinctive among their fellows for their piety.

A century later when the Franciscans were sending mission-

aries to California they followed the same policy as the Jesuits
and as a result Junipero Serra, one of their most distinguished
teachers, found a place among the American missioners, just as
five centuries earlier they had sent Raymond Lully, the Doctor
Sublimis, one of the glories of their Order, as a missionary among
the Moslems. Lullius was one of the most distinguished scholars
in his very scholarly time. It is not surprising, then, that this
distinguished mathematician, Father Kino, who has attracted so
much attention for his intellectual development should be given
the opportunity to go on the missions. Father Kino not long
after his arrival was named with Father Matias Goni missionary
to California.

Because of his mathematical learning the viceroy made him
royal cosmographer, that is astronomer, surveyor and map maker
of the expedition. How well he accomplished this task, the praises
of the geographers tell us. Before leaving Mexico Kino prepared
himself for his scientific task by studying California's geography,
borrowing maps for the purpose from the viceroy's palace, and
taking them to the Jesuit *Colegio Maximo de San Pedro y San
Pablo* to copy.

From this time (1683) for more than twenty-five years, indeed
until 1711, Father Kino was occupied as a missionary among
these Indians of what is now the southwest of the United States.
When he died he was as one of his brethren tells us almost
seventy years old. His many labors and the hardships which
he subjected himself to on his long missionary journeys cannot
be said to have shortened his existence.

Father Kino did marvelous work as a missionary. He recognized that his first task was to win the confidence of the natives
and the direct way to their hearts, according to the old saw, was
through their stomachs. Whenever he made a visit to an outlying
village he carried with him maize, *pinole* and other edibles to
be given to any natives who might be met on the way. Whenever
strangers came from a distance to the mission on a visit they
were given food and presents. It is easy to understand that he
soon secured the confidence of the natives and they were quite
willing to leave their boys with the missionary whose house was

often crowded with them over night. While they were there the Fathers introduced them to the simpler uses of clothing and also to the Spanish language. While they were at the house of the missionary they performed certain domestic duties and they usually took part in prayer and in the singing, in all of which they delighted.

Kino was particularly attractive to the boys and according to tradition whenever he made an excursion he was nearly always followed by a group of Indian boys who would run by the side of his horse and try to keep up with it and would cry if they were left behind. Sometimes one or more weaker boys would be seated behind Father on his horse. Some of the Indian lads learned to love the missionary so much that they did not want to go home to their parents and pleaded to be allowed to stay with Padre Eusebio. Father Kino knew and kept very constantly before him his principal duty which was to make Christians of the Indians. Nothing gave him greater pleasure than to note some index that an Indian was becoming interested in the Faith. He tells many anecdotes to illustrate this.

Of course it is easy to understand that so scholarly a man as he would keep his eyes open for natural curiosities of various kinds and that he would try to learn something about the remedies the Indians used for their ills in the hope that some of them might be found efficacious in the treatment of the same or similar diseases among the Europeans or their descendants.

When he came to instructing the Indians about the Resurrection he found it extremely difficult to pick out a word in their language that would make the Indians understand just what was meant by resurrection, that is that the Lord died and was buried yet rose again from the dead. He found some insects whose eggs hatched into larvæ and these spun a cocoon or shroud for themselves and then came out as winged creatures. Here was a perfect figure of the Resurrection, the larva seemed to die after being wrapped in a winding sheet and then it came forth a winged creature into a glorious resurrection of life very different from the crawling one that it had led until then. When Padre

Kino showed the Indians these details which some of them with acute powers of observation had noted before, he asked them what word they had for the process. They told him and he adopted that word for the Resurrection.

After several years of somewhat wandering missionary life he was sent in 1687 to Pimería Alta and with this he reached the scene where the rest of his life, nearly twenty-five years, was to be spent. Here his life work was to be accomplished. Pimería Alta including what is now northern Sonora, one of the Mexican states, and southern Arizona, formed a large part of the territory which the United States secured after the middle of the nineteenth century by what was known as the Gadsden Purchase.

The inhabitants of this territory and especially the Pimas and Sobaipuris were much more civilized than the Indians of California. Some of them practised irrigation by means of ditches. There were many miles of aqueducts and the huge ruins of cities which as Professor Bolton says [1] had long before been abandoned. These structures are now attributed by scholars to the ancestors of the Pimas. Kino's first church was that of *Neustra Señora de los Dolores* (Our Lady of Sorrows). The site chosen was as for so many of these missions and churches one of special fitness and striking beauty. Many of the houses of religious orders in our time have followed the precious example thus set.

From this outpost at Dolores during the following quarter of a century Kino pushed the frontier of missionary work across the region known as Pimería Alta to the Gila and Colorado Rivers. In the course of the first ten years he had established a chain of missions up and down the Alta and Magdalena rivers. Whenever he went on exploring tours these were really missionary itineraries in the course of which he baptized and taught in many villages up and down the rivers in all parts of northern Pimería. Most of these missions after they were well developed were turned over to other missionaries. Three of them, however, Father Kino built and nurtured and administered personally.

[1] "The Padre on Horseback," p. 47.

They were so complete that even bells were brought from Spain for the churches and the Indians were delighted with the chime of them.

Professor Bolton says: "The establishment under his magic management had become temple, orchard, farm, stock ranch and industrial plant all combined in one." To help him manage this vast establishment Kino organized a select corps of natives to whom he entrusted the civil, educational and industrial life of the place.

Kino's own description of Dolores as given in his autobiography affords one an excellent idea how much he accomplished and how everything was thought of. He wrote of it: "This mission has its church adequately furnished with ornaments, chalices and sacred vessels, bells, choir chapel, etc.; likewise a great many large and small cattle, oxen, fields, a garden with various kinds of garden crop, Castilian fruit trees, grapes, peaches, quinces, figs, pomegranates, pears and apricots." (All these were raised in a part of the southwest not far from what we now know as California and here is the pioneer cultivation of our California fruit which means so much for the United States and a good part of the rest of the world at the present time.) Father Kino continues: "It has a forge for a blacksmith, a carpenter shop, a pack train, water mill, many kinds of grain and provisions from rich and abundant harvests of wheat and maize besides other things including horse and mule herds, all of which serve and are greatly needed for the house as well as for the expeditions and new conquests and conversions, and to purchase a few gifts and attractions with which together with the word of God it is customary to contrive to win the minds and souls of the natives."

One of Kino's highest qualities as it is always of successful men in executive positions such as his was the ability to pick out the men who would serve as his efficient helpers for the performance of the duties which must be delegated to others. He himself has told us of some of the assistants that he had to train to help him. He built up a well-organized corps of native functionaries, civil, educational and industrial, to help him manage his vast establishment. He says: "In Dolores besides the justices, captain,

governor, alcaldes, fiscal mayor, alguacil, topil . . . masters of the
chapel and school and majordomos of the house, there are cowboys, ox drivers, bakers, gardeners and painters."

Kino never spared himself, as he tells us in 1703, "I managed
all the year to go nearly every week through the three pueblos
looking after spiritual and temporal things and the building of
the two new churches," that is to say each week he rode on
horseback to Remedios and Cocóspora and back to Dolores.
The round trip was a good hundred miles. He succeeded in
organizing commerce among the tribes and he was very proud of
his churches.

This was only one phase of Kino's work, however, for his
missionary labors were paralleled by his achievements as explorer
and to him is due the credit for the first mapping of Pimería
Alta on the basis of actual exploration. Here his early mathematical training stood him in good stead. He worked out the
problem as to whether California was an island or a peninsula.
The gulf of California extending between the mainland and what
is known as lower California had given the impression that since
it could only be reached by water that part of California was
itself an island. Father Kino found shells in the possession of
Indians that occurred only on the shores of California and had
been secured by Indians who had not been in boats. He came
to the very definite conclusion that California *no es isla sino
penislo,* "California (meaning the lower part) is not an island
but a peninsula."

Professor Bolton in the introduction to his volume, "Father
Kino's Historical Memoirs of Pimería Alta: 1683-1711," gives
an estimate of the very practical work for the benefit of the
Indians which the Jesuit missionary accomplished as a comple-
ment to his spiritual work among them. He said:

"The work which Father Kino did as a ranchman and a
stockman would alone stamp him as an unusual business man
and make him worthy of remembrance. He was easily the cattle
king of his day and region. From the small outfit supplied him
from the older missions to the East and South within fifteen
years he established the beginnings of ranching in the valleys of

the Magdalena, the Altar, the Santa Cruz, the San Pedro, and the Sonoita. The stock raising industry at nearly twenty places on the modern map owes its beginnings on a considerable scale to this indefatigable man."

After thus describing his work as a ranchman, Professor Bolton says:

"And it must not be supposed that he did this for private gain for he did not own a single animal. It was to furnish a food supply for the Indians of the missions established and to be established and to give these missions a basis of economic prosperity and independence. Stock ranches were established by him at more than twenty places." Bolton proceeds: "And it must not be forgotten that Kino conducted this cattle industry with Indian labor almost without the aid of a single white man."

And yet while he was doing this there was always the danger especially in the earlier time of his missions that the Indians would revolt and run off with the stock as they did in 1695 under the leadership of some troublesome spirits who looked only to the period of idleness and plenty that they would enjoy while their stock lasted. On the other hand there was the danger even more imminent and serious that the hostile Apaches and certain other unconverted Indians of the neighborhood with envious eyes on the stock would secure its possession even at the cost of the lives of the Christian Indians.

While Kino was the original ranchman his endurance in the saddle was, to quote Bolton, "worthy of a seasoned cowboy." When he went to Mexico in the fall of 1695 then past fifty he made the journey in fifty-three days. The distance is more than fifteen hundred miles, so that not counting the stops which he made at Guadalajara and other important places he rode nearly thirty miles a day. Two years later when he went to the Gila he rode about seven or eight hundred miles in thirty days, an average of twenty-five or more miles a day for twenty-six days over an unknown country. In 1701 when he was fifty-six years of age he made over four hundred leagues or more than eleven hundred miles in thirty-five days. The figures are from his actual diaries. In the fall of 1699 he rode two hundred and fifty to three hundred miles, getting in touch with the Indians, preaching to them and baptizing in five villages on the way.

The influence which Father Kino acquired over the Indians was marvelous. No wonder that Bolton calls him "the protector of the border." He says further: "To the Pimas Kino was 'the Great White Father.' They loved him, he loved them and they were ready to die for each other. To him they flocked as if drawn by a magnet. From Northeast, North, Northwest and West they beat trails to the door of the missionary wizard. Chiefs and warriors went to attend councils; to take part in church fiestas; to be baptized; to assist in planting, harvesting and roundups. They had a childish desire to satisfy Kino's every wish. He showed an interest in blue shells. Thereafter delegation after delegation trudged from the far distant Colorado bearing presents of shells in such numbers that Kino's mission must have resembled a museum of conchology."

"Kino's almost hypnotic influence over the Pimas," Bolton proceeds to say, "gave him the position of protector of the Sonora frontier. When they heard that he had been ordered back to California (1697) citizens and soldiers protested, declaring that in defense of the border he was worth more than a garrison."

The Indians who were thus devoted to their missionary were not in any way deteriorations of the most vigorous Indian stock but on the contrary they were some of the bravest of the redskins of that region. They did not dread the Apaches and their aid against the wild Indians of the plains proved very helpful to the Spaniards. As Bolton says: "The Pimas were valiant fighters and every blow they struck for themselves was a blow for the Spaniards themselves. On this help after Kino arrived the Sonorans (the Spanish inhabitants of the district around Sonora) came to rely. The soldiers when they organized a campaign against the Apaches would call for a levy of Pimas. To raise the Indian forces they depended on Kino." On one occasion when the Apaches came down in full force on the settlements the opposing chiefs agreed to fight the battle by champions ten on a side. "After a terrific struggle nine of the Apaches were stretched out on the ground. Then the leader of the Apaches ten fell and the Apache mob fled." These were the sort of men over whom Kino's influence was exerted and who thought of him as their beloved father and brother in Christ.

It is only after learning what sacrifices Father Kino was willing to make and how much he was ready to do for his Indian children, no matter what might be the labor and fatigue involved, that one comes to appreciate just why the Indians thought so much of him. They could not help but have the feeling that he thought at least as much of them. An incident told by Professor Bolton will illustrate this. He calls it: "Another instance of Father Kino's disregard of toil in ministering to others:

"On the morning of May 3, 1700, Father Kino was on his way to Dolores from the founding of Mission San Xavier del Bac. As he was about to say Mass at sunrise he received an urgent message from Father Campos begging him to hasten to San Ignacio to help save a poor Indian whom the soldiers had imprisoned and were about to execute on the following day. Stopping to say Mass and to write a hurried letter to Captain Escalante he rode by midnight to Imuris and arrived at San Ignacio in time to say early Mass and to save the Indian from death. The direct route by rail from Tumacácori (where he started) to Imuris is sixty-two miles and to San Ignacio it is seventy. If Kino went the then usual route by the Santa Cruz River he must have ridden seventy-five or more miles on this errand of mercy *in considerably less than a day.*"

Another feature of Father Kino's character that must have won the hearts of these beloved Indian braves of his who had the courage and the hardihood not only to tackle but to conquer the dreaded Apaches when they were of equal numbers, was his own physical courage which, as Bolton says, "was attested by his whole career in America spent in exploring unknown wilds and laboring among untamed savages." Bolton has given some episodes of Father Kino's life which demonstrate his undaunted courage. Over and over again Jesuit colleagues were sure that he must have met with death. In the early days when the Pimas were not as yet entirely won over to him and later when the growth of the missions attracted raids by neighboring unconverted tribes, he was in the greatest possible peril but always escaped because of his undauntedness. His absolutely unshakable courage carried him through the dangers. He had the modesty of brave men and little is said in his own autobiography about the perils he encountered. Some of the most startling episodes are quite ignored, but fortunately for our due understanding of Kino they have been recorded by his companions who noted in their letters and diaries how utterly fearless he was whenever there was question of danger to himself.

Even stranger Indians, brought in contact with him for the first time, were deeply impressed by his absolute fearlessness. As an illustration of this trait Bolton tells the story of Father Kino's first expedition down the Colorado River below the Yuma junction (1701). This was the first time in almost a hundred years that a white man made this journey. In Father Kino's party of exploration there was but one Spaniard, the only other white man in the party: "As they left the Yuma country and entered that of the Quiquimas the Spaniard, Kino tells us in his diary, 'on seeing such a great number of new people', and such people—that is they were giants in size—became frightened and fled." The missionary thus deserted and left alone with the strange huge Indians instead of turning back went fearlessly on and after a time despatched messengers to tell that he was safe. He continued down the river two days journey and crossed the Colorado guided by gigantic Yumas of awe-inspiring mien into territory never trod by white men since 1540. Bolton comments very pertinently: "Perhaps Father Kino was in no danger, but the situation had proved too much for the nerve of his white companion at least."

Unfortunately there is no portrait of Father Kino extant. There is not even an intimate personal description from someone close to him that would enable us to make a mental picture of him. The question that would inevitably occur to most people would be, was he rugged, coarse-fibred and adapted by nature to such a rough frontier life of exposure, or was he perhaps just the opposite, rather thin, perhaps even somewhat delicate as sometimes such pioneers have been? His companion in many

of his dangers and missionary work, Father Louis Velarde, S.J.
tells us, to quote Bolton whom we are following closely in all
this, that "Kino was a modest, humble, gentle ascetic, drilled by
his religious training to forgetfulness of self, almost to self-
effacement." Bolton adds, "I should not be surprised to find that
like Father Junipero Serra he was slight of body as he was gentle
of mind."

It is probable that further documents may come to light that
will enable us to form a reasonably correct idea of Father Kino's
personal appearance. We know much more of his spiritual,
than we do of his physical, life. He was extremely pious,
devoted several hours every day to prayer and in saying his
breviary, the daily office, a form of prayer which priests are
required to read, his devotion was often so deep that tears came
to his eyes. He liked to read the lives of the saints and nothing
delighted him more than to speak of their virtues: "He neither
smoked nor took snuff nor wine nor slept in a bed." No wonder
Velarde says that Father Kino was considered by his companions
as without fault. They thought of him as a saint and their regard
for him after the most intimate relations with him was very like
that cherished for him by his beloved Indians.

After reading the life of Father De Smet, S.J., of our own
generation or even the chapter we have been able to afford him
in this volume, and thus being made familiar with the astounding
influence that this modern "black-robe" acquired over the
Indians, even the most dangerous tribes among them, the Sioux
and the Blackfeet, it will be easier to understand Father Kino's
career and the success with the Indians which he achieved. Two
centuries apart, the lives of these two Jesuits have many things
in common so that one throws light on the other. This Spanish
Jesuit had a marvelous attraction for the Indians but besides he
was possessed of a personality which gave him something of the
same charm for his white friends. I have often heard those who
knew Father De Smet well in the modern time talk of his light-
heartedness and charm of personality.

Father Velarde tells that it was quite impossible to insult
Father Kino. He was known to embrace one who spoke ill of

him and declare, "You are and ever will be my dearest master." He was himself ever ready to forgive insults and set the veil of charity over men's faults. His Jesuit companions said that he was a man of prayer and by this they meant that he spent long hours at his devotions. Father Velarde says: "After supper when he saw us all already in bed he would enter the church and though I sat up most of the night reading I never heard him come out to get the sleep of which he was very sparing." In addition to all this Father Kino was a man of mortification. That is a word that seems a little bit hard to understand in the modern time. In Father Kino's experiences where he so often had to eat the coarse food of his Indian neophytes one might expect that his mortification would be amply provided for him by his living conditions without adding anything to it voluntarily. We hear of him, however, taking his food without salt and with mixtures of herbs which made it somewhat distasteful. Almost never did he sleep in a bed. On his missionary and exploring expeditions he stretched blankets from his horse for a mattress and a few Indian blankets for covering.

Bolton emphasizes the fact that it is very difficult for our generation, absorbed as we are to a very great extent in material things and with ideals very different from those which occupied the minds and lifted up the hearts of these missionaries, to understand exactly how they set about the accomplishment so successfully of work among the Indians, gave themselves so wholeheartedly to the enterprise of not only making Christians but as far as that might be civilized Christians out of these Indians who were intensely savage in many regards.

Bolton says: "Only with extreme difficulty do we of the twentieth century comprehend the spirit which inspired the first pioneers of the Southwest. We can understand why men should strive to conquer the wilderness for the wealth that it would yield but almost incomprehensible to most of us is the sixteenth century ideal which brought to this region its first adjuncts of civilization—the Jesuit and Franciscan missionaries. These men came single-minded, imbued with zeal for the saving of souls. Most of them were men of liberal education. Many of them were of prominent families and might have occupied positions of honor and distinction in Europe."

After having edited Father Kino's Relacion, the *Favores Celestiales,* Professor Bolton says very straightforwardly, "The problem of the biographer of Father Kino will be to tell much in little, so many and long continued were his activities. He was great not only as missionary and church builder but also as explorer and ranchman. It was from Father Kino that Salvatierra, founder of the permanent California missions, received his inspiration for that work." The Reverend Juan Maria de Salvatierra, S.J., was the Jesuit provincial of that region and spent some time in company with Kino on his visitations and from him absorbed the incentive to go on with further work among the Indians.

Kino died as he had lived in extreme humility and poverty. In token of this during his last illness he did not undress. He could not be induced to sleep on a bed. Death came to him in the house of one of the Fathers where he had gone to dedicate the finely made chapel consecrated to St. Francis Xavier who was his special patron saint and whose missionary labors and life of prayer and mortification were the inspiration for Father Kino's work.

Here indeed was the measure of the man. He might have been the honored professor of mathematics at the University of Ingolstadt, at that time looked upon as one of the most important universities in Germany for the Elector of Bavaria was trying to make it the rival of the universities of neighboring German states, but Father Kino preferred to take up the laborious life of the missionary and give himself whole-heartedly to the hardships and trials that went with that mode of life. He would have had a very peaceful, untroubled, scholarly intellectual life in the Jesuit community in Germany but he preferred to devote himself wholly to others, forgetful of himself and his own comforts and conveniences. He very nobly heads the list of Jesuits who have labored within the territory now embraced in the United States.

CHAPTER II

THE JESUITS AND RELIGIOUS TOLERATION
IN THE UNITED STATES

FOR most people probably the most surprising chapter in the history of the Jesuits in the territory that is now the United States is that which treats of the development of religious toleration under their influence. Whenever religious toleration was put forward as a policy of government in the colonies—with the exception of Rhode Island—Jesuits and students of Jesuits are associated as prominent factors in the movement that proclaims it. In Maryland under the Calverts, in New York under Governor Dongan, in the influence of the Carrolls, Charles and John, in the drawing up of the Constitution of the United States, in the securing of legislation for the upholding of the sacredness of the professional and confessional secret, Jesuits are either prime movers in the matter or are the closest confidential advisers of those whose names are forever identified with this great advance in civilization which came into existence as the result of the foundation of our government on a basis of religious liberty.

The general feeling would be that Jesuits, because of their close identification with the interests and policy of the Roman Catholic Church, and above all their special vow of obedience to the Pope, were not likely to be intimately associated with any movement that would grant freedom of conscience to all those who might differ in religious views from the majority of those around them. Any such presumption with regard to the Jesuits is due entirely to lack of knowledge of the realities of intellectual life within the Order. As a matter of fact university professors in Jesuit institutions and their widely known writers on

35

philosophy at a time when the Jesuits were the schoolmasters of the Catholic world, laid down the principles on which religious toleration is justified, and it is through their teaching more than that of any others that the modern attitude toward tolerance in religion has come into vogue. Such philosophical teaching as religious toleration was almost undreamed of before the foundation of the Jesuits. The policy made but little political headway in Europe but over here in America on this new continent it gradually won its way and it is noteworthy that this progress wherever it occurred almost without exception came about with Jesuits as the close advisers to the leaders in the movement.[1]

RELIGIOUS TOLERATION IN MARYLAND

What has been well termed "the first experiment in religious liberty in the world" was the foundation of the colony of Mary-

[1] As an illustration of how liberal and presumedly modern Jesuit teaching of the great underlying principles of international law was some three hundred years ago, a recent scholastic event in Holland is of special significance. In 1925 the faculty of the University of Leyden organized a celebration of the 300th anniversary of the publication of Hugo Grotius' great work on international law, "De Jure Belli et Pacis." This has often been hailed as the pioneer work of its kind in the world which elaborates to their ultimate conclusion the definite principles and laws which nations must observe with regard to each other in peace and war. While organizing their celebration the Hollanders came to the realization of how much Grotius himself acknowledged that he was indebted to two great Spanish philosophers who preceded him in this department of jurisprudence. To make a definite culmination to their celebration the faculty at Leyden appointed a committee that would carry a share of the honor which they were conferring on their fellow countrymen to his distinguished Spanish teachers. The committee made a pilgrimage to Spain to place wreaths on the graves of Father Vitoria, O.P., the distinguished Spanish Dominican theologian, and on that of Father Francisco Saurez, S.J., the no less distinguished Spanish writer and teacher of philosophy, commonly considered one of the greatest thinkers in the history of the Order. When it is recalled how reactionary Spanish Dominicans were often supposed to be, entrusted as they were with the carrying on of the Inquisition in Spain, and how narrow the Spanish Jesuits might be presumed to be in the matter of such very modern questions as those which constantly crop up in international law and the relations of countries to one another, the mission of this committee of the faculty of Leyden proves to be corrective of many preconceived notions. This tribute from Holland is all the more significant since Holland and especially the University of Leyden has no faintest element of partiality for Catholicity that might have prompted this fine bit of academic courtesy. The leaning was quite the other way so that the tributes paid are all the more deserving of proper appreciation.

land under the very liberal charter obtained for it from the English crown by George Calvert, Lord Baltimore. Of him Bancroft, our American historian, said, "Calvert deserves to be ranked among the most wise and benevolent law givers of all ages. He was the first in the history of the Christian world to seek for religious security and peace by the practice of justice and not by the exercise of power, to plan the establishment of popular institutions for the enjoyment of liberty of conscience." Lord Baltimore was indeed a great pioneer in this extremely important realm of religious toleration and his promulgation in Maryland of a charter to this effect exerted deep influence in securing eventual religious liberty in this country after our independence had been secured. The presence of the Maryland Catholics and their attitude toward religious liberty familiarized colonial minds with the idea that such a policy could be made effective. The Carroll family and especially Charles of Carrollton and Father John Carroll demonstrated how thoroughgoing the patriotism of Catholics was and mollified feelings of intolerance that were rife. Later, religious toleration found its way into the Constitution of the United States as a prime feature of the new government. Lord Baltimore was the leader in this and has deservedly come to be so honored.

The Calverts continued this wise and benevolent policy. To quote Bancroft once more, "Maryland in that day was unsurpassed for happiness and liberty. Conscience was without restraint. A mild and liberal proprietary conceded every measure which the welfare of the colony required; domestic union, a happy concert between all the branches of the government, an increasing immigration, a productive commerce, a fertile soil which heaven had richly favored with rivers and deep bays, united to perfect the scene of colonial felicity and contentment."

Conditions in the colony of Maryland under the proprietary were ideal. It is easy to understand that in such circumstances the liberal enforcement of charter regulations with regard to religious toleration and the absolute liberty of conscience which the provisions of the charter permitted would depend to a very great extent on the clergymen who were closest to the proprietary and on the influence which they exerted on him. The priests

who came over to Maryland with the proprietary were Jesuits,
Father Andrew White and Father Philip Fisher. Father White's
zealous labors for his colonist flock and also for the Indians of
the region won for him the name of apostle of Maryland. His
brother Jesuit, Father Fisher, was only less beloved by the colonists and both were in the closest intimacy with a group of
Englishmen who were in sympathy with Lord Baltimore's
plans for the colony as a refuge for those who over in
England were the subjects of persecution on account of their
religion.

It is no accidental circumstance that brought these two Jesuits
to the colony and if they were not the actual inspirers of Lord
Baltimore's spirit of tolerance at least they were perfectly ready
to second every effort of his in the establishment of this policy
on the American continent. The Jesuits themselves had been
the subject of so much and such bitter persecution on the part
of the English government that they had had the lesson of
toleration brought intimately home to them. Besides the Jesuits
had always been in accordance with their constitutions concilia-
tors in times of religious strife. The more one knows about them
the easier it becomes to understand their association with the men
to whom we owe the foundation of religious liberty in this
country.

It is easy to reach the conclusion that the Jesuits in Maryland
were important elements in the inspiration of Lord Baltimore's
policy of toleration because we have another instance of very
similar character in New York under Governor Dongan some
fifty years later. The story of Dongan's charter, told later in
this chapter, serves to exemplify the fact that where the Jesuits
were in intimate relations with the authorities religious toleration
was quite sure to be the policy adopted.

The Jesuits in Maryland, very soon after landing, manifested
their personal interest in education. In 1638 the Jesuit superior
of the Maryland mission took up the project of founding a school
for the colony. This was about the time of the establishment of
Harvard College. Like other schools in this country, the Jesuit
school did not find a permanent home at once and is noted as

in existence at various places. In 1651 it was at Calvert Manor. In 1677 it was at Newtown Manor. Some seventy-five years later when the Jesuits were compelled to withdraw from southern Maryland, they opened their academy at Bohemia Manor. While never more than a small school with comparatively few in attendance, this academy may be quite willing to submit to the test "by their fruits ye shall know them." It was the Alma Mater of two distinguished Americans, Charles Carroll of Carrollton, signer of the Declaration of Independence, and his cousin, John Carroll, the first Bishop and Archbishop of Baltimore. Those who are at all familiar with the lives of these two men are quite willing to acknowledge that they would have been worthy alumni of any college, however distinguished. Both of them after their preparatory school work at Bohemia Manor went abroad to Jesuit schools on the Continent where they continued their education, always under the tutelage of the Jesuits.

Both were distinguished patriots. Bishop Carroll as a young man received his education in the English Jesuit colleges of St. Omer's and Rheims which had to be situated in Belgium and France because the Jesuits were not allowed to teach in England. Their Jesuit education in no way lessened their love for country as is evident from their careers. Father Carroll, safely ensconced in the position in England in which he might have avoided all the danger to which he was subjected on this side of the water, patriotically returned to his native country just before the Revolution to share the trials and fortunes of his brother Americans. The Continental Congress as well as the leading patriots in the colonies turned confidently to him whenever it was felt that he could be of special service. With his cousin, Charles Carroll of Carrollton, and Benjamin Franklin and Samuel Chase, he was of the committee appointed to secure if possible the cooperation of the Canadians in the Revolution.

His cousin, Charles Carroll of Carrollton, received almost the same education as John except that he finished his course with great éclat at the best known college of the Jesuits, that of Louis-le-Grand in Paris, where he was chosen to make the Grand Act in philosophy. The Jesuit philosophic principles thus imbibed made him all the hardier a patriot.

This is very well illustrated by Charles Carroll's life which exemplifies strikingly the results of Jesuit teaching. There is a well-known letter from the signer to George Washington Parke Custis, the son of the widow Custis whom Washington married, and who had been adopted by Washington as his son. Custis interested himself very much in the history of the development of religious freedom in America and was besides very emphatic in his expression of sympathy for civil and religious liberty in Ireland. Charles Carroll wrote for him a declaration of his attitude toward religious toleration which reveals his ideas on the subject very thoroughly:

"When I signed the Declaration of Independence, I had in view not only our independence from England but the toleration of all sects professing the Christian religion and communicating to them all full rights. Happily this wise and salutary measure has taken place for eradicating religious feuds and persecutions and become a useful lesson to all governments.

"Reflecting as you must on the disabilities, I may truly say, on the proscription of the Roman Catholics in Maryland, you will not be surprised that I had much at heart this grand design founded on mutual charity, the basis of our holy religion." ("National Gazette," Philadelphia, Feb. 26, 1829.)

Lord Baltimore was deeply intent on securing a refuge for English Catholics in America, for at home they were subject to a series of the most stringent and inhuman penal laws. It was no longer treason to say Mass, but any priest discovered was to be fined two hundred marks (a mark was about $3.25) and imprisoned for a year. All those who attended Mass were liable to the same imprisonment with a fine of one hundred marks. Lord Baltimore had become a convert under King James I to whom he was Secretary of State. He resigned his position on his conversion. At that time no Catholic could enter the legal or medical profession or the university or teach school under penalty of perpetual imprisonment. Any priest or prelate born a Briton who returned to England from abroad without renouncing his religion within three days was guilty of high treason, the punishment of which was death.

Lord Baltimore was intent on securing a refuge for his brother Catholics from such exactions but he was quite sincere in his desire to secure for others the same privileges as those enjoyed by the Catholic colonists. He instructed his brother, Cecil Calvert, when he was setting sail to found the colony, "to be very careful to preserve unity and peace and to suffer no scandal nor offense to be given to any of the Protestants." A number of Protestants accompanied the expedition, some of them non-Conformists who were under almost as severe penalties as Catholics. The civil war in England between the Parliament and King Charles I led to the execution of the king in 1649. Meantime (1644) the Puritans under Clayborne invaded Maryland overthrew the government and drove out the governor, Leonard Calvert, the representative of Lord Baltimore. Two years later Calvert returned, defeated the Puritans and regained the colony. It was deemed best under the circumstances to put religious freedom in the form of a law. This was accordingly done and is the first enactment in the land which gave equal rights in religion to all Christians. This act read as follows:

"And whereas the enforcing of the conscience in matters of religion hath frequently fallen out to be of dangerous consequence in those commonwealths where it has been practised and for the more quiet and peaceable government of this province and the better to preserve mutual love and amity among the inhabitants, no person within the province professing to believe in Jesus Christ shall be in any way troubled, molested or discountenanced for his or her religion or in the free exercise thereof."

By this act Jews were excluded from the benefit of the religious toleration and were denied the right of suffrage. This has sometimes seemed narrow and illiberal to modern students of history but a long time had to pass before the feeling with regard to the Jews moderated to such an extent as to permit of their being given rights as citizens. It was actually not until 1826, that is until after an interval of nearly two hundred years, that the Jews were allowed to vote or hold office in Maryland.[2]

GOVERNOR DONGAN AND RELIGIOUS TOLERATION

Just fifty years after Maryland set the example, there was another striking instance of the intimate relationship of the Jesuits with the establishment of religious toleration in this country. It constitutes a parallel landmark in our history to that which happened in Maryland under the Calverts. This occurred in New York under Thomas Dongan, New York's greatest colonial governor. After Dongan had been appointed governor but before he sailed for the colony, the Duke of York who, after the taking over of the colony from the Dutch by the English, became the Proprietor of what had been New Amsterdam but now became in his honor New York, consulted with the Jesuit Fathers in England as to the possibility of sending one or more of their number to his colony in America. The provincial of the Jesuits in England, Father John Warner, S.J., wrote to the General of the Jesuits in Rome in 1683 saying that "Father Thomas Harvey, missioner, passes to New York by consent of the governor of the colony." The English provincial expresses the hope that the presence of Jesuits in New York may lead to the foundation of a Jesuit school for which some of the Jesuits in Maryland may be available as teachers. The special reason for consulting the Gen-

[2] That there was definite opportunity for Jews to practice professions in Maryland in spite of the limitations of this early legislation will be best demonstrated from the fact that one of the earliest practitioners of medicine in his country was Jacob Lumbrozo who settled in Maryland, January 24, 1656. He was described as the "Jew doctor," a native of Lisbon of the kingdom of Portugal. Dr. Solomon R. Kagan in his "Contributions of American Jews to Medicine" relates that he built up a lucrative medical practice in Charles County. Dr. Kagan quotes Hollander, the well known historian of the relations between painting and medicine, "In Lumbrozo first appears, as yet in broken outline, a marked individuality. He is one of the earliest medical practitioners in Maryland, whose arrival forms a distinct event in the life of the province, and who for nearly a decade continued to be an important figure in its economic activity. He died in May, 1666."

eral was this question of the Jesuits in New York getting aid from their brother Jesuits in Maryland.

The English provincial wrote to the General: "In that colony (New York) is a respectable city fit for the foundation of a college, if faculties are given, to which college those who are now scattered throughout Maryland may betake themselves and make excursions from thence into Maryland." The provincial added, "The Duke of York, lord of that colony, greatly encourages the undertaking of a new mission." The General of the Jesuits not only approved of Father Harvey's appointment but also congratulated the English province upon its foundation of this new American mission. It is not surprising, then, to find that a group of Jesuits found their way into New York during Dongan's administration.

This was not the first time that there had been Jesuits in Manhattan. In 1642 Father Isaac Jogues then doing missionary work among the Huron Indians was captured by the Mohawks and carried as a prisoner to their principal fortified town on the Mohawk River. Father Jogues was submitted to severe torture and above all to mutilation by his captors. After he had been condemned to death he succeeded in making his escape and was assisted by the Dutch authorities at Fort Orange [3] in finding his way down to what was then New Amsterdam where he was entertained by Governor Kieft and provided with food, lodging and medical aid and transportation to Europe. Father Jogues was thus the first priest to enter what is now the City of New York. Two years later Father Francis Joseph Bressani, S.J., suffered in very similar fashion. He too was captured by the Mohawks but rescued and aided by the Dutch. He too had the good offices of Governor Kieft, and the Dutch proved themselves thoroughly sympathetic. A dozen years later another Jesuit, Father Simon Le Moyne, visited New Amsterdam (1658) to be of service to some Catholics residing there and especially to the crew of a French privateer which had put into port of New York. These three had somewhat familiarized the Dutch of

[3] Afterwards called Albany because James Duke of York, was also Duke of Albany.

Manhattan with the idea of having Jesuits among them. Later on Governor Dongan proposed to bring over a group of English Jesuits to do missionary work among the Iroquois who had gradually become somewhat civilized and Christianized. His reason for wanting to have English missionaries was that the presence of the French missionaries inevitably impressed the minds of the Indians to a favorable attitude toward the French rather than the English and, as the Iroquois occupied what was considered to be English territory, it seemed well to prevent any development of French leaning because of the French Jesuits with whom they were brought in contact.

Father Thomas Harvey, with at least one Jesuit companion, sailed for New York with Governor Dongan in July, 1683, and arrived there a month later. There is no record of an official chaplaincy being accorded to Father Harvey but there is a record of the yearly payment of sixty pounds to "two Romish priests by Governor Dongan." This was not a salary but a voluntary offering on the part of the colonial government, for the official Jesuit catalog cited by Father Hughes, S.J., states that the priests in New York were supported only by alms.

During the forty years that had elapsed since Father Jogues' visit to Manhattan, there had been a notable increase in the number of Roman Catholics on the island. Father Jogues wrote (Jesuit Relations) that he had found two Catholics on Manhattan, a Portuguese woman and a young Irishman, whose confessions he heard. The increase seemed to justify the provision of a room for a chapel in which Father Harvey said Mass and administered the sacraments. This was in Fort James on the site of which now stands the United States Custom House. The spot is marked by a tablet on the walls of the Custom House placed there by the Knights of Columbus, recording the event with this inscription:

"Within Fort James, located on this site, the sacrifice of the Mass was offered in 1683, in the Governor's residence, by the Reverend Thomas Harvey, S.J., chaplain to Governor Thomas Dongan. Erected by the Order of Alhambra (a branch of the Knights of Columbus), anno Domini MCMXII."

In the meantime some very important developments had taken place in New York. New Amsterdam, as it had been under the Dutch, now became New York in honor of James, Duke of York, the younger brother of King Charles II, afterwards himself to be that King James II whom the English deposed in the revolution of 1688, and replaced by his daughter Mary and her husband William of Orange. The Duke was intent on securing the good feeling of the Dutch inhabitants of the colony as well as of all the colonials in his domain, so he suggested to Dongan that as governor he should summon a meeting of the Provincial Representative Assembly so that the inhabitants might be persuaded that through the favor of the Proprietor they would live under representative government. Shortly after his arrival Dongan convened the first Provincial Assembly of the Province of New York, October 14, 1682. This assembly under his direction and influence passed the well-known Charter of Liberties, the most liberal document in the whole history of religious toleration issued up to that time. This charter solemnly proclaimed the right of religious liberty and freedom of conscience. It is remarkable for a group of propositions proposed and carried by the Assembly which demonstrated that the fundamental principles of democracy were to be maintained vigorously under the new governor.[4]

The Assembly passed an act incorporating that extremely important democratic principle, formulated first in the thirteenth century which afterwards came to be one of the most significant claims of the colonists at the beginning of the American Revolution, one indeed on which they based their right to separate from the mother country: "There shall be no taxation without

---

[4] According to the Ecclesiastical Records of New York (II, 1290), Governor Dongan asked King James II to give a tract of land to the Jesuits for the support of the school. The tract of land mentioned was known as "King's Farm" and was really a part of the estate attached to the Governor's residence. The king refused to grant Dongan's request because he feared that the loss of such land would be an inconvenience to subsequent governors. In Queen Anne's reign, however (1703) this property, King's Farm, was given to the Episcopal Trinity Church of New York. This constituted a large part of the real estate holdings of the church which made it so important a landholder in the southern part of Manhattan Island ever since.

representation." This document announced that, "Taxes can be levied only by the people met in general assembly." Another formula of this basic law in New York was, "Martial law is not to be proclaimed and there is to be no quartering of soldiers on inhabitants without the consent of the people."

The Jesuits who were with Dongan proceeded to fulfill the task which had been suggested for them by the provincial of the Jesuits in England, approved by the General of the Order. They established a classical school in New York situated on what was known as the King's Farm in those days, not far away from Trinity Church at the head of Wall Street as we know it at the present time. Governor Dongan was a patron of the school and the sons of some of the best families on Manhattan were in attendance at the school. The old Dutch burghers proved particularly ready to send their children to the Jesuits. Many of them knew from tradition which had come down to them that the Jesuits had been most successful educators in Europe and even in Holland itself and so they knew that their children were sure to receive the very best education to be had. There were rather intimate relations between the ministers of the Dutch Reformed Church and the Jesuits.

It is easy to understand that under these circumstances the sections of the Charter of Liberties which had to do with religious toleration under Dongan's influence must have been discussed thoroughly with his Jesuit friends and that nothing was done without their approval. Almost needless to say the famous sentence with regard to religious toleration which was incorporated into the Charter of Liberties has very properly given Dongan and his advisers a place for all time in the history of human thought and freedom of conscience: "That no person or persons which profess faith in God by Jesus Christ shall at any time be any ways molested, punished, disquieted or called in question for any difference of opinion or matter of religious concernment who do not actually disturb the civil peace of the province."

Mrs. Schuyler Van Rensselaer in the first volume of her history of the City of New York says: "For this section of the charter there were no precedents in English or English-colonial law or custom." Dongan's governorship of the colony was so well and humanly administered that no wonder historians are agreed in declaring that his conduct "soon won for him the affections of his people and made him one of the most popular of the royal governors."

Dongan was undoubtedly the greatest of the colonial governors. The Dictionary of American Biography says of him: "By his clearness of vision no less than by the vigor of his policy Dongan proved himself one of the race of empire builders. Though himself a Roman Catholic his administration was marked by a broad tolerance in religious matters." The fact that a man of this caliber and wisdom in administration should have turned confidently to the Jesuits to act as his advisers here in America is the best possible demonstration of what was thought of the members of the Order by those who knew them intimately. Dongan was the sort of man who was not likely to be deceived with regard to men. He was astute to the last degree in his dealings with the French and with the Indians. He was noted for his ability to select men to be his agents in important transactions and since he turned with such confidence to the Jesuits we may rest assured that he had never encountered anything but candor and sincerity in them. All the American historians who in recent years have paid particular attention to the career of Governor Dongan are a unit in proclaiming him New York's greatest governor and a man far ahead of his time in all that made for democratic government and religious toleration.

Channing in his "United States" (vol. II, p. 143) says: "Saturday, the 25th of August, 1683, was a memorable day in the history of America for it was then that Colonel Thomas Dongan arrived in New York. . . . With his coming a new epoch opened in the history of the province of New York, in the history of English American colonies, and in the history of the international relations of England and France. . . . To him must be given the credit for first seeing the importance of the position of New York and the Iroquois in the international politics of North America." Other historians may not be quite so enthusiastic with regard to this distinguished governor but all acknowledge his ability and his practical talent for ruling men and above all for securing peace with his neighbors. Dongan settled the boundary disputes with Connecticut, made a peace treaty with the Iroquois Indians who acknowledged themselves as subjects of England, and accomplished an immense amount to prevent the extension southward of the lines already drawn, of French power in North America. Unfortunately his policy of religious toleration was not approved by the Crown but even the gesture in that direction had its influence and a century later was an important factor in bringing about the freedom of worship established in the republic.

Theodore Roosevelt, afterwards President of the United States, in his sketch of New York, called attention particularly to the great work that was accomplished for religious liberty but also for political freedom by the charter which Thomas Dongan granted the city and which has continued to rule the municipality ever since. Mr. Roosevelt said: "Thomas Dongan, the first governor, a Catholic Irish gentleman of good family, the nephew of the Earl of Tyrconnell, acted with wise liberality both in matters political and in matters religious, towards the province he was sent to govern, and was a man of high character and good capacity. He was also vigilant in preserving order, in warding off outside aggression and devoted to the well being of the colony and proved himself perhaps the best colonial governor New York ever had. Dongan reached New York in 1683 and from the first was popular with the colonists. He at once issued writs for the election of members of the long retired Provincial Assembly. With its meeting the province took its first real step— and a very long one—toward self-government."

The tributes paid to Governor Dongan by those who disagreed with him in religious faith and who might be expected to be prejudiced in their judgment of him, demonstrate very clearly the magnanimity of the man and the very practical character of the governor. The historian of the Dutch Reformed Church [5] writes that, "Religious toleration was almost perfect under Dongan. The Puritan governor of the Plymouth colony, Thomas

[5] Corwin, "History of the Reformed Church," New York, 1895, p. 164.

Hinckley, said of Dongan: 'He was of a noble and praiseworthy mind and spirit, taking care that all people in each town knew their duty in maintaining the minister of the place, though himself of a different opinion from their way.' "

When the French Huguenots fled from France after the revocation of the Edict of Nantes (1685) many of them came to New York where Dongan welcomed them and granted them citizenship with all its privileges. They have constituted ever since an important element in New York's population. In September, 1685, the Jews of New York City petitioned Governor Dongan for the right to trade and practice their religion. The Governor recommended their petition to the Mayor and Council of New York City. The petition was refused on the grounds that the Assembly intended freedom of worship and privileges of citizenship and trading only for those who professed faith in Christ. Governor Dongan obtained for the Jews the right to engage in wholesale trade and when the king extended toleration to people of all religious faiths the Governor made it his special purpose to see that the Jews secured their rights. There can be no doubt of this for the names of two Jews, Isaac Henriquez, and Simon Bonan, appear on the rolls of Freemen for 1687-1688, Daly in his "Settlement of Jews in North America" (New York, 1893, pp. 24-27) says that there was a synagogue in New York before the end of Dongan's term.

Although faithful to his duty as a Catholic governor, Dongan never showed undue partiality toward the Catholic Church. He did not hesitate to reprimand and even advise the banishment of French Jesuits from among the Iroquois when he felt that they were using their ministry to the detriment of English interests. Cobb in "The Rise of Religious Liberty in America" (p. 329, New York, 1902) writes with regard to Governor Dongan: "Though a devout Catholic, he showed no strong desire to build up any church but devoted himself to the civil duties in which he proved to be one of the very best governors in the province."

In 1688 King James II united the province of New York to the territory and dominion of New England and appointed Sir

Edmund Andros governor of both provinces. Dongan continued to live in the colony as a private citizen. King James II was deposed by the revolution which brought about a rebellion in Massachusetts and the imprisonment of Andros. A New York merchant, Jacob Leisler, took the opportunity to raise the standard of revolt. He proved fanatically anti-papist. The papists were denied the right to hold office or to vote. Leisler sent raiding parties to Dongan's Staten Island estate but without avail. The governor circulated stories to the effect that the papists were gathering around Dongan on Staten Island so as to terrorize Protestant inhabitants of the island. Besides, he declared that the ex-governor was fitting out vessels with guns, ammunition and provisions and collecting a force of Papists from Boston and elsewhere. Dongan took refuge in Rhode Island, afterwards in New Jersey and finally in Massachusetts. In return for his tolerance, Dongan met with the bitterest intolerance. Roberts expresses it very well in his "Planting and Growth of the Empire State" (vol. I, p. 197) when he says: "Those were evil times which chose such a man for a victim and heaped false charges upon him and drove him even temporarily from the rural home where he was illustrating the modest virtues of a private person."

It is easy to understand that with the removal of Governor Dongan from office in 1688 and the revolution which dethroned James II, the Jesuits in New York were without patrons and soon came to be the special subject of persecution on the part of the new rulers. Fathers Harvey and Harrison barely escaped from Leisler's hands in 1689. Father Harvey went to Maryland but in 1690 returned to New York with a brother Jesuit. Posing as a tutor, Father Harvey ministered surreptitiously to New York Catholics for over thirty years in spite of the risk of severe punishment. He was past seventy by this time and his health broke down so he returned to Maryland to die.

In 1700 an act of the Provincial Assembly was passed under William and Mary which was levelled against Jesuits and papish priests and continued in full force until the Revolution. The wording of that makes it very clear how bitter was the feeling of opposition to Catholicity and especially to Jesuits and other priests:

"Every Jesuit, seminary priest, missionary or other spiritual or ecclesiastical person, made or ordained by any authority, power or jurisdiction derived, challenged or pretended from the Pope or See of Rome, or that shall profess himself or otherwise appear to be such by practising or teaching of others to say any popish prayers, by celebrating of Masses, granting of absolutions, or using any other of the Romish ceremonies or rites of worship by what name, title or degree soever, such persons shall be called or known who shall continue, abide or come into this province or any part thereof after the first day of November (1700) aforesaid; shall be deemed and accounted an incendiary and disturber of the public peace and safety and a disturber of the true Christian religion and shall be adjudged to suffer perpetual punishment.

"And if any person being so sentenced and actually imprisoned shall break prison and make his escape and be afterwards taken; he shall suffer such pain of death, penalties and forfeitures as in case of felony."

It was under this act of the Provincial Assembly that John Ury was brought to trial in 1741, and was condemned to death "for being an ecclesiastical person made by authority pretended from the See of Rome and coming into and abiding in the province of New York."

As Martin I. J. Griffin says in his volume, "The Trial of John Ury" (Philadelphia, 1899) "Ury was believed to be a Roman Catholic priest, was tried as a Roman Catholic priest under a law intended to punish with death any Roman Catholic priest who entered the province of New York." Ury was not a Catholic priest but in the hysteria of that time when there was supposed to be a Negro plot to burn the City of New York in 1741 he was condemned to death and executed. "His trial shows the temper of the time toward Catholics. . . . A holy hatred of the Roman Catholics was inculcated by Church and State."

The state of toleration initiated by Governor Dongan in New

York toward the end of the seventeenth century, like that attempted by Lord Baltimore in Maryland in the first half of that century, was too far ahead of the times in which it was planned. Both Maryland and New York turned out failures as asylums for those persecuted for their faith or as homes of religious toleration for those who were weary of the state of affairs in Europe. After Governor Dongan was relieved from office, penal laws were passed expelling the Jesuits and other Catholic priests and it was enacted that priests "be deemed and accounted incendiaries, disturbers of the peace and safety of the province and enemies to the true Christian religion, and shall be adjudged to suffer perpetual imprisonment."

This law was not allowed to become a dead letter and could not be ignored so the Jesuits had to abandon their schools. New York during the eighteenth century became a hotbed of intolerance and bigotry, and about the middle of that century, in connection with the so-called insurrection of the slaves, poor John Ury, as I have said, was put to death on suspicion of being a priest. He was really, I believe, an Anglican minister but the suspicion of his Catholicity was sufficient to secure his condemnation.

FATHER KOHLMANN, S.J., AND THE PROFESSIONAL SECRET

There were no more Jesuits in New York, then, until after the Revolution, when for some years New York was an out mission from Philadelphia served by the ex-Jesuits from old St. Joseph's. Father Farmer used to come over to New York at regular intervals—it took several days to make the journey, on foot, on horseback and by boat—and he would stay for a time among the New York Catholics, thus affording an opportunity for them to go to Mass and receive the sacraments.

There were very few Catholics in New York at that time and most of them were very poor, many of them having come over as redemptioners, that is as ship passengers who had sold themselves to the captains of vessels to be auctioned off for a term of service to merchants or farmers who might need help for a sum equivalent to what they would have to pay for their passage. Many of these men succeeded admirably in spite of the handicaps under which they began life in America.

In 1808 a second attempt to establish a Jesuit school in New York was made under Father Kohlmann, S.J., who opened a school in Mulberry Street. Father Kohlmann had had some very interesting experiences in life. As a boy he had to leave Alsace, his birthplace, compelled, by the attitude of the French revolutionary government toward the Church, to live in Switzerland, where he made his theological studies and was ordained priest. He joined the Congregation of the Fathers of the Sacred Heart whose institute resembled that of the Jesuits. He labored for two years in Austria and Italy as a military chaplain and then was in Bavaria as a director of an ecclesiastical seminary and afterwards went to Berlin and then to Amsterdam to direct a college established by the fathers at Amsterdam. When Pope Pius VII recognized the Society of Jesus in Russia, Father Kohlmann entered the novitiate there and a year later was sent to Georgetown in the District of Columbia and from here he went on missionary tours to German congregations in Pennsylvania and Maryland.

As affairs in the Church in New York were disturbed, Bishop Carroll picked out Father Kohlmann as the person best qualified to bring about the needed reform. With Father Benedict Fenwick and four scholastics Father Kohlmann took up the work of making New York Catholics faithful. The Catholic population had been growing rapidly, especially by Irish immigration, but there were also some hundreds of French and as many Germans. In all, according to the common estimation, some fourteen thousand souls made up the congregation. Such progress was made under his direction that the cornerstone of old St. Patrick's, the second church erected in New York, was laid on June 8, 1809. He founded a classical school called the New York Literary Institution which he carried on successfully for several years with the aid of Jesuit scholastics. The school was located in what was then a suburban village but is now the site of St. Patrick's Cathedral (50th Street and Fifth Avenue). Some four years later

(1812) he opened a school for girls in the same neighborhood under the Ursuline nuns who came from their convent in Cork, Ireland, at his request. Some twenty years after this the academy of the Ursulines at Charlestown, Massachusetts, was burned down by a mob who came out from Boston for that purpose. Members of this same order founded at the beginning of the twentieth century the College of New Rochelle in which there are now more than eight hundred girls doing college work.

While thus providing facilities for education for both girls and boys in New York at a time when it may be recalled there were no free schools, Father Kohlmann exemplified in another way the application of Jesuit principles to freedom of conscience. A penitent in confession entrusted to him some stolen goods to be returned to their owner. The owner demanded that Father Kohlmann should reveal from whom he had received them. This Father Kohlmann refused to do on the grounds that information received under the seal of confession is privileged. The case was called before the Court of General Sessions where the decision rendered by DeWitt Clinton was in Father Kohlmann's favor.

The privileged character of information obtained through the confessional or in the ministration of clerical duties was some fifteen years later embodied in the State law, passed December 10, 1828, which enacted that: "No minister of the Gospel or priest of any denomination whatsoever shall be allowed to disclose any confession made to him in his professional character in the course of discipline enjoined by the rules or practices of such denomination."

Father Kohlmann took advantage of the publicity afforded by this legal trial and the curiosity aroused by it to publish an exposition of the teaching of the Church on the sacrament of Penance.[6] The book gave rise to a lengthy and quite vigorous controversy with a number of Protestant ministers, and Father Kohlmann followed it up in 1821 by the issuance of a learned theological work: "Unitarianism Theologically and Philosophically Considered." In this work Father Kohlmann replied to the

---

[6] "The Catholic Question in America," Sampson, New York, 1813.

assertions of Dr. Jared Sparks, the well-known American historian and president of Harvard, and other Unitarian leaders, for he had drawn the fire of some of the most distinguished thinkers in the Protestant Church in America.

The thoroughgoing appreciation of the intellectual capacity of Father Kohlmann among his brother Jesuits as well as among the prominent ecclesiastics of that time will be best appreciated from the fact that when Pope Leo XII restored the Gregorian University to the direction of the Society of Jesus, Father Kohlmann was summoned to Rome from Georgetown—where for some years he had been novice master and afterwards president of the college—to take the chair of theology which he filled for five years. This was considered one of the most important teaching positions in theology in all the Christian world. One of his pupils at the Gregorian University subsequently became pope under the title of Leo XIII, and is usually considered one of the greatest intellectual geniuses to occupy the papal chair in modern times.

Pope Leo XIII all during his long life continued to hold his Jesuit professor in high esteem and to praise his ability as a teacher. Both Pope Leo XII and Gregory XVI held Father Kohlmann in lofty estimation and appointed him consultor to several of the most important Congregations of the Church. The last part of his life the worthy Jesuit spent as a confessor in the Church of the Gesu in Rome. Here he was to be found hearing confessions at almost any hour of the day and sometimes well on into the night. His persecution in New York in connection with the sacrament of Penance seemed to have aroused in him a special affection for this work because of the immense consolation which it brought to so many people. The end of his life is said to have been hastened by his utter devotion to this sacred cause.

Father Kohlmann's career has a special interest in modern times because of his securing the privilege of professional secrecy. The incident is the last of a trio of instances in which the exertion of Jesuit influence for securing greater liberty for the mind is brought out very clearly. In each of these instances men were making history of the most significant kind. They were organizing an advance in civilization which was to be of very great importance. In all three the Jesuits were at the very center of the action—the guides, philosophers and friends of those who were accomplishing important steps in human advance.

CHAPTER III

JESUIT MARTYRS IN THE UNITED STATES

In 1930 the American world was not a little startled by the formal announcement from Rome that a group of men whose lives had been spent some two hundred and fifty years ago, mainly in New York and contiguous Canada, had been proclaimed saints by the Church. Their formal process of canonization, that is the definite court procedure conducted under oath by the Congregation of Rites in Rome as to their lives and writings, had been going on for many years but now it was definitely decided that a number of these men had deserved the appellation of martyr, since they had given their lives for their faith.

Most of those who were thus honored by being "raised to the altars" so that they might be invoked as intermediaries to the heavenly powers, were Jesuits, and almost needless to say the Jesuits throughout the world were deeply gratified at and very proud of the honor and distinction that had come to their brother members of the Order. Here were brothers in religion who in their self-sacrificing devotion had faced suffering and death after tortures almost unbelievable in the cause of the spread of Christianity. These men were not only to be admired distantly but to be emulated personally by the Jesuits of our day, two hundred and fifty years later.

Their lives were written once more and were read intensively by Jesuits all over the world. They were true members of the Company of Jesus as their founder had named them, ready like Christ Himself to die for His people who were not yet of the Faith. The Master had said, "If you will be perfect, deny yourself, take up your cross and follow Me." Here was an example, indeed a set of examples of the following of Christ taken very literally to heart by a group of men for whom there was no limit to the sacrifice they were willing to make.

The men thus raised to the dignity of sainthood were Jesuits who had given their lives to the sacred purpose of bringing into the fold of Christianity probably the most savage Indians in the world. It was their definite purpose also to bring earthly peace and happiness into the lives of these barbarous people just as far as that was possible. In the first chapter of this book we have retold Professor Bolton's story of what Father Kino did for the civilization of his Indians in Pimería Alta (Arizona). This was what was done even more splendidly a hundred years later by the Franciscans when they founded the missions in southern California. They wanted to give the Indians an opportunity to have life and have it more abundantly, not only here but hereafter. The Jesuits in northern New York worked among savages more brutal than those encountered by their Jesuit and Franciscan brother missionaries in the distant Southwest. The result was that they suffered awful tortures and eventually death, yet all of them up to the last moment of their lives were ready to say in the words of their Master, "Father forgive them for they know not what they do."

Father Jogues, the best known in the United States of these Jesuit martyrs because of his close relations at one time with the Dutch in New Amsterdam, knew exactly what he might expect on the missions of New York and Canada. He had gone through what was almost worse than death in a preceding experience and yet he was perfectly willing and even anxious to try his fate once more among the Iroquois. He was intent on accomplishing the great purpose of his life—the imitation of Christ in spreading Christianity. What would happen to him in the fulfilment of that purpose, even though it might be death, was a matter of indifference to him; holy indifference this attitude of mind was called in his novitiate years as a Jesuit.

At college he had become very much interested in the heroic deeds of the Jesuit missionaries in many parts of the world. He was impressed above all by the burning to death in Japan of Father Charles Spinola of the Society of Jesus in 1622 for no other reason except the preaching of the Faith. The contemplation of this martyrdom inspired Father Jogues with a strong desire to do missionary work of similar character even though it might cost him his life.

Part of his Jesuit training, as it is of all young scholastics as they are called, was to teach for several years during the period between the completion of his philosophic studies and the beginning of his studies in theology. He became a teacher, then, at the College of Rouen in France in 1629. It so happened that at this particular time there were stationed at the college the three missionaries who had recently returned from Canada, Father Brébeuf, Father Lalemant and Father Massé. All these men had suffered severely in their missionary experiences in the New World but they were not only willing but anxious to return. On his subsequent missionary expedition among the Iroquois Brébeuf was most dreadfully tortured by the savages and put to death before the eyes of Lalemant who had his turn in the sufferings almost immediately afterwards.

Reverend Father Scott, S.J., in his biography, "Isaac Jogues, Missionary and Martyr" (New York, 1927) expresses the thought of the modern Jesuit as to these brothers of the old time: "These ardent apostles of the Gospel were awaiting the opportunity of returning to the scene of their sufferings and labors among the savages in the New World. From their lips Jogues heard of the privations, hardships, treacheries and tortures which ordinarily awaited the missioners who ventured among these cruel dwellers of the forest. Far from discouraging him the recital of the horrible conditions confronting the missioner in these distant lands only served to increase his desire to devote himself to labor there for the conversion and welfare of the natives." He was so intent on the missions that when he was sent for his last studies to the college of Clermont in Paris he asked to be allowed to withdraw from the study of theology under the pretext of want of ability so that he might be sent to America as a lay brother. Shortly after his ordination Jogues received what was for him the grateful news that his prayer was granted and that he was selected as one of the missionaries who were to go to far-off

Canada. He wrote his mother a most touching letter, for he was a son who truly loved his parents and who found the hardest feature of his missionary life the wrench of the home ties. He had tried to console them by saying, "Men for a little gain across the seas endure at least as much as we; shall we not for God's love do what men do for earthly interests?"

Father Jogues was a man of fine taste in literature, studious and talented, selected because of this as the professor of literature in the Jesuit college at Rouen. After his selection as a missionary he came out to America with Montmagny, the immediate successor of Champlain in the governorship of the province. He landed at Quebec and from there went to the distant regions around the Great Lakes where he was in constant danger from the savage Indians who were nearly always at war with one another and whose greatest delight in life was to torture prisoners. Jogues soon became noted for his boldness and hardihood amid the trying conditions but he was an intensely practical man and his great purpose was, if possible, to settle the Indians in more or less permanent habitations where they might practise the Christian religion and gradually advance in civilization. Fathers Jogues and Raymbault succeeded in penetrating through the continent as far as Sault Ste. Marie. Bancroft, the American historian, said of them that "They were the first missionaries to preach the Gospel a thousand miles in the interior five years before John Eliot addressed the Indians six miles from Boston harbor."

There is almost no doubt left that they were not only the first apostles to find their way into this region but also the first white men to reach this outlet of Lake Superior. Jogues proposed not only to convert the Indians at Lake Superior but, going far beyond that to the headwaters of the Mississippi, to convert the Sioux, the immense tribes of the prairies and mountains of whom he had heard traditions. He was actually planning these western expeditions when he was taken prisoner August, 1642, by the Iroquois and after being cruelly tortured was carried to the Indian village which is now known as Auriesville forty miles from Albany. He remained over a year in captivity and slavery, suffering what was apparently beyond the power of natural endurance.

Many other Jesuits suffered as he did, as we learn from the Jesuit Relations, but the Jesuits never despaired and never were ready to give up their work as missionaries. Parkman in "The Jesuits in North America" (Boston, 1867, p. 316) quotes from one of the letters of the Jesuit Father Superior: "Do not imagine that the rage of the Iroquois, the loss of many Christians and many catechumens, can bring to naught the mystery of the Cross of Christ and the efficacy of His blood. We shall die; we shall be captured, burned, butchered; be it so. Those who die in their beds do not always die the best death. I see none of our Company (Jesuits) cast down. On the contrary they ask leave to go up to the Hurons and some of them protest that the fires of the Iroquois are one of their motives for the journey."

At the end of more than a year of imprisonment Father Jogues with the help of the Dutch Calvinists at Fort Orange escaped just after the Indians had in formal council decided to burn him to death. He found refuge in a sailing vessel which carried him to New Amsterdam (New York). The Dutch Calvinist minister, Dominie Megapolensis, proved his best friend. Jogues' description of Manhattan as it was at that time forms an extremely interesting chapter in Dr. O'Callaghan's "Documentary History of New York." From here, after some delay, he found his way in a sailing vessel of only fifty tons burden across the ocean. His hands had been so seriously mutilated by the Iroquois, some of his fingers actually having been burnt off, that it required special permission from Pope Urban VIII for him to celebrate Mass. The pope said, "It would be wrong to prevent the martyr of Christ from drinking the blood of Christ." Reverend Father Campbell, S.J., in his life of Father Jogues in "Pioneer Priests of North America" (Fordham University Press, 1908) says: "It is noteworthy that this quasi-canonization was pronounced by Urban VIII, the very pope who laid down such stringent laws with regard to the canonization of saints," and who forbade the use of terms that would imply sanctity and martyrdom except after due process of investigation and formal canonization.

Parkman in his "Jesuits in North America" (p. 298) tells that when Father Jogues was making up his mind to again offer himself for missionary work among the Iroquois he had a presentiment that he would never return alive: "At first nature asserted itself and he recoiled involuntarily at the thought of the horrors of which his scarred body and his mutilated hands were a living memento." He overcame this by prayer but felt that he would never come back alive. He even went so far as to write to friends, "I shall go and I shall not return."

Two years later Jogues returned to Canada at his own request and in 1646 was sent to negotiate peace with the Iroquois. He followed the same route over which he had been carried as a captive. He passed through Lake George and called it the Lake of the Blessed Sacrament. He reached what is now Auriesville after three weeks' journey from the St. Lawrence. He was well received by his former captors and a treaty of peace between them and the French Canadians was successfully concluded. On his return to Quebec Father Jogues asked to be sent back to the Iroquois as a missionary. Only after much hesitation did his superiors consent. When he reached the Iroquois they were in a very different mood from that in which he had left them at the time of the treaty. Sickness had broken out and a blight had fallen on their crops. The Indians regarded Jogues as a sorcerer and blamed their misfortunes on him. The Iroquois met him near Lake George, stripped him naked, slashed him with their knives, beat him and then led him to the village. On October 18, 1646, entering a cabin, he was struck with a tomahawk and afterwards decapitated. His head was fixed on the palisade and his body was thrown into the Mohawk.

After giving the details of Jogues' death, Parkman (p. 304) said: "Thus died Jogues, one of the purest examples of Roman Catholic virtue which the western continent has seen. The priests, his associates, praise his humility and tell us that it reached the point of self-contempt—a crowning virtue in their eyes; that he regarded himself as nothing and lived solely to do the will of God as uttered by his superiors. They add that when left to the guidance of his own judgment his self-distrust made him very slow of decision but that when acting under orders he knew neither hesitation nor fear."

The Jesuits all look upon themselves as soldiers in an army. St. Ignatius, who was thoroughly military in his outlook upon the world, called his associates not the Society of Jesus but the Company of Jesus—he even used to like to talk of it as the Little Company. It is easy to understand, though Parkham finds it difficult to comprehend, that Jogues was the perfect soldier in his thoroughgoing compliance with orders as issued to him and with his distrust of himself when not under orders.

Parkman has made up for his lack of understanding in another passage: "With all his gentleness Jogues had a certain warmth or vivacity of temperament; and we have seen how during his first captivity while humbly submitting to every caprice of his tyrants and appearing to rejoice in abasement, a derisive word against his Faith would change the lamb into the lion and his lips that seemed so tame would speak in sharp bold tones of menace and reproof."

Jogues' martyrdom is only a type of what happened to the other Jesuit martyrs. One of the most striking among them was Father Jean de Brébeuf, who displayed all the fortitude of the early Christian martyrs in the midst of the tortures that the Iroquois inflicted on them. When captured by the Iroquois he made it his main occupation to encourage the others and the Christian Hurons around him assured him that they would be faithful. Campbell in his "Pioneer Priests in North America" (vol. 2, p. 171) describes the torture that ended his life. Brébeuf had experienced the awful savagery of the Iroquois, had been sent back to France to recuperate where his meeting with Jogues, as we have told, sent that indomitable soul on the American missions. Brébeuf pleaded to be allowed to go back to the dangers and hardships of the missions and find the martyrdom he craved.

The influence that Brébeuf had come to exercise over the

Indians has been told very well by Parkman in his "Jesuits in North America." On returning from one of his expeditions he came to one of the Huron villages: "A crowd ran out to meet him. Echom (their name for him) has come again! Echom has come again! they cried, recognizing in the distance the stately figure robed in black that advanced from the border of the woods. They led him to the town and the whole population swarmed about him. After a short rest he set out with a number of young Indians in quest of his baggage which he had hidden away. There was a certain Awandoay in the village noted as one of the richest and most hospitable of the Hurons—a distinction not easily won where hospitality was universal. His house was large and amply stored with beans and corn; and though his prosperity had excited the jealousy of the villagers he had recovered their good will by his generosity. With him Brébeuf made his abode anxiously waiting week after week the arrival of his companions. One by one they appeared, Daniel weary and worn, Davost half dead with famine and fatigue, and their French attendants, each with his tale of hardship and indignity. At length all were assembled under the roof of the hospitable Indian and once more the Huron mission was begun."

Brébeuf came of a noble race—the same, it is said, from which sprang the English Earls of Arundel—but never had the male barons of his line confronted a fate so appalling with so prodigious a constancy. To the last he refused to flinch, and his death was the astonishment of his murderers. They came in a crowd to drink the blood of so valiant an enemy, thinking to imbibe with it some portion of his courage. . . . A chief tore out his heart and devoured it. (Parkman.)

Parkman, who probably never met a Jesuit in the flesh in his life, cannot keep himself from uttering the slur that comes to him with regard to a state of mind that he manifestly cannot understand. The details of his life which Parkman knew very well made him realize that Brébeuf was a very practical man and yet he could not help but think, since he risked his life among the savages and since his religious training enabled him to withstand all torments without a cringe, that there must be something uncanny about him. As Parkman puts it, "Extravagant as were the chimeras which fed the fires of his soul, they were consistent with the soberest of good sense in matters of practical bearing."

Parkman has given a brief résumé of the characters of these French Jesuits who were so willing to devote themselves to the missions among the Indians of North America. He has been particularly enthusiastic over the character of Father Charles Garnier, who was such a contrast to Brébeuf—"that masculine apostle of the Faith, the Ajax of the mission." Parkman says: "Nature had given Brébeuf all the passions of a vigorous manhood and religion had crushed them, curbed them or tamed them to do her work—like a dammed up torrent sluiced and guided to grind and saw and weave for the good of man."

The characterization of Garnier which follows is a striking contrast:

"Both were of noble birth and gentle nurture; but here the parallel ends. Garnier's face was beardless though he was above thirty years old. For this he was laughed at by his friends in Paris but admired by the Indians who thought him handsome. His constitution bodily or mental was by no means robust. From boyhood he had shown a delicate and sensitive nature, a tender conscience and a proneness to religious emotion. He had never gone with his schoolmates to inns and other places of amusement but kept his pocket money to give to beggars. One of his brothers relates of him that seeing an obscene book he bought and destroyed it lest other boys should be injured by it."

Garnier was born in Paris and went to the Jesuit colleges. From early years he wished to become a Jesuit and at the age of eighteen entered the order. He desired above all to be sent on the foreign missions so after his ordination he was sent to Canada where he spent some fourteen years and then was slain during the Iroquois attack on St. John's village.

Parkman says of him: "The Church indeed absorbed the greater part if not the whole of this pious Garnier family,—one brother being a Carmelite, another a Capuchin and a third a Jesuit while a fourth seems to have also taken vows." Of the twenty-four letters that were written by Father Garnier at various times to his father and brothers, it may be said that they are models of missionary fervor: "They breathe the deepest and most intense Roman Catholic piety and a spirit enthusiastic yet sad as of one renouncing all the hopes and prizes of the world and living for heaven alone. The affections of his sensitive nature severed from earthly objects found relief in an ardent adoration of the Virgin Mary. With none of the bone and sinew of rugged manhood he entered not only without hesitation but with eagerness on a life which would have tried the boldest; and sustained by the spirit within him he was more than equal to it. His fellow missionaries thought him a saint; and had he lived a century or two earlier he would have perhaps been canonized." (Parkman in his time was inclined to think that canonization was a thing of the past, but had he lived into another generation he would have been among those who heard the news of Garnier's canonization.)

Parkman says further of him, "While all his life was a willing martyrdom, one can discern amid his admirable virtues some slight lingerings of mortal vanity. Thus in three several letters he speaks of his great success in baptizing and plainly intimates that he had sent more souls to heaven than the other Jesuits." It is rather amusing to have Parkman find almost a serious fault in such a harmless bit of vanity—if indeed it can be called vanity under the circumstances. Surely that may be excused in a man who made such sacrifices as Garnier, whose family was wealthy as well as noble, and who might have lived a life of ease and comfort at home had he wished it. The members of the family, as always happens when there are members of religious orders among them, were strongly attached to one another. The young man's father was greatly distressed at his departure for Canada. The family knew what he must endure in his missionary labors, they felt for him deeply but he himself was intent on only one thing, the making of sacrifices for others regardless of himself. He knew that he faced martyrdom and it came to him in its own time.

Brébeuf and Garnier were sons of the nobility. The next of the Jesuits whom Parkman considers is Joseph Marie Chaumo-

not, who unlike Brébeuf and Garnier was of humble origin, his
father being a vine dresser and his mother the daughter of a
poor village schoolmaster. At an early age his family sent him
to Chatillon on the Seine where he lived with his uncle a priest
who taught him to speak Latin and who cultivated in him a
spirit of piety that was already strong in his soul. He had the
spirit of adventure in him and wandered off from his uncle's
house through many towns begging from door to door, sleeping
under sheds by the waysides or in haystacks, now and then
securing lodging and a meal at a convent. He had heard of the
Holy House of Loretto and he set out for that shrine. After
his pilgrimage there was over in the course of his further wanderings he made his confession in Latin to a Jesuit priest and the
Jesuit finding that his acquirements were considerable employed
him as an assistant teacher in the Jesuit school. A strong desire
grew up within Chaumonot to become a Jesuit and at the age
of twenty-one he was admitted to the Jesuit novitiate. While
there he read one of the Jesuit Relations from the Canadian missions and burning to share in those glorious sufferings of the
missionaries he asked to be sent to Canada after his ordination
and his request was granted. In spite of all his labors and hardships he lived to be seventy-two years of age and accomplished
an immense amount of good on the missions.

Another of these Jesuit martyrs was Gabriel Lalemant who
was born at Paris in 1610 and died in Canada in 1649. At the
age of twenty he entered the Society of Jesus (1630) and after
his ordination in 1646 he came to Canada as assistant to Father
Brébeuf. With him he suffered a horrible martyrdom, the hideous
details of which are almost incredible. He was to be burned to
death but when fastened to the stake as he still continued to
turn his gaze toward heaven and seemed to derive some consolation from that, his eyes were torn out and burning coals thrust
into the sockets; in order to prevent him from speaking or pray-
ing firebrands were not only placed in his mouth but forced
down into his throat. When he lifted his hands in prayer they
beat them down with clubs and forced him to his feet again
when he attempted to kneel. They refrained while torturing

him from touching any vital part but of course the prolongation
of his agony was worse than death itself. The Indians did not
permit their victims to die between sunset and sunrise, but after
having been under torture from six A. M. to nine P. M. the
Indians wearied of their work and crushed his skull with the
blow of a tomahawk.

Father Lalemant was the greatest possible contrast to Father
Brébeuf and yet he met the fate that was in store for him with
a steadfastness that was even more admirable than that of
Brébeuf because it was more human and he could not suppress
all evidences of the pain that the torture of his enemies inflicted
on him. Lalemant had been physically delicate from his childhood, indeed it was scarcely expected that he would live to
manhood, yet though he was slender almost to emaciation, his
missionary experiences in the woods and along the rivers and
lakes proved beneficial rather than harmful to him. The Indians
compelled him to look on while they were torturing Brébeuf to
death. Brébeuf's hardihood and unflinching tolerance of the worst
suffering that the Iroquois Indians could invent, tempted the
Indians to try such extreme cruelties on him that death came at
the end of four hours. Recognizing the delicacy of Lalemant,
they were more careful in their choice of torments and he is said
to have survived under the torture for nearly seventeen hours.

Some idea of the sort of life that these French missionaries, so
many of them gently born and delicately brought up, had to
stand among the Indians is very well illustrated by a paragraph
from Campbell's first volume "Pioneer Priests of North America" in the introduction:

"The Indians' personal habits were filthy in the extreme.
Bruyas speaks of that as one of his tortures. They ate the most
disgusting things and boasted of their prowess in this regard.
Yet though voracious gluttons they starved uncomplainingly
when food was lacking—which was often. They knew nothing
of the laws of health though Lafitau tells us of their use of
lotions and poultices and attributes to them some skill in setting
bones and in making incisions with their stone knives, but the
reader of the Relations will find such medical treatment rare.

Incantations are mostly in evidence and some of the results achieved by the medicine men as well as some of their predictions were so startling that they were attributed by the missionaries to diabolical intervention. Mostly, however, their sorcerers were ridiculous charlatans."

Father Campbell pictures also the moral side of the Iroquois which it is easy to understand must have proved quite as disgusting to the good Jesuits as the ugly physical life which the Indians lived:

"Morally the Iroquois were very degraded and the abominations of the villages are only hinted at in the Relations. They were thieves and gamblers of course. There was no reason for their being polygamists because their marriages which the mothers of the parties concerned generally arranged could be broken at will. The women were corrupt from girlhood and after a few years became degraded and hideous drudges. At times, however, the girls were consulted by the council and in certain contingencies could nominate a chief. The children were never punished and were allowed to grow up like animals.

"Their cruelty which was fiendish in the extreme was made worse by an affectation of tenderness for their victim even while they were burning and gashing his limbs or making him writhe in agony at the stake. It is not generally adverted to, but they were atrocious cannibals. De Lamberville informs us that six hundred captives were killed and eaten in a single expedition against the Illinois. Even little children would be plucked from the mother's breast and boiled and eaten. Radisson gives us some details which the priests do not dare to describe. The head and heart of the victim was the portion of the chief, the carcass was tossed to the crowd."

Hardships quite literally meant nothing to these Jesuits though so often they had been brought up in rather affluent or at least comfortable circumstances and many of them had been for years teachers in some of the best known colleges of Europe. Reverend James J. O'Brien in his story of "The Louisiana and Mississippi Martyrs" (New York, 1933) quotes the expressions of a naval officer of the time which has been preserved for us in the

"Relation de la Louisiane au Mississippi." He understood thoroughly how much they had to go through and he had had some of these experiences himself so that he was poignantly aware of how much courage and hardihood it required to go on with work of this kind. He said: "I cannot help doing justice to the Jesuit Fathers in regard to their missions. Nothing is more edifying to religion than their conduct and the unwearied zeal with which they labor for the conversion of these nations. Picture to yourself a Jesuit four hundred leagues away in the forest, with no conveniences, no provisions, and most frequently with no resources but the liberality of the people who know not God, compelled to live like them, to pass whole years without receiving any tidings of his country, with savages who have only the countenances of human beings, among whom instead of finding society and relief in sickness he is daily exposed to perish and be massacred. This is done daily by these fathers in Louisiana and Canada where many have shed their blood for their faith."

At least five of the Jesuits who were working in the Louisiana district were martyred, that is were put to death by the Indians because of their faith and their teaching of religion which aroused bitter enmity in the minds of the Indians, especially the medicine men. Father Paul du Poisson was tomahawked, Father John Souel was shot to death, Father Anthony Sénat was burned at the stake. These men knew that they were running danger of death at all times. They were prepared for it but that did not make them any the less ready to proceed with their missionary labors and do whatever they could to lift the Indians out of the barbarism and superstition in which they were sunk. We may make a simple biographic sketch of one of them, Father Paul Du Poisson, which may serve as a symbol of the others. He entered the Society of Jesus at Nancy September 11, 1711, at the age of nineteen. For some five years he studied at the College of Charleville and the College of Metz. Then he taught at Chalons-sur-Marne for some five years until 1722 when he was at the College of La Fleche for some two years. Then he was several years in Paris. In a word, he had had study and teaching experiences at the most important French colleges. He asked to be sent to Louisiana and reached there at the age of thirty-six, only to meet his death the following year.

No wonder that we hear that the cause of canonization of such men has been opened, that is that the ecclesiastical and legal process of securing testimony to the fact that they lived lives of heroic virtue has been begun and that the formal inquest as to whether definite special favors have been granted through their intercession was initiated. These men were not fanatics in any sense of the word. They were, on the contrary, very lovable individuals who lived the community life of the Jesuits for years and who had won the golden opinion of those intimately associated with them. They were often the best liked in the community. We hear, for instance, of Father Du Poisson, that he was one of the most amiable of priests, in the flower of his age, noted for his intellectual capacity as well as for his readiness to be helpful to others whenever opportunity offered. A bystander reports that as he fell he was heard to utter the words, "Ah my God! Ah my God!" just before he expired.

What has been said of Father Du Poisson in this regard might be said of Fathers Souel and Sénat. They were picked men of the choicest members of their Order, known for their mental powers but particularly for their virtue and piety. They had asked to be sent on the missions knowing that the fate of martyred Brébeuf and Jogues might be in store for them but they were only tempted the more by that thought, for they deliberately courted martyrdom in the hope that their bloodshed would bring about the conversion of the Indians, for they took Tertullian's apothegm quite literally "the blood of martyrs is the seed of Christianity."

Thus to the ignorant savages the Jesuits devoted their lives. Themselves men sometimes of noble birth, often of good breeding and scholarly education, trained by more than a dozen years of study that fitted them to be teachers in the colleges and universities of Europe, they were now giving their time and mental energy to the Indians. Their experiences told in simple letters home were read to the communities of all the important Jesuit houses in Europe. Instead of deterring the young members of the Order from risking such possibilities of serious suffering and even of death, the tales told by the missionaries aroused them to emulate their brothers in the foreign missionary field. This was the Jesuit spirit. These men who suffered so much were the most admired members of the Order whose deeds were in benediction among their co-members everywhere throughout the world. Candidates came forward to join the Order in ever-increasing numbers, and one of the incentives to this growth was undoubtedly the stories from the distant missions which stimulated young men to take up their cross and follow the Master in the glorious Company of Jesus which had achieved such wonderful things all over the world.

CHAPTER IV

THE JESUIT RELATIONS

The Jesuit missionaries were all men of trained intelligence, most of them representing the pick of the Jesuit schools, for one of the most significant features of the growth of the Jesuits is that not a few of their best students join the Order. This is the heartiest compliment they could pay to their masters whom they learned to respect during the years when they were in intimate contact with them. It is not surprising to find that in the course of their missionary work in distant countries and among strange peoples these men made original observations that were of special significance from many social and scientific standpoints. Very often they were the first white men to have prolonged contacts with the natives among whom their missionary labors were accomplished. The Jesuits knew their neophytes very well before they came under the influence of artificial civilization and the disturbing ways of civilized men.

The missionaries were accustomed to send letters home to their superiors containing intimate details of their experiences on the missions. These were familiar but not trivial. They told of everything that attracted the attention of the Fathers. When these "Edifying Letters," or as they were called later, "Jesuit Relations," were published they came to be looked upon not only as precious historical documents but also as contributions to science and literature because of the original observations on natural history and on the ways of men which they contained. As a result of the recognition of this fact the "Jesuit Relations" have been issued in a number of complete and condensed editions and have proved valuable source books of materials for American ethnology and anthropology, for botany, folklore, geography, as well as for the history and especially the languages of the people with whom the Jesuits were brought in contact in the course of their missionary labors.

The letters sent by Father Kino, S.J., and other missionaries from the southwest of what is now the United States to their superiors in Rome nearly three centuries ago are striking examples of these "Jesuit Relations" as they concern our American history. On the other hand the letters sent by the French Jesuit missionaries who devoted themselves to the conversion of the savage Iroquois and others of the Six Nations in New York and Canada are among the impressive adventure stories of the world.

This custom of having the missionaries write letters home to their brother Jesuits in their native country has continued down to the present time. There are letters from Alaska and from various missions under the equator in the Philippines and in the West Indies, written in our generation, that are as full of adventure and stories of peril to life as those from the Spanish or French missionaries over two hundred and fifty years ago. The Jesuits have not changed in any way, they continue to do their missionary work in the same spirit, and the notes of their adventures as read to their brother Jesuits in the refectories and recreation rooms in the distant homelands attract just as much attention now as they did in the older time.

In spite of the hardships which they chronicle and the tales of the trials through which the missionaries are compelled to go in the course of their labors, these letters of theirs evoke as many vocations to the missions as they did in the long ago. Many a young man who entered the Jesuits with the definite idea that his life was to be spent in quiet havens of peace for study and teaching finds himself stirred a few years later to emulation of the self-sacrificing devotion to the cause of Christianity of his brother Jesuits. After careful consideration in thoughtful prayer and consultation over the subject he offers himself for the distant difficult missions. Youth—women as well as men—when the idea suggests itself of taking up hard tasks for an ideal, responds as well now as at any time in the history of Christianity.

The "Jesuit Relations" originated as the result of instructions given by St. Francis Xavier, the great Jesuit missionary, to his missionary companions in the Far East. He directed Father Beira to send to Ignatius in Rome and Rodriguez in Lisbon, that is to the Father General and Father Provincial "such news as when known in Europe would make everyone that heard it give glory to God." Whenever these letters were not in Latin they were translated into that language and extracts from them were published as "Annual Letters of the Society of Jesus to the Fathers and Brothers of the Same Society." These constitute what are generally known as the "Relations." [1]

The best known of these missionary communications to their superiors, then, are the letters of the French missionaries to Canada, some few of which were written by missionaries among the Indians in what is now New York State. These have proved a rich mine of information in early American history. Practically all our historical writers have taken advantage of the information they afford. Parkman declares, "They hold a high place as authentic and trustworthy documents." Parkman himself, Bancroft, Kip, Field, Dr. John Finlay and other well-known historical writers, have drawn freely from them and they are looked

[1] These earliest "Edifying Letters" or Jesuit Relations now command very high prices in the book stores. Maggs Bros., the well-known London booksellers, in one of their recent catalogs, advertise "Early Jesuit Mission Letters from Japan and China" (Lisbon, 1598). This work is in two volumes bound in one thick quarto and the price is £225 which at the present value of exchange is well above $1,000. The catalog states that the only copies of the work that are known beside this one which they offer for sale are in Lisbon, Evora, Coimbra, Oporto, in the British Museum, and the Library of King Manuel of Portugal, at Fullwell Park in England. A single other copy, location unascertained, is known to be in existence in Brazil. The letters are declared to be a rich mine of valuable information on the Far East, such as had not until then reached Europe. The catalog adds:

"The literary style of the writers and their shrewd observations on the facts which they relate make the work an interesting study of Oriental affairs in the sixteenth century."

The letters are from St. Francis Xavier, the apostle of the East; Father Cosme de Torres; Padre Alexandro Valeguano, the provincial for India, and others. Some of the letters were addressed to Ignatius, the founder and General of the Jesuits, and some of them to Don Theatino de Braganza, archbishop of Evora, at whose instance the work was published. These were the first Jesuit Relations and they served as a model for the others.

upon as the most authentic historical documents with regard to the Indians before and after the coming of the white man to this continent.

The letters written by Jesuit missionaries among the Indians of New York and Canada were sent to their superiors in Montreal and were forwarded by them to the provincial of the Jesuits in France. Beginning with 1632 these were published annually for some forty years (1632-1673) through Cramoisy, the well-known publisher of Paris, under the title "Jesuit Relations." The books came to be popular reading during the latter half of the seventeenth century and then as books have their fates disappeared from view to a very great extent until about the middle of the nineteenth century when attention was called to their great value as historical authorities. They had been read in the seventeenth century almost as romances or tales of the wide open spaces, and they lend themselves effectively to that sort of reading, but they are ever so much more than that for they give first-hand personal accounts of the Indians as they lived in what is now the United States and Canada before the coming of the white man to settle the country and during the years before the white man in his advance westward pushed the Indians ahead of him off their ancestral domains.

Modern interest in the "Jesuit Relations" is due more to Dr. Edmund Bailey O'Callaghan than to any other. He was a graduate of the University of Bordeaux to which he had gone because the penal laws forbade opportunities for medical education for Catholics in his native Ireland. He settled in Montreal and built up a successful practice, but he had to flee from Canada with a price on his head as a traitor because of the part that he took in the Papineau rebellion of 1837, precipitated by the impositions of the English government on the French Canadian population. Dr. O'Callaghan settled in Albany, New York, and became the historian of the State of New York and of the City of New York, issuing altogether some twenty volumes on these subjects. His researches very soon brought him to recognize the value of the "Jesuit Relations" as providing the material for the background of the history of New York. He called the attention of

Mr. James Lenox, founder of the Lenox Library, to the value of these books and Mr. Lenox proceeded to gather the best collection of them in the world in the Lenox Library which has since become part of the Tilden-Astor-Lenox Foundation which merged into the New York Public Library.[2]

Dr. O'Callaghan made a special study of these volumes and published "Jesuit Relations (A Descriptive Pamphlet)" (New York, 1847). It was subsequently published as a small volume in French in Montreal in 1850. This attracted the attention of historical students generally to these precious Americana and the "Jesuit Relations" came to be known all over the world. Dr. O'Callaghan gave in his pamphlet a succinct account not only of the contents of the separate volumes but he also indicated where the rare volumes might be found in this country. A few of them existed practically in single copies in private libraries and their owners began to be disturbed by historical students who wanted to consult them. Dr. O'Callaghan's essay was read before the New York Historical Society. It remains to this day the best introduction to the "Jesuit Relations" that we have.

From his studies Dr. O'Callaghan pointed out that the Jesuits were well and intimately acquainted with the country from the Delaware and the Susquehanna on the south up to the St. Law-

---

[2] Some idea of the money value which has been placed on the American "Jesuit Relations" as the result of the recognition of their worth as original historical documents in American history, may be gathered from the prices which copies of the earlier "Relations" command in the auction rooms and at private sales. After the O'Callaghan sale in which these volumes of Relations went for good substantial prices, some of them even to $100 or more, the special attention of bibliographers and book-lovers was called to them. The Church collection next caught the public eye and passed into the hands of Mr. Dodd of Dodd Mead & Co. to be sold subsequently to Mr. Huntington for his library in Pasadena at a price that was not made public but that was understood to be much higher than the average prices up to that time. Prices for the various issues have more than doubled. The American Prices Current (1930), an annual for booksellers, shows prices still mounting. Special copies of the "Jesuit Relations" were sold that year for $175, $265, and even $290. This last was bid for "La Vie de la Venerable Mere Marie de l'Incarnation." Miss Agnes Repplier, well-known American essayist, used a subsequent edition of this for a biographical sketch of Mere Marie which was selected for distribution by the Book of the Month Club and which proved to be a best seller because of the life of adventure and charity which is told so vividly.

rence and from the Great Lakes to the Atlantic sea coast. He says:

"Such a field could not but afford abundant material for the reflective mind and observant eye. New men in an unknown country, new languages and strange manners, all were to be studied, analyzed, explored and noted down and every favorable circumstance and event was at the same time to be taken advantage of to wean the wild inhabitants from their wandering ways and draw them insensibly to the practices of civilized life."

The Jesuits were eminently well qualified by their previous college and university training for this work and they came to it developed in such a way as to make the opportunity for original observation prove a factor in enabling them to put before their young men the great task of disseminating knowledge. Dr. O'Callaghan realized what thoroughly educated and trained observers the Jesuits were—he had known them by personal acquaintance in Canada, and therefore appreciated that their documentary evidence as to what they had seen and experienced among the Indians could not fail but prove very precious for subsequent generations. He said of them: "Fortunately the early Jesuits were men of learning and observation. They felt deeply the importance of their position and while acquitting themselves thoroughly of the duties of their calling as missionaries carefully recorded whatever they saw novel in the country or its inhabitants. We are thus made acquainted with the actual condition of the aborigines (at the time when the whites first came in contact with them) and are enabled to trace distinctively the causes which led to their gradual but natural disappearance from this continent."

Dr. O'Callaghan dwelt on the discoveries which had been made by these Jesuits but pointed out also how careful they were to substantiate whenever it was possible the stories told them by the Indians. When they accepted tales on hearsay they noted that fact as carefully as Herodotus in his history and left them, as did the great father of history, to be authenticated by subsequent observations:

"It is to one of these that we owe the discovery of the rich

and inexhaustible salt springs of Onondaga, an event so unexpected by the Dutch in New Amsterdam that they pronounced
the story of it when they first heard it a 'Jesuit lie.'"

The Jesuits were right, however, and the Dutch wrong, but
then they were used to getting a supply of salt from the ocean
and could scarcely think of salt sources so far inland from the
sea.

Dr. O'Callaghan notes others of the Jesuit achievements and
among other things said: "Five years before Eliot of New England (the Puritan Indian missionary) had said a single word to
the Indians within six miles of Boston harbor, the French missionaries planted the Cross at Sault Ste. Marie on Lake Superior.
From here they looked down on the Sioux country in the valley
of the Mississippi. The vast and unknown west now opened its
prairies before them. The Wisconsin and Fox rivers are discovered. The Illinois country and its vast tribes are visited.
Finally in 1673 the Jesuit Marquette crowned the labors of his
Order and his age by the discovery of the Father of Waters, the
mighty Mississippi."

After O'Callaghan's renewal of interest in them, the Canadian
government in 1858 reissued the Cramoisy series of "Jesuit Relations," and not quite ten years later Parkman in his volume,
"The Jesuits in North America," which was Part II of "France
and England in North America" (Boston, 1867) drew on the
"Jesuit Relations" very abundantly for his history. Miss Edna
Kenton in her "The Indians of North America" (Harcourt Brace
& Co., New York, 1927) says that Parkman "retold the story of
these explorers, ethnologists, anthropologists, scientists, astronomers, linguists, economists, historians, essayists, martyrs and
saints,"—for such these Jesuits proved to be to anyone who read
the "Jesuit Relations" with an eye to the scientific and human
value of their contents.

Soon this Canadian Cramoisy reprint was almost as difficult
to secure as the original edition of the "Relations." The Burrows
Bros. Co. of Cleveland, Ohio, took up in 1894 the huge task of
reprinting all of the "Jesuit Relations" and allied documents
under the editorship of Reuben Gold Thwaites, the secretary of

the State Historical Society of Wisconsin. He included all the Relations that had been edited by Dr. O'Callaghan, Gilmary Shea, Lenox, Martin, Rochemonteix, Father Jones and others, together with some additional material obtained from the "Lettres Édifiantes," the "Litteræ Annuæ," "Le Journal des Jesuites," and other sources that would serve to throw light on the history of the Jesuit missions in New York and Canada.

Burrows Bros. edition consisted of seventy-three octavo volumes of which altogether only seven hundred and fifty copies were issued. They appeared about a volume a month from 1896 to 1901. This edition has now become very difficult to obtain but it is looked upon as a most valuable source of information with regard to the Indians and the environment in which they were placed. Miss Edna Kenton in her abbreviation of these Jesuit Relations in two volumes under the title "The Indians of North America" has described very well all that the Jesuits did. The Jesuits began their work when the two Jesuit fathers, Biard and Massé, on June 12, 1611, landed at Annapolis in Nova Scotia. In the course of the next hundred and fifty years over three hundred members of the Society of Jesus came from France to North America.

In the introduction of her book Miss Kenton said of these Jesuits:

"The first, they are easily the best historians of the Indian; for they came to North America not only to convert him but to know him. This was the second nature of their missions; and beginning with Biard they began to write his history, while he was still overlord of virgin forests and netted waterways with no enemies to conquer or to fall before but those of his own red blood."

It is easy to understand that men educated so thoroughly as the Jesuits had been, many of them trained observers, all of them educated in the best traditions of the European universities and colleges of that day, would find very much of highest academic as well as practical interest in the lives of these Indians whom they looked upon as human beings with souls to save, for that was the one reason why they had come all this long distance

across the stormy Atlantic to get in touch with them. Miss
Kenton said:

"Jesuits, trained in all the arts that make for intelligence, were
endlessly curious, and forever alert in their quest after knowledge. Having come to North America to know the aborigine,
they took a strangely royal road to that end. They deliberately
went with him into his wilderness, paddled for him on his
waterways, foraged with him for food, endured his filth, sickened
with his diseases, and, although amazingly seldom, died his
death. They learned his languages, spelled his so-far unspelled
words, delved into the mysteries of his syntax, and put them into
grammars and dictionaries. Sitting with him in his Councils,
they listened to his oratory, noted his native trends, collected his
extravagant metaphors, took over his symbols, his logic and form
of reasoning, and later, in his Councils, matched harangue with
harangue. They fraternized with his Sorcerers and his Jugglers
and his Medicine-men, and with a daredeviltry that gave all to
win all, staked miracle against 'miracle,' magic against 'magic,'
wit against wit."

There was literally no end to the interest which the Jesuits
had as regards the nature and ways of the Indians. They were
writing for brother Jesuits whom they knew would be deeply
interested in what they had to say. On account of their thorough
Jesuit education they were men who eminently responded to
Terence's exemplification of civilized man: "I am a man and
nothing that is human is without interest for me." Miss Kenton
has summed this up in admirable fashion:

"They drew slowly from him the slender thread of his traditions, dug after the strata underlying his superstitions, listened
to his folklore and noted his morality, his immorality, his
unmorality. They investigated his religion and beliefs, became
familiar with his divinities and his deities, his stories of the
deluge and of the recreation of the world. They wrote at length
about his Khichikouai, Genii of light or air; of his Okis, his
Manitous, and his Aaskwandics. They set down his speculations
regarding the nature and condition of the soul both in this life
and after death; his extraordinary theories regarding the origin

of disease and the various manifestations of his captivity to
dreams, [anticipating our modern Freudianism and some features
of psychoanalysis and forestalling what is most recent in psycho-
therapy]. They studied his polity, his government, his modes of
warfare and his weapons, his marriage and divorce customs, his
laws governing legacy and inheritance, his preparations for death,
his funeral rites and burial. It would be difficult to find in
ethnological—or for that matter in any other literature, finer art
than shines through the last chapter of Brébeuf's Huron 'Relation' of 1636,—'Of the solemn Feast of the Dead.' For these
missioners were not only trained observers, but adventurous
scholars who could write, and who sent 'letters home' packed
with first-hand notes on the American aborigines, that are, like
the pearl of pearls, without price. Since their purpose was to
know the Indian, they let no chance go by for adding to their
store of facts. They attended his dances, and took down his
music and the chanted words of his songs; they ate at his feasts,
and described informally, for friend or brother, his foods, his
tastes, his cooking. Ever-imminent victims of his tortures, they
were invited spectators of incredible cruelties which they made
credible. And, insatiably lying in wait for whatever crumb of
knowledge might blow their way, they were constantly incorporating in their letters, or journals, or 'Relations,' bits of information at large on their 'man under observation',—of his poisons,
his medicines, his dress, crafts, arts and ornaments, his fishing
and hunting, his charms and fetishes and cunnings and superstitions, his philosophy and religion and mythology and folk-lore.
They compared their Micmac with their Montagnais, their
Huron with their Iroquois, and all of these, later on, with their
specimens from Western and Southern tribes,—by comparing
him, they might come to know him. And they sent also to
Europe, as by no means unrelated matter, notes on his flora and
fauna,—perhaps the first observers of a stranger-race to count as
pertinent to their problem its observed environment."

In his "Historical Introduction to the Jesuit Relations and
Allied Documents" in the Burrows Bros'. (seventy-three volume)
set, Reuben Gold Thwaites summed up succinctly the intellectual

qualities which enabled the Jesuit missionaries to make of their letters to their superiors scientific documents of distinct value, possessed of literary qualities that have made them of great human interest two centuries later. Their value as historical material is almost beyond computation:

"The authors of the journals which formed the basis of the 'Relations' were for the most part men of trained intellect, acute observers, and practiced in the art of keeping records of their experiences. They had left the most highly civilized country of their times, to plunge at once into the heart of the American wilderness, and attempt to win to the Christian faith the fiercest savages known to history. To gain these savages, it was first necessary to know them intimately,—their speech, their habits, their manner of thought, their strong points and their weak. These first students of the North American Indian were not only amply fitted for their undertaking, but none have since had better opportunity for its prosecution. They were explorers as well as priests. Bancroft was inexact when he said, in oft-quoted phrase, 'Not a cape was turned, not a river entered, but a Jesuit led the way.' The actual pioneers of New France were almost always *coureurs de bois,* couriers of the woods, in the prosecution of the fur trade; but *coureurs de bois,* for obvious reasons, seldom kept records, even when capable of doing so, and as a rule we learn of their previous appearance on the scene only through chance allusions in the 'Relations.' The Jesuits performed a great service to mankind in publishing their annals, which are, for historian, geographer, and ethnologist, among our first and best authorities."

Mr. Thwaites in this same introduction to the "Jesuit Relations" (Burrows Bros. 1896-1901) has detailed the almost impossible conditions in the midst of which the "Relations" were composed by their authors. These would seem to make it quite out of the question for men to have written as lucidly and accurately as the Jesuits have done. Their accomplishment shows how superior to circumstances the Jesuits could rise and how thoroughly these men could triumph over difficulties. They far outran the ethnological and anthropological science of their day in

what they noted about the Indians. Their notes were so true
to life that now two centuries and a half later they fit in with
the advance of these sciences and enable our generation to
understand the Indians of that distant date:

"Many of the 'Relations' were written in Indian camps, amid
a chaos of distractions. Insects innumerable tormented the journalists; they were immersed in scenes of squalor and degrada-
tion, overcome by fatigue and lack of proper sustenance, often
suffering from wounds and disease, maltreated in a hundred
ways by hosts who, at times, might more properly be called
jailers; and not seldom had savage superstition risen to such a
height, that to be seen making a memorandum was certain to
arouse the ferocious enmity of the band."

Mr. Thwaites continues: "Not only do these devoted missionaries—never in any field has been witnessed greater personal heroism than theirs—live and breathe before us in the 'Relations';
but we have in them our first competent account of the red
Indian at a time when relatively uncontaminated by contact with
Europeans. . . . The photographic reports in the 'Relations' help
the student to an accurate picture of the untamed aborigine and
much that mystified the fathers, is now, by aid of their careful
journals, easily susceptible of explanation." Indeed anyone who
is familiar with the accounts written in the Jesuit Letters will
agree with Mr. Thwaites that "few periods of history are so
well illumined as the French regime in North America. This we
owe in large measure to the existence of the 'Jesuit Relations.'"

A typical example of the sort of information that the "Jesuit
Relations" may carry with them and which serves to show how
valuable were the observations made by these Jesuits, is to be
found in the monograph of Father Jogues, the martyred Jesuit
of Auriesville. He had been captured by the Mohawks, as told
in a previous chapter, and was sentenced to death, but succeeded
in escaping to Albany whence the Dutch sent him down to New
Amsterdam. He is the first priest known to have visited Manhattan. He wrote a monograph of his experiences which is
included among the "Jesuit Relations" and he calls attention to
the fact that already as many as eighteen languages were spoken

on the polyglot island of Manhattan and that there were as many different churches. Even then some two hundred and fifty years ago, New York was the melting pot of races and nations almost as it is today. This account of the inhabitants of Manhattan is the best background for the understanding of the Chapter of Liberties granted by Governor Dongan that there is and enables the writer of the history of this time to appreciate the difficulties that the new governor had to encounter and the problems that he had to solve.

There are some very surprising things to be found in these "Jesuit Relations." Some of the Indian ideas anticipate thoughts supposed to be much more modern in origin. For instance, the letters of Père Jouvency show that the Indians were persuaded that there are two main sources of disease. One of these is in the mind of the patient himself which *unwittingly* craves something and will vex the body of the sick man until he possesses it. Père Jouvency goes on to say, "For they hold that there are in every man certain inborn desires often unknown to himself upon which his happiness depends. For the purpose of ascertaining such innate and ungratified desires they summon soothsayers who as they are quite convinced have a power imparted to them from on High to look into the inmost recesses of the mind."

This sounds like and is indeed a definite anticipation of Freud's doctrine of the influence of the subconscious. There is only one thing lacking and that is that the Indian medicine men did not place so much emphasis on sex as the modern neurologists and psychiatrists do. There is another difference in the situation which Miss Repplier has pointed out in her life of Père Marquette. That is that the braves were the only ones to be affected by such suppressed desires and unconscious influence. The squaws were entirely too busy with their work to suffer in that way though in the modern time it is the women who crowd the consulting rooms of the psychoanalysts and find ever so many things the matter with them.

Some idea of the estimation in which manuscript materials with regard to the languages of the Indians written in the midst of such trials and hardships by these Jesuit missionaries during the seventeenth century, are held, can be secured from the Annual Report of the John Carter Brown Library (July 1, 1933). The John Carter Brown Library is a collection of Americana housed in a special building on Brown University campus with an endowment of $500,000 devoted to the preservation of works relating to America. The report says: "Chief among the books purchased during the year were two manuscripts in the Huron and Iroquois tongues which give better balance than has previously existed to the linguistic sources in our possession." The first of these is a seventeenth-century French-Huron dictionary presumably from the pen of the Jesuit missionary, Father Pierre Marie Joseph Chaumonot. The two others are of later origin. Chaumonot missed the martyr's crown so harshly thrust upon the heads of some of his associates, but shared to the full the labors and dangers of their mission among the Hurons of Canada and the Iroquois of New York. It was said by the Indians that he spoke their language better than they did themselves. The John Carter Brown Library Report goes on to say that it considers that it has acquired a very precious bibliographic treasure in this manuscript.

But there are other "Jesuit Relations" to be discussed besides those of the French Jesuits of New York and Canada. The Spanish members of the Order in the territory now represented by the territory that is New Mexico, Arizona and California, were also writing "Relations" to their home audiences. Professor Bolton of the University of California ferreting through the archives of Mexico found Father Kino's "Relacion," the Spanish account of that great missionary's life among the Indians. The manuscript bears the title, "Favores Celestiales," though the Spanish title "Relacion" is also used.

Professor Bolton has made a careful study of the work and has established beyond all doubt the identity of it with what is called the "history" or "Relacion" attributed to Father Kino. This was referred to by a number of Spanish-American historical writers and was manifestly considered a source of as reliable information with regard to the ways of these Indians of the Southwest and the country in which they lived as were the letters of the French

Jesuits in eastern America which are held in such high esteem by modern historians. Father Kino's "Relacion" or "Historia" was written at the request of the Father General of the Order and was done as a labor of love. Professor Bolton's work in rescuing it from oblivion is looked upon by historians not only in the United States but in Europe as one of the most important triumphs of historical research in this country in the twentieth century.

In the course of historical research further "Relations" have come to light. The immense value of the French "Lettres Édifiantes" has set historians on the track of others. A group of letters written by Father Adam Gilg, S.J., to his Father Superior at the College of the Society of Jesus at Brünn in Moravia, February, 1692, show that the Jesuits in the Southwest were just as observant and as faithful in recording their observations as the French Jesuits in New York and Canada. Father Gilg wrote from Populo in the domain of the Seri Indians in the district of Sonora. His letters were translated for the Historical Records and Studies (vol. VIII, New York, June, 1915) of the United States Catholic Historical Society. Father Gilg was born at Rumerstadt in Moravia and became a Jesuit at the age of seventeen. He left for the missions of America when he was past thirty-three. Upon his arrival in Mexico he was appointed to the mission among the Seri and Topocas Indians at Populo in Sonora. He was an assistant to Father Kino.

After settling down here he writes to his superior apologizing for not keeping his promise to write sooner but unlike many travelers who have written over-hasty descriptions of their travels and their experiences in the modern time, Father Gilg felt that he ought to be sure of his ground before he described conditions: "I could not and would not write until I had in my mind and experience become sufficiently familiar with this part of the world to give my statements proper authority. If then my report is somewhat late it is so much the more complete."

Father Gilg has no illusions with regard to the possibility of accomplishing very great things immediately among the Indians and declares that patient work is required: "The greatest and almost the only miracle that a missionary can at all times perform here is his own pious and in every way blameless conduct, in addition to an insatiable zeal, generosity toward the needy and a tender though purely fatherly affection for his Indians, so that with the apostle he not only gives for nothing that which he received for nothing, but also endeavors to aid those in poverty and distress out of his own resources and without recompense." He says that the greatest obstacles to the spread of Christianity among the Indians is the existence of hostilities among the various tribes. The missionaries succeeded in overcoming this difficulty, however. He adds that there is no peculiar danger there although "not long ago two of our fathers were put to death by the Tarahumares." His experience shows that not everyone is fitted for mission work among the Indians but that these letters may serve the purpose "that our novices in Germany may from the very beginning be intent upon magnanimous deeds and consequently may bear with so much greater patience the lesser dangers and hardships in their fatherland."

Father Gilg presents a number of acute observations which indicate very clearly that his eyes were open for anything and everything of interest. He tells the story, for instance, of the first visit that he paid to the sea coast when he found a giant rib of incredible size. Apparently he must have come across one of the bones of the huge extinct animals, the brontosaurs of the pre-glacial period, so many remains of which have since been found in the Southwest. He describes in detail how cruelly the Indians treat their children by piercing not only their ears but also the septums of their noses in order that ornaments may be suspended from them. It was a fashion in the tribe and the Indians followed it quite as regardless of any injury it might do as the women of our times do with regard to high heels and corsets when these are the fashion. They also puncture the faces of growing youth about the eyes and mouth with thorns so that when the wounds have stopped bleeding the scars from them may leave black dots or spots (the black patches of our day) which they consider their greatest adornments.

The young men like to deck themselves out with all sorts of

colors, feathers and childish baubles, "the more ridiculously a young man is decked out the more beautiful and distinguished he appears to his fellows." The reader is inevitably reminded that fashions almost equally harmful are still in existence in our time among the whites, only it is the young women and not the young men who have to submit to them or at least feel that they have to submit. The Indian squaws were too busy at their work to have any time for this sort of thing. Father Gilg says: "Among other unnatural customs is that no father-in-law may speak or come near to his son-in-law or vice versa." This social usage is more likely to be observed in our time among the women two hundred years later as regards the mother-in-law and daughter-in-law, than among the men. The emancipation of women has been achieved among us.

A number of the children died as the result of this piercing of ears and noses and puncturing of faces and it represented evidently one way of getting rid of weakling children, though there was probably no such conscious purpose. It was just a following of tribal fashion and fashion was at least as arbitrary and imperative in this matter as it is with regard to so many other matters in our time. On the other hand, Father Gilg says that, "The Creator has revealed to them certain remedies with which they easily cure themselves of diseases and especially of the bites of the numerous poison snakes that exist around them, as I have learned in my own person in the case of a scorpion sting."

If they survived the mutilations of childhood they were very likely to attain ripe old age though they were very often treacherously killed at night by other members of their tribe or by enemies. A vendetta existed among them so that whenever a person had been murdered treacherously his friends but above all the old women of the family mourned for him continuously until one of his relatives avenged his death in the same dastardly manner.

Father Gilg tells of the Indians making cactus wine and drinking it to excess. He also tells of their eating carrion and almost any kind of animal food, crawling things of all kinds. They were used to that sort of diet and they were inclined to be critical of many of the things that the whites ate: "One of my Indians dared to tell me that all that they consumed in the way of food was clean while we Europeans on the contrary swallowed all kinds of trash, by which he meant mutton and all spiced dishes; nor was it possible to dissuade him from this silly conceit." The special diet of one people, even their favorite dishes, often seem to others to consist of materials that arouse disgust until accustomedness has made them palatable or hunger has driven one to the eating of them. The surprise is to find this principle applied also to the Indians as regards their attitude toward the white man's food.

These letters of Father Gilg as well as some of Father Kino were published originally in a German missionary journal, "Der Neue Welt-Bott," ("The New World Messenger"). This was a somewhat irregularly published magazine containing news from the missions, which comprised not only "Relations" from the French but also from the Spanish and German Jesuits at work in this country at that time. The missionaries gathered material of various kinds, anticipating not a little of what has since come to be called ethnology and anthropology as well as some of the botany and zoölogy of the modern times.

The Jesuits manifestly made it a point to make close observation on things around them in order that they might be able to tell their brother Jesuits at home about them.[8]

The Jesuits, as we have said, still continue to write letters from their missions all over the world to their superiors and these continue to be valuable from a scientific and historical standpoint for the information contained in them as well as for the reflections on conditions as they exist among the people to whom the missionaries are ministers. In a number of the Jesuit provinces magazines are published, the main contents of which consist of these letters from distant brethren. These publications

[8] We owe the knowledge of these German writers here in America to Professor Charles Herberman, editor-in-chief of the Catholic Encyclopedia and professor of Latin at the College of the City of New York who called attention to the extremely valuable character of these Relations and did for the Jesuits in the Southwest in this regard what Dr. O'Callaghan had done for the French Jesuit Relations about the middle of the nineteenth century.

are not meant for the general public though special permission to see them can be readily obtained by those who wish to consult them for any educational or scientific purpose. They are meant for distribution to the various houses throughout the world and some of the letters are read in the refectory during meal time in order to enable those at home without any waste of time to get a definite idea of the work that is being accomplished by Jesuit missions at a distance. These letters are especially interesting to those who have known personally missionaries who have sent them.

As we have seen, the reading of these letters often prompts young men to offer themselves to the missions. They envy their distant brethren their opportunities for special accomplishments in the Lord's service. Sometimes there may be an element of the craving for adventure in the minds of those who make applications, but as such applications are never responded to at once and applicants are kept waiting until their characters can be properly judged, only those whose motives have been purified of anything like personal satisfaction are eventually granted permission to go into missionary work. Those who go are following Christ's admonition to teach all nations, taking up His cross and following Him.

Sometimes what are really "Jesuit Relations" are in somewhat different form from the missionary letters that originated in the early history of the Jesuits and have continued ever since. A good example of the modification of these letters to suit the modern spirit better is to be found in the books of Reverend Joseph J. Williams, S.J. He spent some five years on the missions in Jamaica (West Indies) and during that time came intimately in contact with the Negroes of what is called the Jamaica bush.

He retells the folklore of the West Indian Negroes in his volume "Whisperings of the Carribean" which has the subtitle, "Reflections of a Missionary" (New York, 1925). He says that, "For one who is familiar with the amusing escapades of Brer Rabbit as told by Joel Chandler Harris in his inimitable way the Anancy stories of the Jamaica 'bush' must inevitably hold a special charm. This word Anancy originally meant a spider; as the chief character in the Tales he plays a rôle similar to that of Brer Rabbit in the Uncle Remus Stories. With Brer Rabbit, too, Anancy shows great cunning and ingenuity in circumventing his enemies and in overreaching the other animals." Almost needless to say the spider of these stories is not the comparatively small insect to which we are accustomed but one of the huge spiders of the tropics with round shining eyes, eight legs more than an inch long and hairy with black spots on them. It is very common to all houses, running about even in their ceilings. Sir Hans Sloane said of them long ago, "They are not venomous nor do they any hurt but hunt and kill cockroaches and they are carefully defended from injuries." Father Williams has also told in this volume the story of "bush" funerals and other features of Negro life in the West Indies.

During the five years in Jamaica Father Williams began the collection of the material for his work on "Hebrewisms of West Africa" with the secondary title "From Nile to Niger with the Jews" (New York, 1931). This is not another attempt to find the so-called "lost tribes" but a serious effort to trace through diffusion from the Nile to the Niger the many Hebrewisms real or apparent which are to be found among distinctively Negro tribes in West Africa in general but particularly among the Ashanti. Because of their strength and stature, though they were by far the most restless and untamable of the Negroes, a great many of the Coromantyns, the Ashantis and the Fans, were imported into Jamaica where they became the instigators and leaders of every rebellion. Those who escaped to the bush maintained many of their African customs and it is these that Father Williams studied for his octavo volume of 400 pages.

For that volume a number of distinguished ethnologists, philologists and anthropologists have expressed their high esteem. Dr. Westerman of the University of Berlin who is director of the International Institute of African Languages and Cultures in Africa says that the "full quotations and almost numberless references to works on West African ethnology and history are a special feature of the work and make it particularly valuable."

He adds: "It deserves careful study and can be of material help to all those who are interested in this problem." Dr. Eduard König of the University of Bonn, Germany, who has long been occupied with cognate subjects says: "You have with tireless patience gathered together some extremely valuable material and in exact fashion with accurate listing of the sources have set it before the reader. Science owes you a debt of deep gratitude for that work."

Not only the Germans but also the French have recognized the value of this modern "Jesuit Relation" and there is a tradition well authenticated now that whenever the Germans and French agree about anything there is sure to be something in it. Charles de la Roncière, Custodian of Documents at the National Library of Paris, wrote to the author: "I have read with the greatest interest your 'Hebrewisms of West Africa.' I think so much of it that this very day I shall present an abstract *(compte rendu)* of it to our committee of geography at the Ministry of Public Instruction. Tomorrow if they have not already done so the Bibliothèque Nationale will buy your work for it is important that this new interpretation of the Diaspora (the dispersion of the Jews) should be distributed to the world of scholarship."

Dr. Stanley A. Cook of Cambridge University, England, wrote to the author, "Let me congratulate you on the book. . . . The whole question of Jewish relationship and influence is one that interests me very much and you have certainly dealt with it in a very full and attractive manner." Many compliments of similar kind received from distinguished scholars in various parts of the world might be added to these but at least these will serve to show that the modern Jesuit missionary succeeds in securing in the midst of his missionary labors material that proves as interesting to his contemporaries as any that the Jesuits in the olden time accumulated for their "Relations."

A third volume by Father Williams bears the title, "Black Irish of Jamaica" (New York, 1932). In his arduous missionary work in Jamaica Father Williams found in even the remotest sections of the "bush" and among the darkest of the Negroes who clearly trace their ancestry back to the earliest slaves from Africa, distinctively Irish names so common that in an unguarded moment one is apt to give flight to the imagination and claim that he has actually encountered a touch of the "brogue."

Father Williams himself found "a few years ago in one school in Kingston such names as Burke, Collins, Mackay, McDermott, McKeon and Walsh, and with one exception, the last-named who was a dusky brown, they were to all appearances full-blooded Negroes. In a single classroom of another school there were Collins, Kennedy, McCormick and O'Hare. And here again in only one case did the features or complexion indicate any infusion of Caucasian blood; although this one too was as black as the rest."

Father Williams took up then the riddle, "whence the black Irish in Jamaica," and found that a great many of the Irish had been transported to the Barbados and Jamaica and that in the seventeenth century they had owned slaves who came to be named after them. In the course of his investigation of that Father Williams came across the historical question involved in the transport under Cromwell of a great many Irish men and women to the West Indies to enable the English to keep up the sugar plantations there and above all to supply wives for the planters, for miscegenation with the Negroes was working sad havoc with the English strain.

The most popular of Father Williams' books is likely to be the latest one, "Voodoos and Obeahs: Phases of West India Witchcraft" (New York, 1933.) In this volume Father Williams' experience in Jamaica combined with years of research with regard to voodooism has enabled him to write what is a very valuable book. Some five years ago a reviewer of a sensational publication on the voodoo cult among the blacks in Haiti said in "The Nation": "It is time for a tempered, intelligent presentation of the manner in which the Haitians who are addicted to voodooism live. This presentation staying close to facts yet probing under the surface and eschewing rumors will make quite as fascinating a tale as the sensational fiction on the subject that has been published."

Father Williams would seem to have supplied that long-felt want.

The exotic cults of Voodoo and Obeah are traced back to their origin on the "slave coast" of Africa in the seventeenth century. The deterioration of the religious ceremonial from genuine worship of the Deity to a mere fantastic round of superstition and black magic is narrated with scholarly care and thoroughness. Striking examples are given of the fearful excesses to which the adherents of both cults have gone. The evidence adduced is authenticated by the statements of travelers and students. Voodooism represents any practice of malicious, defensive, amatory, healing or soothsaying enchantments in the West Indies or in our own southern States when they are tinctured with African superstitions and customs. The name Voodoo is sometimes given to the personal spirit of evil supposed to be supreme among the evil powers. Obeah, sometimes spelled Obi, is not quite so much a religion as it is a species of magical art introduced into the West Indies by African slaves. This found its way also into the United States. It is a religion of charms and the charms are made of all sorts of materials. The Negroes have recourse to the Obi for the cure of disease, for securing revenge, for the telling of fortunes and the discovery of theft.

Father Williams has explained the uncanny ritual connected with the gatherings in which these magical or superstitious exercises are practised. He points out the terrible mischief that has resulted in the West Indian settlements through the machinations of the Voodoo and Obeah men. He is engaged in gathering materials for the proper understanding of further practices and beliefs, folklore and religious tradition among the Negroes. His work is a typical illustration of what the old "Jesuit Relations" represented. Two hundred and fifty years later, the modern members of the old Order are demonstrating that the scientific and inquisitive spirit of the Jesuit missionaries is still the same. Times have changed but their zeal for understanding the neophytes among whom their lot is cast remains what it was long ago.

For over three hundred years, then, the Jesuits have been enriching the field of history and of science on this continent by the observations which they made in the course of their missionary work and which they wrote down for the benefit of brother Jesuits at home so that they might be in touch with all the features of interest with which distant members of the Order were being brought in contact. Their letters were supposed to be just friendly communications passing between men who had a community of interest but because they were written by scholars who were themselves of trained intelligence and powers of observation they proved to be of very great value both as regards history and science. Undoubtedly many more of them will come to light for unfortunately the suppression of the Jesuits and their exile from various countries which so often led to the dispersion of their libraries have scattered precious documents of this kind into almost inaccessible archives and collections of manuscripts as is well illustrated by Professor Bolton's discoveries with regard to Father Kino and his companions in the Southwest. Whenever discoveries are made they will prove, as in the case of Father Kino's autobiography, to be extremely valuable for the historian and the scientist of the future.

Perhaps the best way for modern readers to appreciate properly the old "Jesuit Relations" and how much of interest there was in them is to take up a modern "Jesuit Relation" published in our own day. The best example of that would very probably be the book of Father Hubbard, S.J., "Mush, You Malemutes!" This is a description of missionary experiences combined with scientific expeditions and observations of various kinds made in Alaska. A number of the chapters in the book proved to have so much human interest that they were accepted for publication by the editor of the "Saturday Evening Post." This would surely stamp them as of very definite popular interest for almost needless to say the editor of the "Post" has a flair for what will catch readers' attention that is seldom deceived.

Father Hubbard, as professor at Santa Clara College, California, went up to Alaska with a trio of students from Jesuit colleges mainly on science bent but he devoted himself to priestly work of various kinds while up there. His companions, students of the Jesuit universities of Georgetown, D. C., Santa Clara, Cal., and San Francisco, accompanied him in the investigation of the great volcano of Aniakchak, one of the greatest in the world. They gathered an immense amount of information with regard to volcanic phenomena and succeeded in obtaining hundreds of pictures of scenes in the frozen north in connection with the eruption of the volcano. The dangers were very different from those which the Jesuits of the older time encountered because of the barbarity of the savages among whom their lives were spent, but the perils were almost as great as in the older time. The group penetrated into the crater of the volcano under such circumstances that there was constant risk of penetration of the lava crust and where only the most careful precautions enabled them to avoid serious burns from lava still in the heated state and scalds from boiling springs of many kinds on the edges of which they walked. The thoroughgoing sense of humor with which the modern Jesuit enriches his descriptions of the various incidents on their trip furnishes us with an excellent demonstration of how the Jesuits of the older time enabled themselves to go on with their work in spite of the dangers and difficulties encountered.

Some of these scenes make it easy to understand why the editor of the "Saturday Evening Post" felt that the articles would be popular. There was the description of the bear, for instance, which looked up so erectly into the heavens to get a view of the aeroplane that it fell over backwards. Then there were the caribou and other animals which were very much disturbed by the approach of this huge bird and were inclined to go into stampede. Even the birds themselves were startled at this monstrous intruder in their world of the air. Some of the experiences the explorers encountered, as for instance the cooking of meals by volcanic fire or over fumeroles of hot lava, must have afforded a thrill of excitement beyond almost anything that adventurous travelers to a distance can describe for us any more. Father Hubbard confirmed the scientific conclusion that observations of volcanos have now reached a point where successful prophecy of future events demonstrates that the science of volcanos has received a definite initiative. Valuable warnings may now be given from impending dangers of volcanic action. This indicates beyond a doubt that such cataclysms as happened at Krakatoa in Japan (1882) which killed many thousands of people, and Mount Pelee in the West Indies (1902) which wiped out a whole city, may now be foretold with such reasonable accuracy as to make the loss of life in such immense numbers definitely a thing of the past.

CHAPTER V

A JESUIT STUDENT: CHARLES CARROLL
OF CARROLLTON

THE first student of the Jesuits to come into prominence in this country was Charles Carroll of Carrollton, the distinguished signer of the Declaration of Independence from Maryland. He had spent altogether more than ten years in their schools. So far as unselfish patriotism, abiding love of country, self-sacrificing devotion to the cause of his fellow men, and the securing of their rights to life, liberty and the pursuit of happiness, are concerned, he deservedly came to be looked upon as one of the Fathers of the nation. He was willing to put all that he had— and he was with the possible exception of Washington the richest man in the colonies—to the hazard so that there might be government of the people, by the people and for the people in this country so far as that ideal was possible of realization.

He was the intimate friend of Washington, one of his firmest supporters in time of trial, whether at Valley Forge in the darkest hours of the Revolution or when the Conway Cabal came so near to ousting the Commander-in-Chief of the Continental Army— a commander whose military genius has in later years come to be appreciated by all military experts and whose replacement by any other of the generals of the Revolutionary army would almost inevitably have proved extremely detrimental if not absolutely fatal to the success of the colonial cause.

It has been said that to Charles Carroll more than to any other single individual in this country is owed the alliance of France with the colonies which eventually brought about the success of the patriot arms. He had many friends in France, he had acquired distinguished scholastic prestige that made his name familiar to the scholarship of France, and his thoroughgoing adhesion to the patriot cause deeply influenced a great many Frenchmen in the direction of alliance with the colonies. Without that alliance American independence would have been won, if at all, only at the cost of many more men and such severe financial sacrifices as would have been almost impossible for the colonists to make by themselves.

Charles Carroll's first schooling with the Jesuits was in their academy at Bohemia Manor on the eastern shore of Maryland. There he received some of that intensive training in Latin, customary in the Jesuit schools of that time, which brought the boys of fourteen or fifteen a talking knowledge of Latin. This attainment was required in all the colleges of that day and all the classes here in the colonies as in Europe were held in Latin and there was actually a fine for anyone who spoke anything but Latin except during recreation. Though he left Bohemia Manor at the age of eleven Charles Carroll had been drilled in some unforgettable knowledge in this pioneer Jesuit institution.

Before he was twelve, in spite of the fact that he was a rather delicate boy, with his cousin "Jackie" Carroll who was to be later the first Catholic bishop of the United States, Charles was sent by his thoroughly Catholic father on the long difficult voyage—as it was in those days—across the Atlantic in order that he might have the benefit of Jesuit education.[1]

[1] The reason for this foreign excursion is told by Reverend Dr. Peter Guilday in his "Life and Times of John Carroll, Archbishop of Baltimore":

"The chief problem in the Catholic homes of colonial Maryland as in all Catholic homes within the British dominions during the post-Reformation period was the Catholic education of the children. As the cleavage with the Catholic past widened in England the education of Catholic boys and girls became more and more difficult and an outlaw race of schools, colleges and seminaries was begun 'beyond the seas.' The schools in the English colonies were regulated by the same penal code as prevailed in England and Catholic children could enter only at the price of their faith. It was against the law to employ a Catholic tutor, though as the years went by the law fell into abeyance, especially toward the end of the eighteenth century. It was equally unlawful, in fact treasonable, for the Catholics to send their children to the English Catholic colleges on the continent; but it is well known that Catholic parents felt no hesitation in allowing their boys and girls despite their tender years to run the risk of capture on the seas in order that they might receive a Catholic education. In structure the anti-Catholic laws of the colonies in educational matters were practically identical with those of the mother country."

Charles' father was proud to confess his own obligations to his teachers, the Jesuits. In one of his earliest letters to his son he said: "I have, I thank God, been bred among them, and if you do what they have taught you and nothing contrary to it, you will be happy here and hereafter." That was the way that the vast majority of Jesuit students felt with regard to their teachers at this time and men who had themselves been educated among the Jesuits were the readiest to send their sons to Jesuit colleges because they knew how satisfactory Jesuit education was.

Charles Carroll's first school in Europe was the College of St. Omer where he received so good a grounding in the classics, Latin and Greek, that during his long life of over ninety years he always retained his partiality for the classic authors and especially the Latin writers. During his stay in France he became thoroughly conversant with French literature also and with the European thought of the time as it focused itself in Paris which was the intellectual capital of Europe.

In attendance at St. Omer's there were other Maryland boys sent across the ocean for the sake of a Catholic education with whom Carroll was acquainted or at least with their families. He found at St. Omer's an older cousin, Anthony Carroll, who came from Ireland, and who later became a Jesuit as did John Carroll, the future American bishop. From St. Omer's Charles Carroll went to the college at Rheims, and then later to the great Paris college of Louis-le-Grand, one of the best known schools of the Jesuits at that time, and they were looked upon as the best teachers in Europe with altogether some two hundred thousand pupils in attendance at their schools.

At the end of his course at Louis-le-Grand, Charles Carroll took part in what was known as a Public Act, that is he presented himself for the public defense of a series of propositions in philosophy against all comers. These propositions included all the great theses of scholastic philosophy as they were studied in the *trivium* and *quadrivium,* logic, rhetoric and grammar, and the three philosophies, mental (metaphysics), moral (ethics), and natural (physics), as well as mathematics which constituted the basis of the college curriculum in those days.

Tested competency in these gave the right to the degree of Bachelor of Arts. Charles Carroll had done special graduate work, and his public examination was the equivalent of the test for the doctorate. He emerged from this severe public ordeal which was taken quite seriously and was no mere closing exercises' formality, with great academic *kudos*. The event was widely heralded in university and collegiate circles in France at least and he acquired a very enviable reputation for accurate and thoughtful scholarship.[2]

Many years afterwards when emigrés from France became exiles in this country in their flight from the atrocities of the French Revolution, the one name in America that was familiar to many of them was that of Charles Carroll. Fortunately he was in a position owing to his substantial wealth to be of assistance to many of them in that very trying period and he exercised his charity, as was the case at all times during his long life, very generously and effectively.

To most people, and this would be particularly true for a great many American educators, it would have seemed that the kind of education which Charles Carroll received at Bohemia Manor Academy and in the Jesuit colleges in Europe would be very different from that afforded by the colonial schools and colleges in this country, three of which were already in existence—Harvard, William and Mary, and Yale—at the time of Carroll's birth, while Princeton, the University of Pennsylvania, King's College and Brown came into existence during his student years. As a matter of fact all of these colonial colleges in America, as

[2] At the College of Louis-le-Grand, probably the Jesuits' largest school, while Charles Carroll was in attendance there, there were nearly three thousand students. It is easy to understand what an honor it was under these circumstances to be chosen to be the champion of his college and in what high esteem his Jesuit teachers must have held his intellectual attainments. He must have become thoroughly saturated with philosophy as it was taught by the Jesuits in those days. Almost needless to say everywhere throughout the world they taught the same philosophy. They must have been thoroughly assured of his competency before they would have permitted him to be the protagonist of their philosophic teaching, ready to defend it against all comers at a time in academic history when this defense demanded a real battle of wits and when failure in it would have marked a man for life.

I pointed out in an article in the July number of the "New England Quarterly" (1932), had the same curriculum as the Jesuit colleges of that time and their courses were organized around the trivium and quadrivium of the old medieval schools. The students of these colonial Latin schools came up from the Latin schools supposed to be able to talk Latin just as were the students of the Jesuits. In this language all of their studies even mathematics and astronomy as well as physics were made, and in this language the theses, that is the various propositions that formulated their knowledge of all subjects, were defended in the weekly disputations during the year as well as in the Public Act at the end of the year.

Carroll was given, then, the same education that he would have received at home only that he had the advantage of a European background as well as a thorough acquaintance with the French language and the French people which was to mean so much for him when he was devoting himself to helping the colonists in every way in their struggle with the mother country during the Revolution. Carroll studied law for four years at Bourges in France and then read law at the Temple in England though with no thought of practising the legal profession for, as an orthodox Catholic, he would have been unable to subscribe to the required test oath. While in London he came in intimate contact with a number of students from the American colonies. Unlike him, they were almost without exception reading for the bar and most of them returned to America to take up their profession and not a few of them were co-signers with him of the Declaration of Independence. Carroll himself attended debates in Parliament and made himself as thoroughly familiar as possible with the English Constitution. It is easy to understand from all this study how eminently he was prepared for the position of leadership which he came to hold in colonial affairs in America beside such men as Washington, Jefferson and Adams.

Charles Carroll returned to America in 1765 and at once entered into sympathetic relations with the men in the various colonies who were insisting that there must be no levying of taxes on the colonists without representation in Parliament and who just at that time were creating in the minds of the colonists intense dissatisfaction with the Stamp Act. Carroll took part on the popular side of a public controversy by pamphlet over the questions at issue between the governor and the legislature and proved a valuable spokesman for the patriots. These pamphlets attracted all the more attention as Carroll was very temperate in his statements, thoroughly judicial to the point of conservatism and was manifestly well versed not only in the law but also the English practices and the colonial customs. His long years of training in French and English law were now put at the services of the colonies. He signed himself "First Citizen" but was soon identified and his success in the controversy brought him into great prominence. It is sometimes thought that the Boston tea party as a protest against the tax on tea was unique but it must not be forgotten that Annapolis, New York and other colonial ports had their tea parties as well as Boston. Carroll continued to be for the next fifty years a leader in Maryland political opinion, thoroughly trusted, indeed almost revered by his fellow colonists and fellow citizens of Maryland.

He gave himself and his time wholeheartedly to what he considered his patriotic duty at this time and he was willing to accept various positions in the Revolutionary government. In the midst of all this he was thoroughly aware that if the dissatisfaction that was gradually being intensified among the colonists were to proceed to the extent of hostility he was risking his patrimony as well as life. He knew very well from the study of English law and still more from his study of English history just how the leaders of such movements were likely to be treated. Besides the Carrolls were deeply sympathetic with the Irish and they must have known from that source how heartlessly the British government would proceed against revolutionists. If the movement in the colonies were to be declared treasonable by the British government as came actually to be the case when the Revolution broke out, Carroll and the other patriots, declared traitors, would have had their estates confiscated to the Crown and such properties as those of Carrollton or Mount Vernon would have been fat plums for the British generals who had been sent over here or would have enriched the friends of the Crown in the colonies or in England.

He was one of those who foresaw, years before the Revolution, that an appeal to arms would probably have to be made and so he prepared for armed defense of what he considered colonial rights. He had been his father's business manager for some years and this included the superintendency of the Patapsco Iron Works. His thoroughgoing practical knowledge of the iron business was a very valuable asset to the colonials and the Patapsco Iron Works turned out excellent military supplies. In spite of the danger involved in all this Carroll with his relatives, Daniel Carroll and Charles Carroll, served on the local committee of correspondence and of safety as well as on the provincial committee of correspondence, and in the Maryland convention where he supported the non-importations agreement which the other colonies were considering. That agreement would put an end to all imports of British goods into the colonies.

Charles Carroll was thoroughly appreciated by his brother patriots of the other colonies. In a letter to a friend, John Adams, who was not over given to enthusiasm especially for those who were not New Englanders, said of Carroll's membership on this commission sent to Canada consisting of Franklin, Chase of Maryland and Carroll: "The characters of the two first you know. The last is not a member of Congress, but a gentleman of independent fortune, perhaps the largest in America—a hundred and fifty or two hundred thousand pounds sterling; educated in some university in France, though a native of America; of great abilities and learning, complete master of the French language, and a professor of the Roman Catholic religion, yet a warm, a firm, a zealous supporter of the rights of America, in whose cause he has hazarded his all."

Everywhere that he was called upon for his services he gave himself wholeheartedly to the work. In the Continental Congress he served among other committees on the Board of War, by far the most important of the committees during the Revolution. He had for companions on the committee men like John Adams and Benjamin Harrison, the father of one President of the United

States and the great-grandfather of another. By education and environment no two men among the colonists could possibly be more different from each other than Carroll and Adams and yet we have Adams' testimony to the fact that Carroll proved "an excellent member whose education, manners and application to business and to study did honor to his fortune, the first in America." There are many other tributes to Carroll in Adams' letters in which the sole reason for his praise was that it was forced from him by his profound appreciation of Carroll's character and activity in the patriotic cause.

The commission to Canada failed of its specific purpose but then what else could have been expected? The Canadian habitants were quite satisfied with the liberal privileges which had been granted to them by the Quebec Act. This was almost unexampled in British history for its tolerant liberality. It had been in effect for some years and its enforcement had afforded the Canadians full religious toleration. They had no reason to be disloyal to the British crown. On the other hand they had every cause to distrust the rebel colonies and above all New England. If there were but the two reasons, the utterly heartless treatment of the Acadians and the exaggerated Puritan outburst against the Quebec Act as granting freedom of religious worship to Catholics on the American continent, these had served to show how extremely bitter still were the feelings of New Englanders against their Canadian neighbors. John Jay's protest with regard to the toleration thus enacted into law by the British government in what was known as the Quebec Act put a climax on this situation and made the Canadians feel how little assurance there was that they would have anything like corresponding religious toleration under the colonists to that which they now enjoyed under the British. They were quite willing to let well enough alone and not subject themselves to conditions they knew not of but that might prove intolerable. As it was, as we shall see in the chapter "A Jesuit Patriot," the commission had a favorable effect on the attitude of the Canadians toward the Revolution that proved of great value.

In the meantime it is well to realize what that journey to

Quebec on foot and on horseback with many nights in the open air, sleeping wrapped in a blanket, paddling in canoes, tramping portages and on horseback riding on Indian trails, meant for a man like Carroll, never rugged in health, indeed always rather delicate, one of those thin light men, small in stature who so often live to good round old age, though they often feel that they are destined to short life. All his life Carroll, while at his own home in this country or in many places in Europe, had dwelt under the most comfortable—indeed for that day almost luxurious circumstances. He had none of that liking for the great outdoors that makes some people delight in such adventures though all his life he was a devoted horseback rider. He knew very well just what hardships he would have to go through as did his cousin, Father John Carroll, who went with the commission as secretary and aid; but they both felt that they should be ready to make sacrifices of this kind and go through hardships for the good of their native country and for the benefit of their fellow countrymen. Theirs was no frigid patriotism that satisfies itself with political addresses or even with monetary contributions but was quite willing to give personal service.

As to Charles Carroll's religion his contemporaries afford the best evidence. Father John McCaffrey in a panegyric at Mt. St. Mary's College (Emmitsburg) gave first-hand evidence as to the thoroughness of his belief and of his efforts to make that belief as intellectually well-founded as possible. He dwelt on the fact that Carroll had insisted on having his grandchildren educated in the Faith because he knew from his own experience how much of happiness and satisfaction in life that would afford them. He dwells on the thought that patriotism and religion were to him the two great virtues that made life have a meaning and a purpose. Father McCaffrey said (Gurn: "Charles Carroll of Carrollton," New York, 1932, p. 189):

"As honor and patriotism were not with him words of pretty sound and profitable use, so neither were his religion and morality mere subjects of philosophic speculation or commonplace eulogy, but living, active principles of conduct, influencing him in all his relations, civil, social and domestic. . . . Nor be it said that he blindly acquiesced in the dogmas of an hereditary creed. If any man's faith was deeply laid in rational conviction it was that of Charles Carroll. The advantages of his excellent classical and philosophical education, his extensive and acute observations on events and on men, his familiarity with languages and books, and the leisure which an independent fortune permitted him to enjoy, prepared and enabled him to make the study of religion in the fullest, fairest and most satisfactory manner; and I have it on unquestionable authority that he did at one period in his life, by the advice and with the aid of his illustrious relative, the first Archbishop of Baltimore, make it his chief occupation and delight for three successive years, pursuing in the most regular manner a course of theological investigation.... New strength was added to his reasons and motives for remaining in communion with the great majority of Christians, and professing the faith of Fenelon and Columbus."

Toward the end of his life extremely significant tributes were paid to Carroll by the statesmen of his day who felt deeply that here was a model citizen, worthy to be held up to the emulation of his fellow citizens throughout the country. When on July 4, 1826, two of the three surviving signers of the Declaration, Thomas Jefferson and John Adams, passed away on the fiftieth anniversary of the drawing up of that document, they left only one of their number alive, and this was Charles Carroll. Their deaths, so dramatically placed, proved the signal for a series of orations, one of which by Daniel Webster delivered at Faneuil Hall in Boston on August 2, 1826, is one of the greatest examples of American eloquence. In this eulogy Webster pictured Charles Carroll, the last of the fifty-seven, as only our greatest American orator could have done it. It is a marvelous tribute to this worthy citizen and founder of the American republic. Webster said of Carroll:

"Of the illustrious signers of the Declaration of Independence there now remains only Charles Carroll. He seems an aged oak, standing alone on the plain, which time has spared a little longer after all its contemporaries have been leveled with the dust.

Venerable object! We delight to gather around its trunk while it yet stands, and to dwell beneath its shadow. Sole survivor of an assembly of as great men as the world has witnessed, in a transaction one of the most important that history records, what thoughts, what interesting reflections, must fill his elevated and devout soul! If to dwell on the past, how touching its recollections; if to survey the present, how happy, how joyous, how full of the fruition of that hope which his ardent patriotism indulged; if he glance at the future, how does the prospect of his country's advancement almost bewilder his weakened conception! Fortunate, distinguished patriot! Interesting relic of the past! Let him know that while we honor the dead we do not forget the living, and that there is not a heart here which does not fervently pray that Heaven may keep him yet back from the society of his companions."

In his "Life of Charles Carroll," Joseph Gurn (New York, 1932), brings out very well the homage and veneration which were paid to Carroll during the six years that he remained alive as the only surviving signer of the Declaration of Independence:

"During the years in which Charles Carroll of Carrollton lived as the last of the signers he was venerated as 'Pater Patriæ' with a universality and a warmth which left no doubt as to the place he occupied in the hearts of the American people. 'His star continued bright after all the others had set, and the rising generation looked up to it with an almost religious veneration,' we read in 'The United States and Canada' by C. D. Arfwedson, a foreign traveler who was in Baltimore when Carroll passed away. After the death of Jefferson and Adams the 'National Journal' declared, in July, 1826, that 'every expression, every fragment of a phrase from such a man, is now of inestimable value.' William Wirt, Attorney-General of the United States, in delivering a eulogy on Jefferson and Adams in the House of Representatives, October 19, 1826, left no misgivings as to Carroll's status, when he declared: 'That brave and animated band who signed it (the Declaration)—where are they now? What heart does not sink at the question? Only one survives—Charles Carroll of Carrollton—a noble specimen of the age that is gone by, and now the single object of that age, on whom the veneration and prayers of his country are concentrated.' "

A tribute to him in the form of an unusual honor conferred upon him by Congress touched Charles Carroll very deeply. This was the granting to him of the same franking privileges through the mails as that enjoyed by the President of the United States. In reply to the resolution passed by the House Carroll said: "This privilege I consider an honorable approbation of the part I took in the Revolution and commands my grateful acknowledgment and thanks." The official communication in the matter from the Speaker of the House gives an excellent idea of the tender feelings that the representatives of the people had at this time for their living *pater patriæ:*

"I have the honor to communicate to you, by direction of the House of Representatives, the enclosed joint resolution of both Houses of Congress, extending to you, as the only surviving signer of the Declaration of Independence, the privilege of franking. You will be pleased, sir, to receive it as a token of the distinguished respect and veneration which Congress entertain towards an early and devoted friend to liberty, and one who stood eminently forward in the purest and noblest band of patriots that the world has ever seen. I cannot resist the gratification which this opportunity affords of publicity testifying the strong sentiments of esteem and veneration which, individually, I entertain for your character and services, and expressing an earnest hope that the evening of your long life may be as peaceful and happy as it has been active and useful."

Even though well past ninety years of age, Charles Carroll did not allow himself to drift into inactivity but continued to take an active interest in affairs around him. On the 4th of July, 1828, Charles Carroll took part in a ceremony which he himself regarded as only second in importance to his signing of the Declaration of Independence. This was his formal participation in the laying of the cornerstone of the Balitmore & Ohio Railroad. This was the first formal railroad project to be launched in the United States and as a member of the original board of directors he occupied a post of honor at the ceremonies on that occasion. First came the recital of prayer followed by the reading of the Declaration of Independence, and then the orator of the day referred to him:

"The existence which he contributed to give to the United States on the Fourth of July, 1776, on the Fourth of July, 1828, he perpetuates. Ninety-one summers have passed over him. Those who stood with him in the Hall of Independence have left him solitary upon the earth—'the Father of his Country.' In the full possession of his powers, with his feelings and affections still buoyant and warm, he now declares that the proudest act of his life, and the most important in its consequences to his country, was the signature of the Declaration of Independence; the next the laying of the first stone of the work which is to perpetuate the union of the American States, to make the east and the west as one household in the facilities of intercourse and the feelings of mutual affection."

One of the hardest things to understand in the lives of the signers of the Declaration of Independence who set their signatures to the proposition that all men are born free and equal is the fact that so many of them owned Negro slaves. In all the colonies at this time there were slaves of one kind or another and most of the northern colonies had at least a few Negro slaves. Jefferson who wrote the Declaration of Independence was a large slave holder but while still a young man he offered a resolution in the House of Burgesses of Virginia granting freedom to the slaves. At that time it seemed quite impossible for the southern planters to cultivate their crops of corn and tobacco unless the institution of slavery was continued and unless they had the opportunity to own a number of slaves. There were serious abuses connected with the institution of slavery but then there are abuses connected with most of the good things of the world and as slavery had existed for thousands of years and as it seemed to be commended or at least not condemned by the Scriptures, it was continued.

Like Jefferson, Carroll was a slave holder but like him he **had great sympathy with the slaves** and he hoped that in this free country the institution would disappear. On the death of Carroll his son-in-law, Richard Caton (after whom Catonsville in Maryland is named) in a letter addressed to the president of the select and common councils of the city acknowledging in behalf of the Carroll family the condolences of the city on the death of the last of the signers, sets forth the views that he had heard expressed by his father-in-law on many occasions on the subject of slavery:

"There is one trait of character in the history of Mr. Carroll's life which is not known generally, and I hope you will pardon me in taking this occasion to mention it. He bitterly lamented the existence of slavery, which British laws and policy had rooted in Maryland. He held many slaves, and he would gladly have adopted any means by which the country could have been relieved from the evil, without inflicting a greater one in the attempt. To accomplish this, he in 1797 introduced into the Senate of Maryland a bill for a gradual abolition, the provisions of which were that the State should buy up all the female children, educate them for freedom and usefulness and bind them out, to be free at twenty-eight years of age, when habits of order would have befitted them for a state of liberty. At a given period all males, and others under forty-five years, were to be free. Unhappily the law did not prevail. Had it prevailed, the measure at this period would nearly have extinguished slavery in Maryland. He never was an advocate for letting loose on society a race of beings, who, nine out of ten, are incapable of providing for themselves, as he knew the experiment, often tried, but never succeeded, and he thought no one had a right to do an evil to society by such a measure. But he did all that could be done to the African race whilst in servitude; he had them protected with humanity, and he elevated their characters by religious instruction, which was daily administered by persons appointed for that purpose. The children of his colored females were daily congregated and taught their catechism, and received moral instruction. These preparatory measures he thought would advance them for a state of manumission, which must soon take place in Maryland."

We have first-hand testimony as to his relations toward his

colored servants who called him master but to whom he stood much more in the light of a beneficent father. The Reverend Constantine Pise, the first Catholic chaplain to the United States Senate, says of him after knowing from intimate intercourse with his household just exactly what his feelings and relations to his colored servants were:

"As a master he was kind, lenient and generous, feeling for the condition of those beings whose color excluded them from the privileges of their fellowmen and whose destiny had made them his slaves. He clothed them well, provided carefully for their comfort and health, and treated them with parental attention when sick; and I feel convinced that no matter how much the country may lament the decease of the patriot and the statesman she cannot do so more deeply than his slaves bewail the loss of their 'Old Master.'"

What his Jesuit education meant for Carroll at the end of his life is told us very well by Father Pise, the Senate chaplain, and himself one of the memorable men of that first half of the nineteenth century. His thorough study of the classics gave Carroll a great resource in those last years of his life when naturally he had a great deal of leisure and when to a great extent life had become sedentary. We are intent at the present time on the question whether education is to enable men to make a living or to make something out of life. We have been educating men to a great extent for their employment, but as time goes on it is evident that we should educate them for the leisure that is sure to come to them in connection with the lengthening of the average of life from less than forty years to more than sixty years, and in consideration of the unemployment which is developing and that will give men leisure for hours every day.

Father Pise said with regard to the ultimate years of the signer:

"The retired life of Mr. Carroll was a literal translation of the *otium cum dignitate*. I love to bring this period of his life before your consideration; for, honored as I was during the last ten years with a familiar acquaintance with him and his delightful family, I can speak from my own observation, from my own personal knowledge; of all those who once shared the dangers and the honors of his public life, not one now remains to tell of him; but of his venerable and serene old age, there are thousands to bear witness; of those rare virtues which adorned him, of his simplicity of heart and manner, urbanity, elegant hospitality, social intercourse with his friends, solicitude and care for his domestics and slaves, suavity, alacrity, charity, liberality, piety, religion, thousands can bear testimony.

"I have seen him, and it is delightful to me to represent him to you, spending his summers under the shade of those trees which his father's hands had planted nearly a century and a half ago, and which *consociari amant,* which love to twine their hospitable boughs over the venerable mansion of Doughoregan. The manner in which he there spent his time resembled the *mitis sapientia Laeli.* He rose very early to enjoy the fresh breezes of the morning, plunged into a cold bath, mounted his horse and rode a certain number of miles; spent some time at prayer and, if the chaplain of the Manor was there, heard Mass in the chapel; varied the long days in reading and conversing, and indulging in those meditations which the scenes of his past life, and the circumstances of the present period, were calculated to awaken in his philosophic mind. The Manor was never without some visitors, whom it was Mr. Carroll's delight to entertain and to put upon the most agreeable familiarity. He paid equal attention to all alike, and all left him not only full of admiration for his character, but veneration for his virtues and attachment to his person."

As to Charles Carroll's firm and faithful adhesion to his religion, we have the testimony in this regard furnished by Father Pise. Father Pise like Charles Carroll himself had been educated by the Jesuits graduating at Georgetown College in the District of Columbia. After graduation Pise entered the Jesuits but left the Jesuits after two years to become a secular priest and developed into a distinguished lecturer and preacher. He was very well acquainted with the Carroll family and was a special intimate friend of the signer of the Declaration during his last years. He quotes Carroll as saying toward the end of his life:

"I have lived to my ninety-sixth year. I have enjoyed continued health; I have been blessed with great wealth, prosperity and most of the good things which the world can bestow—public approbation, esteem, applause. But what I now look back on with greatest satisfaction to myself in life is that I have practised the duties of my religion." He had seen enough of the world and had had experiences of all kinds so that this review of his career is a very definite index of what the experiences of life had brought him.

Fortunately we have the detailed account of his last hours from his physician, Dr. Stewart, who felt that his patient was so important an individual in the history of this country that it would be of value to have everything that happened in the sick room during the terminal hours of his existence definitely recorded. Shortly after his attendance on his patient, then, he wrote down what he had observed and this account has been preserved for us. Dr. Stewart's description of the reception of the Holy Eucharist as a Viaticum is particularly interesting because it is seen through the eyes of a non-Catholic:

"The venerable old man was in a large easy chair; in the center before him a table with blessed candles, an antique silver bowl of holy water and a crucifix. By his side the priest, Reverend John C. Chaunce, president of St. Mary's College and afterwards bishop of Natchez, in his rich robes about to offer him the last rites of the holy Catholic Church. On each side of his chair knelt the daughter and grandchildren with some friends making a complete semicircle; and just in the rear three or four old Negro servants, all of the same faith, knelt in the most venerable manner. The whole assemblage made up a picture never to be forgotten.

"The old gentleman had been for a long time suffering from weak eyes and could not endure the proximity of the light immediately before him. His eyes were three-fourths kept closed but he was so familiar with the forms of this solemn ceremony that he responded and acted as if he saw everything passing around. At the moment of offering him the Host (the Communion) he leaned forward without opening his eyes yet responsive to the word of the administration of the Holy Offering. It was done with so much intelligence and grace that no one could doubt for a moment how fully his soul was alive to the act."

After the Communion service was over Dr. Stewart, aware that Carroll had been fasting many hours, suggested that he must be very weak and must be in need of sustenance. The doctor therefore offered him something to eat but Charles Carroll's response, to quote once more from Dr. Stewart's record, made "in the most gentle and intelligent manner" was, "Thank you, doctor, not just now; this ceremony is so deeply interesting to the Christian that it supplies all the wants of nature. I feel no desire for food." Not long afterwards his granddaughter and the doctor raised him from his chair and laid him once more in his bed and in appreciation of their act he said to them: "Thank you, that is nicely done."

With regard to the hours of leisure so well filled as he grew older, his biographer has said, "His learning proved a treasure in his declining years." He makes the comment, "Indeed it would not be over much to say that it added to the span of his life. His books were friends, indeed a source of inspiration and enjoyment of which he availed himself to the fullest." The satisfaction that accrued from the reading of the best literature undoubtedly made life well worth the while during those years when so many men who have never been properly naturalized in the realm of books find so many hours that are wearisome and monotonous. Undoubtedly as was quite true of Adams and Jefferson these surviving signers of the Declaration of Independence owed much of their happiness in their declining years to all that books signified for them as the result of deep and broad education in their younger years. Father Pise tells us:

"Mr. Carroll delighted in reading. His library was composed of the most valuable and beautiful editions of the classics which up to his ninety-third year he understood with the greatest facility and pleasure."

Toward the end of his life he found the philosophic works of Cicero, the "De Amicitia" (On Friendship), the "De Senectute" (On Old Age), and the "Somnium Scipionis de Immortalitate," (The Dream of Scipio on Immortality) particularly to his liking.

Unfortunately for most of us the reading of these philosophic essays on friendship, old age and immortality, comes at a time when we are but very little interested in these subjects and some of us may remember only the difficulties of the construction of Cicero's rather idiomatic Latin. Those of us who live on, however, to the time when old age and friendship and immortality have come to be the most important subjects for thought, are likely to find it a distinctive pleasure to go back and work out of their idiomatic Latin some of Cicero's deep thoughts with regard to these extremely interesting subjects. That proved to be the case with Charles Carroll and Father Pise tells of discussions on these subjects he had with him during the months just preceding the time when there would come for the old patriarch in another world the solution of these problems.

Charles Carroll illustrated very well those traits of character which Matthew Arnold collected together under the term sweet reasonableness. He was an exemplification of the sweetness and light that meant so much for life according to the English literary man. While Carroll was a devout practical Catholic deeply religious he was not at all bigoted but had as his biographer has said of him, "an exceeding charity toward those of other faith or no faith at all." Father Pise once more must be the source from which we learn the reality and intensity as well as the reasonableness of Carroll's spiritual convictions and to these Father Pise bears eloquent testimony:

"His attachment to the Roman Catholic faith was firm and unchanging. He was a Catholic not merely by birth, felt himself bound to that creed not merely by the pride of family and honor, but from a thorough investigation into religious matters. He had read much on all subjects, had examined the objections started and ingeniously supported by the French and English infidels. He had perused the great masters of the English Church. And after all his researches, he himself declared that his convictions as a Roman Catholic were only the more solidly established. But he was an enlightened Christian. He did not object to any on account of controverted principles. He loved all and entertained for all that pure and ethereal charity which is the first of virtues. For he was well aware that in a country like ours, in a republic of the first and purest nature, toleration of all creeds and denominations is the vital principle of her constitution, and the very essence of her existence. He lamented, however, the disingenuous attempts that have been made to prejudice his countrymen against the Roman Catholic. He attributed them not to malice, or even to interest, but to the ignorance of our tenets and an unwillingness to investigate them. He was not only a Catholic in theory—he was so in practice. He confessed and received Communion monthly, attended Mass every Sunday and holyday of obligation, observed all the minutest rules and customs of the Church. He was first on every good work, first to subscribe to the relief of the poor, the education of the orphan, the erection of churches; first to appear on Good Friday at the ceremony of kissing the Cross; first to receive the ashes on Ash Wednesday, and first to receive the palms on Palm Sunday. And all this he performed with the utmost simplicity and humility, perfectly removed from anything like show or ostentation."

CHAPTER VI

A JESUIT PATRIOT: ARCHBISHOP CARROLL

ONE of the men whose name is almost as intimately associated with the cause of independence as that of Charles Carroll of Carrollton, the signer of the Declaration, is his cousin, John Carroll, who afterwards became the first Catholic bishop and archbishop in the United States. He had been a Jesuit for some twenty years until the suppression of the Order by the pope and then he came over to America when the politics of the colonies were very much disturbed and when a revolution was manifestly imminent because he wanted to share with his fellow countrymen in the effort that they were making for freedom.

With his cousin, Charles, John Carroll took the long trip across the Atlantic, a perilous crossing in those days, to St. Omer's in France, the college founded by the English Jesuits, themselves exiled from their country, for the purpose of enabling English Catholics to secure education for their children. Owing to the test oaths that were administered at the English universities, the sons of the English nobility or gentry could not go to Oxford or Cambridge, and had to take the trip over to France to secure higher education. The Catholic colonists here in America, though of course there were only a few of the families that could afford to do so, took advantage of the foundation of this English college to secure a Catholic education for their sons.

Charles Carroll spent some ten years in study in the Jesuit colleges of France and Flanders and graduated with high honors at the College Louis-le-Grand in Paris. He devoted some years to further study in London before returning to America. John Carroll, however, after spending some six years as a student, decided to spend the rest of his life with the Jesuits, so he entered the Jesuit Order. After having been for some years a professor at St. Omer's and at Bruges he became a teacher of the younger Jesuits, a position assigned as a rule only to those who were themselves brilliant teachers and who were, as far as possible, model Jesuits after the heart of their founder. It looked as though all his life would be spent amid the scholarly peace and hospitable obscurity of Jesuit college life but fate was mapping out a very different destiny for him and he was to have a career with many vicissitudes in it and with the necessity for the exercise of fine executive ability and knowledge of men in order to be of help to his Catholic fellow countrymen on this side of the water. He would have gladly remained a Jesuit but instead he was to be a bishop and archbishop, in our primitive conditions bearing a burden that almost shrouded the dignity.

In 1762 the Parliament of Paris ordered the expulsion of the Jesuits from France and the English Fathers at St. Omer had to take the road into exile. They accepted the hospitality tendered them by the Belgian Jesuits at Bruges. Father Carroll continued his work as a teacher here and he must have seen that the storm clouds were gathering over the Order. As a professor of English boys at St. Omer's, Father Carroll had come to be very well known by many of the English nobility and gentry and in 1772 Lord Stourton requested him to make a tour of the continent as tutor to his son. On this journey and especially while at Rome, Father Carroll must have come to realize that the enemies of the Jesuits were gaining the upper hand and the outlook was far from favorable. He was still at Bruges after his return when the papal brief suppressing the Jesuits throughout the world was issued. The civic authorities at Bruges seized the English college in October, 1773, and held Father Carroll and his fellow Jesuits as prisoners after stripping them of all means and even of their private papers. When the English Jesuits were allowed to return to England Father Carroll accepted the hospitality offered to him by Lord Arundel of Wardour. Here he came to realize the disturbed state of the relations between the colonies and the mother country.

Following the suppression of the Jesuits by the pope in 1773,

Father John Carroll after a year of waiting in England to orient himself, threw in his lot with the colonists in America though he was well aware of the fact that trouble was stirring, that the colonies would probably be embroiled in war with the mother country before long and that living conditions would become rather difficult across the Atlantic because of the developments necessarily attending the Revolution. Friends among the nobility in England whose sons he had taught would have welcomed his stay among them as a chaplain. His English friends made his residence in England very pleasant and he might have had a life of scholarly leisure, intent on the cultivation of his own mind and occupied with the things of the intellect to which he had devoted so many years of his life. He was deeply interested in the classics, was well acquainted with both Latin and Greek and above all had Cicero's feeling that he was "never less alone than when alone" so long as he had books to occupy him. He chose instead to take up a life work of activity among his fellow countrymen here in America and to be of whatever help he might be to them during the struggle that he saw impending.

He had been in Maryland less than a year when he was asked, indeed urged by the personal request of Washington and Franklin and others among colonist leaders, notably his cousin Charles Carroll, to go as secretary to the Mission consisting of Benjamin Franklin, Samuel Chase of Maryland and Carroll of Carrollton, which took the long journey to Quebec with the purpose of winning the French Canadians if possible to the cause of the colonists farther south along the Atlantic seaboard. It was a long and tedious journey which began on April 2, 1776, and formally ended only when Chase and Charles Carroll reached Philadelphia to render their report to Congress on June 11 of that same year. Franklin was already feeling the weight of years and in one of his letters he paid a high tribute of praise to Father Carroll for his attention to him during the journey: "As to myself I find I grow daily more feeble and think I could hardly have got so far but for Mr. Carroll's friendly assistance and tender care of me." (Mr. was the title applied to priests in England in those days because any ecclesiastical title would betray them to the English authorities and Franklin followed the English custom in this regard.)

The Canadian mission was in one sense a failure. It could scarcely have been otherwise. Russell writes: "It is difficult to understand how the people of the colonies could have imagined it possible to win over Canada to a union with them against Great Britain when at every turn they outraged her people on what was dearer to them than life." In another sense the mission was far from a failure. It failed so far as its main objects were concerned, the securing of military cooperation or even a declaration of neutrality from Canada, but its ultimate effect proved extremely favorable to the colonists.

As Martin F. Morris said in his address at the centennial celebration of Georgetown College: "The Mission was more successful than is usually supposed. The assistance or alliance of Canada, it is true, was not secured to the thirteen colonies. After the bitter enmities of two centuries of strife and conflict it was impossible so far to reconcile hostile feelings as to bring Canada into an alliance that would place her side by side with New England. Canada had no such grievance against England as the revolted colonies had, and she had been granted civil and religious freedom; and the guaranty it must be said had been faithfully preserved. John Carroll did, however, secure the substantial neutrality of the French Canadians; and it is a fact that very few of them were found in the armies of Clinton and Burgoyne."

The only ecclesiastic in Canada who showed any favor to the American Mission and whose attitude was complacent to the American cause, was Reverend Pierre Floquet, like Father Carroll himself, an involuntary ex-Jesuit, indeed the last of the Canadian superiors of the Jesuit missions. Father Carroll on his way up to Canada stopped with Father Farmer in Philadelphia, another ex-Jesuit, but solely through the suppression and not by his own will, who presented him a letter of introduction to the Canadian Jesuit. As the result of this Father Carroll was permitted to say Mass in Father Floquet's house while he was in Quebec. Because of the favor shown to Father Carroll, his host was drawn into disgrace with his bishop Briand because of his welcome to the Americans. Floquet had disobeyed Briand's order that no courtesy should be shown to the American priest and he was suspended *a divinis* by the bishop. He made an ample apology and then was restored to his priestly functions. Floquet lived to be not only the last of the superiors but the last of the Canadian ex-Jesuits.

During the Revolution Father Carroll stayed at Rock Creek, the guest of his mother, devoting himself to his priestly duties and attending to the spiritual wants of Catholics of whom there were a good many in that neighborhood. At Rock Creek as Gilmary Shea says, he "beheld a field of labor where much could be accomplished. There were Catholics in the neighborhood and many at greater or less distance which could be reached by a priest willing to devote himself to their service. There were stations in Virginia which had occasionally been attended by the fathers, till the difficulties of the Order diminished the number of missioners." As Reverend Dr. Guilday says, "Father John Carroll could easily have travelled all over southern Maryland and the northern part of Virginia and pass his days in visiting relatives of both sides of his family, the Carrolls, the Darnalls, the Youngs and the Brents." As the active field of battle in the Revolution shifted toward the South, Carroll's ministrations were a great source of encouragement and consolation to the fighting men and their families in that region. If his visits had only encouraged the families of his relatives all over these two colonies, that would have meant very much for strengthening the patriotism of a great many people, whose allegiance to the cause of the colonists was a significant factor for the cause of independence.

One of the most important incidents in Father Carroll's career just after the Revolution was his controversy with the Reverend Charles Wharton. Wharton was a cousin of the Carroll family who had been educated at St. Omer's, like Carroll himself, and like him too entered the Jesuits, and finished his studies at Bruges and Liège, being ordained a priest September 19, 1772. July of the following year he was appointed professor of mathematics in the English college at Liège but the suppression of the

Society deprived him of his teaching position and of his status as a Jesuit. Like John Carroll he took refuge in England and there he became permanent chaplain to the Catholics of Worcester, England. He gradually became unsettled in his faith and wrote after some five years of occupancy of the chaplainship a "Letter to the Roman Catholics of the City of Worcester," announcing his resignation of the chaplaincy and his defection from the Church. He returned to Maryland in June, 1783, after the Revolution, and for a year lived on his estate. While here he published his "Letter to the Roman Catholics of the City of Worcester."

The publication of the letter aroused a strong spirit of hostility to the Church in Pennsylvania and Maryland so that the American clergy felt that an answer was called for. This duty would seem to devolve on Carroll, both because of his education and his long years of teaching. The response was difficult, however, not because of the arguments advanced but because of the quotations from many sources that would have to be looked up. Books were scarce in America and particularly copies of the works of the Fathers of the Church. While preparing his letter in England, Reverend Mr. Wharton had had access to these without difficulty.

Carroll was invited to come to Philadelphia where Father Molyneux wrote:—"I have a snug chamber to rest you in and a library well fitted up in a choir of the old chapel and partitioned off from the same where you might spend many agreeable hours in study and application free from noise." When he wrote in reply asking for certain authors and for verification of the many quotations in Wharton's Letter, it became very clear that even the library of James Logan in Philadelphia would not prove adequate or available.

Fortunately Father Carroll found not far from him at Annapolis a valuable public library and it was here that he composed the greater part of his reply which is entitled: "Address to the Roman Catholics of the United States of America." It was published at Annapolis by the firm of Frederick Green in the autumn of 1784. Dr. Wharton was an antagonist worthy of Father John

Carroll and his Letter received much attention both in this country and in England where it had been written. On both sides of the Atlantic the Catholic reply was awaited with interest. As Reverend Dr. Guilday says: "Wharton's display of learning was pedantic, caught the fancy of the intellectual groups in the republic and it was in this display that Carroll proved him to have overreached himself and many of Wharton's quotations not only from the Fathers and theologians but from Protestant authors were found to be inaccurate and erroneous. John Carroll's Address is twice as long as the Wharton Letter and is written in a style as dignified and lofty [an unusual thing in the controversies of that time] as that of his apostate cousin. . . . The old hackneyed arguments against the Church Carroll refutes with a logic that reveals the power of the teacher in the days when he taught at Liège and Bruges."

Above all those who have made comments on Bishop Carroll's answer to Wharton have emphasized the fact that his address as Gilmary Shea says "had a peculiar dignity and equanimity, was free from all acerbity and harshness and was admirably fitted to exercise a beneficial influence on the public mind." Carroll himself was afraid that controversy might stir up bigotry and arouse the intolerance which he knew existed in the minds of so many of his fellow citizens here in America. He knew too that these existed not alone in the minds of the uneducated but in those also of the educated and that indeed many of the ecclesiastics of the Anglican Church in this country who represented the best there was of mental development among the clergy were thoroughly convinced that the Catholic Church represented the fulfillment of the prophecies of the Apocalypse and was the Beast of the Revelations and the Scarlet Woman of Babylon.

Wharton's objections to the Church are those which have been urged for centuries since the beginning of Protestantism and are still urged though they have been answered many times. Wharton, for instance, insisted that only the ignorant continue to belong to the Church and that knowledge always takes people out. After all the "Catholic Encyclopedia" was published in our generation for the purpose of answering that objection almost as the principal reason. Wharton labored the phrase, *extra ecclesiam nulla salus,* "outside the Church there is no salvation." How many times in the hundred and fifty years since Carroll answered that objection has it had to be answered again. Carroll shows that the rigorous interpretation of that phrase insisted on by Wharton is nowhere held by the Fathers or the theologians.

Rev. Mr. Wharton had appealed to Protestants by insisting on the Bible as the sole rule of faith. Father Carroll emphasizes in reply to the other points at issue that the Church can teach nothing that is contrary to the Holy Scripture. The Holy Scriptures properly interpreted are the rule of Faith in the Catholic Church quite as much as in any other, though Tradition is also a source of Revelation, and he convicts Wharton of deliberate misapplication of Scripture to the tenets of the Catholic Church.

The most important part of Carroll's answer, however, was his demonstration that Wharton garbled texts from Bellarmine and misquoted the Councils of the Church but also misquoted the Fathers. Here is a striking instance of Carroll's method and the content of his answer:

"I will not deny that I was surprised when I read the first passage cited by the chaplain (Wharton); it appeared so opposite to the principles which St. Chrysostom had laid down in several parts of his works. It was a mortifying circumstance that I could not conveniently have recourse to that holy Doctor's writings nor minutely examine the passage objected to together with its context. I procured a friend to examine the edition of Chrysostom's works belonging in the public library at Annapolis; he has carefully and repeatedly read the forty-ninth homily on St. Matthew; and not one syllable of the chaplain's citation is to be found. After receiving this notice I was for sometime doubtful whether it might not be owing to a difference of the editions. I could not persuade myself that he who so solemnly called heaven to witness of the impartiality and integrity of his inquiry, would publicly expose himself to a well-grounded implication of unpardonable negligence in a matter of such serious concern.

But I have now the fullest evidence that the passage for which Chrysostom on Matthew (Homily 49) is quoted is not taken from that Father. It is extracted from a work of no credit supposed to be written in the sixth century entitled 'The Unfinished Work of Matthew,' but had it even been fairly quoted the chaplain would not have had so much cause for triumph as he imagines, for the passage he adduces carries with it equal condemnation of the Protestant and Catholic rule of Faith."

It is easy to understand that the Wharton-Carroll controversy gave the new prefect apostolic who had only just been advanced to that post by the pope a position of prominence in the scholarly circles of the new republic. His address was just being read and favorably commented upon among Catholics and non-Catholics alike when the news became public that he had been chosen head of the Church in the United States. Father Plowden, S.J., who knew Carroll very well during his stay in England and who was himself a very scholarly man wrote to Carroll the following year: "You have written as a scholar, a Christian, a gentleman and a man of feeling.... When I read your work I easily foresaw the good effect which it would produce in strengthening the faith of the North American Catholics who must be too well apprised of the artifices of your antagonist to need a rejoinder to his Reply." Reverend Mr. Wharton did make a reply but it fell quite flat. During Carroll's lifetime no member of the Protestant clergy ventured to come out in print in favor of Dr. Wharton.[1]

Meantime Wharton was accepted by the Episcopalian church as a minister and sat in the first General Convention of that body in New York in the fall of 1784. Toward the end of the century

---

[1] There is a curiously interesting sequel to the controversy. After the resignation of Dr. Samuel Johnson II as president of Columbia College in New York, Reverend Mr. Wharton was elected the fourth president on May 25, 1801. His Jesuit training had fitted him for an academic career and he had secured a prestige for scholarship that brought about his election to this position. He probably found it impossible to fulfill his duties as pastor while acting as president, so after but three months' occupation of the position he resigned in August of the same year.

he was elected principal of an academy at Burlington, N. J. In 1798 he became the rector of St. Mary's Church in Burlington, a position which he held until his death in 1833. Wharton married twice, his first wife not long after his acceptance by the Episcopalian church. She was Mary Weems of Maryland. When Mary died June 2, 1798, Wharton published an elegy on her expressive of his grief but his mourning was not prolonged for he married shortly afterwards Anna Kinsey, daughter of the Chief Justice of New Jersey who long survived him.

In one way Father John Carroll had a distinct advantage over Wharton in his appeal to the fair-mindedness of the American people. Wharton had stayed over in England until the Revolution was over enjoying the peace and quiet of English homes. Carroll, on the other hand, while he might have spent his time in the houses of English nobility because of his intimate relationship with their sons at college, preferred to make his way over to America in order that he might share the dangers and the efforts of his fellow countrymen during the revolution that was just impending. He became the friend and admirer of Washington and was himself deeply respected by the Commander-in-Chief of the Revolutionary Army and by that great leader of men in that disturbed time, Benjamin Franklin. Readers of the two pamphlets could scarcely fail to recall these facts when reading the documents.

John Carroll's prestige helped the Catholic Church in the United States through the critical period of American Catholic history which is synchronous with the five years of his occupancy of the position of Prefect Apostolic. The feeling of freedom among the people led a number of Catholics to refuse that obedience to their religious superiors which means most for the success of the Church's work. The spirit of independence made itself felt in every aspect of American life,—in literature, in social customs, in politics and even in religion. To have a man like Carroll so completely trusted by the most distinguished American statesmen, so thoroughly American in his own sentiments, so exquisitely patriotic when the opportunity came to do things for the country, was of itself a great factor in making the Church respected in this country in spite of the disturbances of various kinds that occurred among the Catholic people and that sometimes involved also their clergy.

That was one of the serious difficulties in the Church at that time. Unfortunately a number of priests who had not been able to get on with their bishops or their religious superiors in Europe found their way to America and in the great need for priests that there was they were accepted by the ecclesiastical authorities and proved after a time to be anything but desirable pastors of flocks still less as roving missionaries among the people. As Dr. Guilday says in his life of John Carroll, "It was not that the private lives of these men were always morally reprehensible, for the Catholic laity could be trusted to repudiate the administrations of the hireling, but the truth is that it was open season with ecclesiastics many of whom left their dioceses in Europe for their dioceses' good; and turbulent men loving more the adventure of the times and yielding to a desire for change found their way here and in spite of canon law and the Church authority set up their standard in the midst of flocks whose rejoicing in their presence for eagerness to hear the Word of God and to receive the sacraments clouded their judgment on the caliber of the shepherds who came unasked and in so many cases unannounced." As Prefect Apostolic John Carroll had the difficult task of winning these men back to ecclesiastical discipline; he had the severer task of controlling those among the laity who were led astray by the intruders.

There was a very definite tendency among the American people generally to take sides with these disturbers against constituted authority in the Church and this feeling would have been greatly increased and would have been even more widespread than it was only for the fact that John Carroll himself both for his own sake and for his cousin the signer was so much respected by the American people. His reputation then was a very valuable asset, his character and judgment which had been so thoroughly trained by the Jesuits enabled him to accomplish ever so much more in eliminating disturbers of the peace in the Church than would otherwise have been possible.

As it was, in the three largest cities, Philadelphia, New York and Boston, there developed during the years after the Revolution and those of the beginning of the nineteenth century Church scandals which proved very seriously detrimental to the Church and led to the departure from the Church of a number of Catholic families, some of them the most prominent in these cities. Carroll solved many of these problems and he accomplished wonders in securing more and more of the clergy for his little flock and at the same time succeeded in lessening the number of recalcitrant clergymen who were leading their flocks into positions dangerous to their adhesion to the Church. The extent to which these scandals developed can be best appreciated from the fact that for a full generation after this they were thought of as having seriously hampered Church development.

During his Prefecture Apostolic conditions in the United States which were not as yet the United States but only the Confederation were very much disturbed. It has been said that life under the Articles of Confederation was little better than organized anarchy. No wonder these years (1783-1789) have been called critical and the State as well as the Church passed through perilous days. Reverend Dr. Guilday says: "It is significant that about the very time the Catholic clergy had decided to petition the Holy See for a bishop the delegates of the several States were in session in Philadelphia drafting the Constitution of the United States which was to give unity to the republic, stability to its government, and an acknowledged leader in George Washington, its first president." One thing Carroll had not, he had no Tory or Loyalist problem to solve as had the leaders of some of the non-Catholic religious bodies. The Catholics, few though they were in number, were practically all on the side of independence from the mother country. The Catholic Church in the rebelling colonies had become closely identified with the spirit and with the purpose of the Revolution especially after the support of a great Catholic country like France had been cast into the balance in favor of American independence.

Carroll's prestige had much to do with the securing of religious liberty for Catholics. There was grave danger owing to the fewness of Catholics in the country, less than one in one hundred in the population of all the colonies taken together, that this privilege so devoutly to be wished might not be secured. Fortunately there were some very representative Catholics besides Carroll. His cousin, Charles of Carrollton, was the only Catholic signer of the Declaration of Independence, and Thomas Fitz-Simons and Daniel Carroll were the only two Catholic signers of the Constitution of the United States. These with another, Dominick Lynch, and Bishop Carroll himself were the signers of the Catholic Address to Washington on his election in 1789 and fortunately the great father of his country was lacking in the bigotry and religious intolerance which characterized so many of the prominent men of New England and even of New York. The presence of two leading American Catholics, Thomas Fitz-Simons of Philadelphia and Daniel Carroll of Maryland, the brother of the Prefect Apostolic, in the Constitutional Convention of 1787, heartened the little groups of Catholics in the several states.

The address to Washington by the Catholics on his election as president of the United States attracted very favorable attention throughout the country. It is usually considered to have been almost entirely written by Father Carroll for the memory of his response to Wharton made everyone realize that he was the representative Catholic writer of the day. Together with Washington's answer it was published in London in order to call attention to the fact that the new republic of the West was beginning its career under such happy auspices so far as religious toleration was concerned. As the London publisher said, the address from the Roman Catholics to the incoming president "breathes fidelity to the States which protect them, asserts with decency the common rights of mankind; and the answer of the president truly merits that esteem which his liberal sentiments, mild administration and prudent justice have obtained him. . . . Is this not a lesson?"

The English Catholic subjects of the king were hoping that the example so nobly set and the lesson so well taught in America would be followed in the mother country. The lesson was not taken for some forty years in England, however, and Catholic emancipation did not come until 1829. The happy conditions which developed in the United States were largely the result of the favorable impression created by the Carrolls and other Catholics with whom American statesmen became intimate. Knowledge is all that is necessary to destroy prejudice.

Washington's reply to the letter addressed to him by the prominent Catholics mentioned shows how grateful he felt to their co-religionists for the help afforded the patriots in many ways by the Catholics during the Revolution and his personal appreciation of their allegiance to the cause of independence. He said: "I presume that your fellow citizens would not forget the patriotic part which you took in the accomplishment of their revolution and the establishment of their government—or the important assistance which they received from a nation in which the Roman Catholic faith is professed.... May the members of your society (the Friendly Sons of St. Patrick) in America, animated alone by the pure spirit of Christianity and still conducting themselves as faithful subjects of our free government enjoy every temporal and spiritual felicity."

One of the very interesting developments of religion here in America brought about by Bishop Carroll was the introduction of a community of Carmelite nuns from Antwerp into his diocesan city of Baltimore. While their brothers were sent on the long voyage to St. Omer's and other Catholic colleges in France from Maryland, some of the daughters of prominent Maryland Catholic families found their way over to enter the Carmelites in Antwerp. These nuns find their satisfaction in life and the solution of the problems of existence in a life of contemplation and prayer. Bishop Carroll wanted to have this phase of Catholicity represented in his diocese, hence his invitation to them to found a house in Baltimore. They took up the practice of the mystical life on this continent and their prayers continued to be felt as important auxiliaries for the success of the work of the Church in this country. There were not a few people even among Catholics in this country at that time who felt that our climate would not be suitable for a mode of life so severe as that of the Carmelites. They sleep very little, they are extremely sparing in their diet both as to quantity and variety and they are absolutely confined to their convent enclosure. Prophecies were rife that surely the lives of members of the Order would, because of their practice of mortification, be brief beyond the average. As a matter of fact so many of the Carmelites have lived to advanced years that regulations had to be made to increase the number of younger members of the community by special indult.

CHAPTER VII

GEORGETOWN UNIVERSITY AND HER SONS

THE year after the end of the Revolution, as the unanimous choice of his associates among the clergy in this country, Reverend John Carroll was appointed by the pope Prefect Apostolic of the Catholic Church in the United States.

He was an ideal personage to be selected for the position of Prefect Apostolic of the new nation that had come to life in America, and his wisdom and patriotism were largely instrumental in reorganizing the Catholic Church in the United States, setting it free from the jurisdiction of the Vicar General of London, under which it had been for centuries, and making it independent of any foreign power. Some French ecclesiastics had suggested that it would be better to keep the infant church in the new republic under French jurisdiction, but Carroll asked for absolute freedom for the Church in the United States within the pale of the Roman Catholic Church, and in this he was strongly seconded by Benjamin Franklin. They achieved ecclesiastical independence for the new nation and that meant much for the struggling Church.

During the Revolution Father Carroll occupied himself with his priestly duties and his Plan of Organization, issued in 1782, shows that he was thinking broadly and deeply in terms of the Catholic problem in this country. As time went on it began to he realized, as Reverend Dr. Guilday points out in his life of Archbishop Carroll, that "no one appreciated more keenly than Carroll the necessity of spiritual independence from every foreign court, the Holy See alone excepted." The French intrigue particularly, while it accidentally hastened his own appointment, became very distasteful to him. He was evidently the man for the position but no one knew better than he what an immense task there was before him in trying to organize the Church in America. Scattered along the Atlantic seaboard there were altogether some 30,000 Catholics among the 2,500,000 inhabitants. The task of affording opportunity for as many of these as possible to get to Mass on Sunday in places where there were a number of Catholics, and at least sometimes during the year where they were few in number, with the chance to make their Easter duty so far as that might be possible, was indeed difficult; but Father Carroll as Prefect Apostolic accomplished it to general satisfaction. It is not surprising, then, that five years later his name was submitted to Rome as an episcopal candidate by twenty-four out of twenty-six of the assembled priests, and he was named by the pope Bishop of Baltimore. His diocese reached from Georgia to Maine and westward to the Mississippi.

The new bishop, who was himself an ex-Jesuit, because of the suppression of the Society, had been a teacher in Jesuit colleges for many years, and it was his deep conviction that the one hope for the conservation and healthy growth of Catholicity in this country was the foundation of a Catholic college. This would provide for an educated priesthood—worthy leaders of their people—and also for a mentally developed laity, who would know the reasons for the faith that was in them.

All the colleges founded in America, that is in English-speaking colonies before the Revolution, had expressed this same religious purpose in their charters.[1] The colonists who themselves had had the benefit of education wanted above all to have the clergy educated men and faithful leaders of the people, but their purpose also was to graduate lay students who would make worthy magistrates, political officials whose principal purpose in life as the result of their liberal education would be not their own selfish advancement but the benefit of the community. All seven of the pre-Revolutionary colonial colleges emphasized in their charters and announcements the necessity for religious teaching and the making of better citizens.

[1] James J. Walsh, "Education of the Founding Fathers of the Republic," New York, 1934.

It is not surprising, then, that Bishop Carroll grasped at the opportunity afforded because of the guarantee of religious toleration in the Bill of Rights to take up the problem of founding the first Catholic college in the United States. In 1789 the cornerstone of the college was laid at Georgetown in what was afterwards to be the District of Columbia, on ground that is now actually within the limits of the city of Washington. Two years later, in 1791, the college was opened for the reception of its first students. The growth of the college was very slow. The number of students in attendance at the opening was very small, though it is to be noted that the number at the opening of the various colonial colleges founded before that time was not larger on the average than that of Georgetown.

The remote foundation of Georgetown College can be traced much farther back than its location in what is now the District of Columbia. The Jesuits founded schools which were expected to develop into colleges at various places in Maryland. Because of religious intolerance there was enforced migration from one location to the other. Others of the early American colleges, notably Yale and Princeton, though for quite different reasons, had similar experiences in migration, so that the college authorities felt justified in tracing their origin to places remote from the present location of the institutions.

Among the companions of Cecil Calvert there came with the Catholic pilgrims to Maryland two Jesuit fathers to take their part in the great work of colonization in America under a policy of religious toleration. They began their ministry as priests in missionary work and education at once. J. Fairfax McLaughlin in addressing the alumni on the occasion of the centenary celebration at Georgetown said:

"It has been a favorite study with me to trace the beginnings of Georgetown College back to their source—the landing of the Pilgrim Fathers of 1634 upon the shores of Maryland. . . . I traced the origin of Georgetown College to a period in colonial history as remote as that of Harvard College itself which has long boasted preeminence as the oldest English institution of learning on this continent. Father Poulton, S.J., had been sent out as superior of the Maryland mission in 1638. One of his first acts was to project a seat of learning. At or about the same period the initial movement was made in the colony of Massachusetts to establish Harvard College."

The first Jesuit academy had come into existence in the neighborhood of Calverton Manor on the Wicomico River in 1651 with Mr. Ralph Crouch, himself a Jesuit pupil, as the principal. This had existed for some twenty years. It was suppressed by the intolerance of the Protestants who in Maryland ousted the proprietor and established Protestant rule. Less than ten years later the Jesuit Academy was in operation in 1677 near New Town Manor. Father Foster, S.J., and Mr. Thomas Hothersell, a Jesuit scholastic, conducted the school and taught the humanities so well that two of the pupils, both native Marylanders, were admitted to advanced standing at St. Omer's the Jesuit college of northern France. Further intolerance necessitated the closing of this school after some years, so the Jesuits crossed Chesapeake Bay and established a famous classical academy at Bohemia Manor on the eastern shore of Maryland in which to teach the scattered sons of the persecuted Catholics. Sixteen years after the close of the academy at Bohemia Manor, the Jesuits were back once more at the spot where Fathers White and Poulton labored among the tribes of the Piskatoways and Anacostans some hundred and fifty years before. Their foundation at this point proved to be more enduring, and Georgetown College came to be an institution close to the capital of the nation when Washington was founded.

Fortunately Bishop Carroll had continued his relations with some of his English friends and they proved of help to him in the foundation of Georgetown. Father Plowden, the ex-Jesuit, was one of these. He was a learned man and for a time it seemed as though Carroll might secure him as the president of the new institution. Carroll wrote to him: "How often have I said to myself: 'What a blessing to this country would my friend Plowden be. What reputation and social advantage would accrue to the academy from such a director.'" When Carroll came to realize that it would be impossible for Plowden to leave his friends in England, he asked him to suggest someone capable of being the first director or president of the college. He even said, "I trust this important concern almost entirely to your hands." While Plowden refused to come as president or superintendent, when after his consecration Dr. Carroll appealed for help for the college to some English Catholics, it is worthy of notice that the list of benefactors included many of the former English Jesuits. Father Charles Plowden's name is in the list for a substantial sum.[2]

The site selected for Georgetown College was one described by the founder, afterwards Archbishop Carroll, as "one of the most lovely situations that imagination can frame." His residence at Rock Creek had familiarized him with the shores of the Potomac and the comparative importance of Alexandria and Georgetown at the time doubtless influenced his views. West of the knoll at Georgetown on which Mr. Alexander Doyle was erecting old Trinity Church there was "a point jutting out into the Potomac, finely elevated, free from malaria, and swept by every breeze from above or below." This was the site chosen by Reverend Father Carroll, and, as early as December 15, 1785, we find him writing, "The object nearest my heart and the only one that can give consistency to our religious views in this country is the establishment of a school and afterwards of a seminary for young clergymen."

The first pupil to be registered was William Gaston of North Carolina, destined to become a distinguished jurist, well known over most of the country for his oratory at a time when oratory was so thoroughly appreciated that men took particular pains to cultivate the faculty. His education devolved on his mother, his father having been killed during the Revolution, and she was a devout Catholic Englishwoman who welcomed the opportunity to send her boy to a Catholic college. Young Gaston remained at Georgetown for four years and attracted attention

---

[2] One is reminded that in the preceding generation Benjamin Franklin at the University of Pennsylvania had chosen Dr. William Smith of Aberdeen as Provost, Princeton had invited Witherspoon from Edinburgh to be president, just as Harvard in the early days had asked Comenius to take charge of the organization of Harvard's curriculum as president.

by his ability and success in his studies. After completing the course as far as it was organized at that time at Georgetown, he entered Princeton College, New Jersey, where he was graduated with first honors in 1796.

Though North Carolina, settled to a great extent by the Scotch Presbyterians, was rather intolerant especially in so far as Catholics were concerned, Gaston entered the field of politics when he was twenty-two and was elected to the Senate of his native State in spite of the fact that the constitution of North Carolina at that time contained a clause excluding Catholics from office. His service in the Senate proved so satisfactory to his electorate that when he offered himself for election to the Congress of the United States in 1813 he was elected. He was reelected in 1815 and came to be the close friend of many of the Federalists of that time. His career in Washington was active and brilliant as one of the influencial leaders of that party.

After his Congressional experience he resumed the practice of the law with such success and dignity that in 1833 he was elected Justice of the Supreme Court of North Carolina, an office which he held for the remainder of his life. When the Constitutional Convention for the amendment of the original constitution of North Carolina assembled in 1835, Justice Gaston exerted all his influence and his eloquence in securing the repeal of the article of the first constitution which practically disfranchised Catholics. Gaston was the intimate friend of Bishop England, the Irish priest who had been chosen bishop of Charleston, South Carolina, and who in the course of the years developed intense patriotism for the land of his adoption. The distinguished jurist proved a great encouragement to the bishop in the many controversies that he carried on and which had to be maintained in order to make the people of the South understand the real truth about the Church so as to eradicate bitter, old-fashioned intolerance. Gaston's influence meant very much in the southern states for correcting the bigotry so rife there and, when he stood shoulder to shoulder with Bishop England, they exerted great power over the minds of non-Catholics who had been brought up on—

drinking in almost with their mother's milk—the deepest intolerance with regard to Catholicity.

After all, this was the period when, as I pointed out in the Introduction to my volume, "A Catholic Looks at Life," (Boston, 1928) nearly every Anglican bishop is on record in an official episcopal document with expressions which show that he was quite convinced that the Roman Catholic Church was Anti-Christ and that the Pope of Rome was the Scarlet Woman of Babylon. All of these bishops were university men, thoroughly educated, well aware of the awful meaning of their words, and they employed such expressions on the most solemn occasions. One Anglican bishop declared, "Catholics are enemies of all law human and divine." Another said, "Catholicity is a religion fit only for persons weak in body and mind." A third said, "The Catholic Church stands convicted of idolatry, blasphemy and sacrilege." If educated bishops felt this way toward the Church, it is easy to understand how bitterly bigoted the uneducated members of their flocks were and therefore what a hard task men like Bishop England and Justice Gaston had in making their fellow citizens understand the true inwardness of the Catholic Church and the place that should be accorded her in the history of the times.

Among the other very earliest students at Georgetown was Robert Walsh, the well-known writer and member of the diplomatic service, who attracted so much attention not only here but also in Europe and who did probably more than any other in the early years of the American Republic to foster good will and understanding between the European countries and the new republic across the Atlantic. He graduated at Georgetown in 1801. When, in 1798, Washington after his retirement from the presidency visited Georgetown formally—for he was a close friend of the Jesuits there and particularly of Bishop Carroll— Robert Walsh was chosen to make the student address to him, and according to tradition made an excellent impression by his mature and thoughtful eloquence. After graduation he followed the old-fashioned custom of making the grand tour in Europe for several years and during that time he contributed a series of articles on the institutions and laws of the United States to the Paris and London papers.

Europeans generally were quite convinced that this noble experiment of ours in America of government of the people, by the people and for the people, was an idle dream that might last for a time but would surely prove a failure. Monarchs of all kinds were in the ascendant in Europe and the only democracy that had been tried seriously over there was the French republic which had disgraced humanity by its atrocities and which had ended up—as Europeans insisted all such experiments must—in a military dictatorship if political chaos did not intervene before that. Under the circumstances it is not surprising that Walsh's articles on the political situation here in America were read with great attention and provided for Europeans a better understanding of conditions over here than they had ever been able to secure before. His work came to be recognized and appreciated in this country also.

Walsh did not return to the United States until 1808 and then took up the practice of the law, though his literary tendencies were too compelling to allow him to devote himself to his legal practices exclusively. Three years after his settling down in Philadelphia he established in that city the "American Review of History and Politics," the first American quarterly to be published in this country. Literature proved so attractive that he soon came to devote himself entirely to it. The law is a jealous mistress and usually demands and enforces the demand that her favors be paid for by the strictest exclusive attention. Walsh made his literary career of great value to his country by his contributions to the better understanding of American political affairs both at home and abroad. Some of his works attracted wide attention. His "Appeal from the Judgment of Great Britain Respecting the United States" (1819) proved an important contribution to the political literature of that time and secured for him by formal resolution the thanks of the legislature of the State of Pennsylvania.

In 1821 Walsh followed up his earlier journalistic adventure by founding the "National Gazette." He continued to be the editor of this in Philadelphia for the next fifteen years. The periodical was devoted to politics, science, letters and the fine arts. His wide knowledge and liberal taste as well as his critical ability gave a hearty initiative and a striking impulse to American journalism. Lord Jeffrey of the "Edinburgh Review," who could be so bitter in critical castigation when it pleased him to be so, read Walsh's book, "Letters on the Genius and Disposition of the French Government," with cordial interest and felt that it represented an important contribution to the political literature of that day. At a time when Douglas Jerrold and other distinguished English literary men were demanding, "Who ever reads an American book?" Lord Jeffrey said of this book by Walsh, "We must learn to love the Americans when they send us such books as this." So, far from Jeffrey being alone in this opinion, there were many others who felt that here indeed was a very valuable work on a difficult subject.

Walsh was for the greater part of a generation one of the best known men in our western civilization so far at least as the literary folk of that era and the outstanding political personages were concerned. He was known widely in France and in England and it goes without saying at home here in America. No wonder that one of his biographers (Fry) said of him: "Probably no citizen of the United States of his age ever personally and immediately knew so many celebrated men and women. It was the social worth and enjoyment of literature that he chiefly prized; a more disinterested votary of knowledge it would be difficult to find in our day." When he became a resident of Paris he "habitually associated with the authors, statesmen and scholars who rally round the Institute, the Academy and the libraries, lectures and salons of that brilliant capital."

His intimate relation with prominent Americans is best demonstrated by the letters that passed between him and some of our most distinguished men. At the Library of Congress they have fourteen letters written by Walsh to Jefferson, (1817-23); ten letters from Jefferson to Walsh, (1817-24); three from Walsh to Madison, (1831-36); and ten from Madison to Walsh, (1819-31), but he was also in close touch with the Adamses. When his book appeared "Appeal Against the Judgment of England on the United States" (1819) its publication drew forth letters of congratulation from Thomas Jefferson, John Adams as well as John Quincy Adams, and many of the most prominent politicians and learned bodies. He wrote a sketch of General Andrew Jackson in order to oppose the torrent of abuse poured on the General and though he himself would have preferred to have John Quincy Adams reelected his sketch had much to do with the election of Jackson.

It was in literature rather than in politics, however, that Walsh was prominent. He was a trustee of the University of Pennsylvania and a chair of belles-lettres was held for him for years. John Quincy Adams considered him at the head of the profession of letters in America. Poe got along better with Walsh than with any other of the litterateurs of the time. He said with regard to some of Walsh's writings that in them he experienced "that thrill of pleasure with which I always welcome my own long cherished opinions when I meet them unexpectedly in the language of another." Poe felt that Walsh was one "to whom I might speak with the perfect certainty of being understood." As has been said by a recent biographer of Walsh [3] "that is a compliment that one is disposed to think the irascible genius never paid to another writer of his time."

The copy of the first number of the "American Quarterly Review," founded by Walsh, lists among other contributors Renwick, Bancroft, Hopkinson, Paulding and Rawle, so that the editor was evidently in touch with our most prominent American writers. He himself wrote for that number a review of the recently published life of Napoleon by "the author of Waverly" which attracted no little attention. This review lasted for ten years, that is until the author left to reside in Paris. Walsh was always intent on having the civilized peoples of the world understand one another as far as possible. He knew how many national prejudices there were and how unfortunate their continuance was for the fostering of enmity between countries.

[3] J. C. Walsh in his paper in the "American Irish Historical Society Journal," 1927.

He was in himself for his time a whole Society of Foreign Affairs. He thought that knowledge meant more than anything else to keep peace between civilized people. For him "to know all is to forgive all." He was one of the editorial directors and an important factor in the foundation of the "American Magazine of Foreign Literature," the forerunner of that very useful compilation which still continues to be published, Littell's "Living Age."

Walsh was to occupy another very enviable place in international relations before his life span was over. He was appointed Consul General of the United States in Paris, a position which he continued to occupy for the next seven years until his death. His house became, in a comparatively short time after he took up the consulship, the favorite rendezvous of the learned and distinguished men of France and also a popular recourse for literary or political visitors from England and the United States. His widespread interests, never superficial, but often profound, in politics, literature and science, made contact with him a pleasure at all times. His vivacity of mind and intellectual enterprise made people who had the opportunity of visiting his house to meet the men who were the leaders of thought and action of that time, feel that they had had an unforgettable social opportunity.

Robert Walsh was a social being in the best sense of that term and he accomplished an immense amount in enabling people of various nations with very different ways and modes of thought to understand each other or at least become very much better acquainted. At his death a distinguished American writer who knew him well declared that he was "the literary and intrinsical link between Jefferson, Madison and Hamilton, and the men of the present day."

Gaston and Walsh and Charles Carroll and his cousin John are very interesting examples of Jesuit college training. They prove beyond a doubt that Jesuit education and patriotism go hand in hand. Besides they make it very clear that students of the Jesuits can be distinctive leaders in democracy. Ordinarily it might be assumed that, as government in the Society of Jesus is of monarchic character, the products of the Jesuit schools would be definitely influenced in this direction. Many of the European graduates of Jesuit schools rose to hold important posts under European monarchs. Manifestly they are not committed to favoritism for any mode of government and our American exemplars of Jesuit education are counted amongst our worthiest patriots in the early days. Dean West at Princeton once said, "Let us make men and they will find their work." It would seem to be very clear that the Jesuits produced graduates who could think for themselves and they proceeded therefore to find their work and use their influence to the best advantage.

Georgetown College had at the beginning scarcely more than a score of students. It grew slowly until the beginning of the nineteenth century when it doubled in numbers. In 1850 the first catalog was published listing 125 students, all of them in the Arts (Classical) department. By the end of the century this number nearly doubled. In 1920 there were 300 and in 1927 over 900 in the college departments. Overcrowding of accommo-dations led to refusal of applicants and a reduction to 800 and then to 625. Each student entering is required to be in the first third of his class in high school.

The college buildings include: the Infirmary, the Faculty Building, Copley Hall which contains the Coleman Museum, Ryan Hall, the Maguire Building, the Healy Building, the Old and New North Buildings, the White-Gravenor Building, the Ryan Gymnasium, the Dahlgren Chapel, the Astronomical Observatory, and the Seismic Observatory. The buildings present an aggregate frontage of about three thousand feet. They are surrounded by grounds comprising nearly one hundred acres, a large part of which is occupied by the "Walks," the woodland scenery of which is famous.

These buildings house, besides the scientific museums, a valuable collection of works of art and a number of Maryland colonial relics. The Riggs Memorial Library has 166,247 volumes, among them many rare and curious works including nearly one hundred incunabula. This library incorporates that of the historian, John Gilmary Shea, which is particularly valuable for the Americana it contains as well as the volumes on the Indian languages.

The astronomical observatory has been in existence some ninety years and at the time of the centennial celebration in 1889 the main purpose of the observatory was changed from student instruction to scientific research work. While Father Secchi, S.J., and Father Hagen, S.J., both afterwards to be directors of the Vatican Observatory in Rome, were in charge at Georgetown Observatory, some excellent original scientific work was done. The seismological observatory, founded in 1911, has always been a favorite department at Georgetown and has been looked to by the press of the country for announcements with regard to the occurrence of earthquakes all over the world. Under Reverend Francis Tondorf, S.J., this department came to be very well known throughout the country, and its equipment has been kept up to date in spite of expense. A list of all seismic disturbances received at this station are, through the courtesy of the Associated Press and other news agencies in the United States and abroad, sent to more than one hundred and fifty observatories all over the world. There is special communication with the Jesuit seismological stations which are distributed over the globe. Immediate records are also sent to Science Service for distribution by cable and radio.

Among the distinguished alumni of Georgetown who are commemorated on the North Bay Window of Copley Hall, besides Judge Gaston and Chief Justice White—as well as Robert Walsh already mentioned—there are some men who reached distinction in civil and ecclesiastical life. Bishop Northrop, fourth bishop of Charleston, S. C., was one of the great churchmen of the South. He built the Cathedral of St. John, one of the most beautiful in the southern states. Edwin Kavanagh became prominent in his native state, Maine, of which he was a member of the state legislature, Secretary of the State Senate, United States Congressman, president of the State Senate, and Governor of Maine. He was an intimate friend of Longfellow, one of whose books bears the title "Kavanagh." Benjamin A. Young, both a student and professor at Georgetown, studied

philosophy and theology at Ferraro in Italy and later was professor of theology at Viterbo. Salvator Tongiorgi was a student
for two years at Georgetown and later held the chair of philosophy at the Roman College. He was a leader in the revival of
scholastic philosophy and his textbook in philosophy went
through nine editions in less than twenty years. Colonel Julius
P. Garesché reached distinction in the Civil War and was killed
in action at Stone River. A fort was named after him as a
special mark of honor. Charles Boarman, Georgetown's son in
the navy, became Rear Admiral. James Ryder Randall, so well
known because of his song, "Maryland My Maryland," is sometimes called "the poet laureate of the lost cause." His later
poems were deeply religious in tone and deserve to be better
known. William W. Corcoran, who founded in Washington the
Corcoran Art Gallery "for the perpetual establishment and
encouragement of the Fine Arts," was the first president of
Georgetown Alumni Association and at that time the oldest living alumnus. His art gallery, visited by practically all sightseers
in the national capital, has been an extremely important factor
for the cultivation of art among people generally in the United
States. Dr. Thomas Herran, a native of Colombia, was sent to
Georgetown at the advice of President Buchanan, an intimate
friend of his father, General Herran, ambassador to the United
States. He was in his country's diplomatic service in London,
Washington, as well as at Hamburg, Germany, and at one time
was president of Medellin University and Minister of Education
in Colombia.

No less than thirteen students of Georgetown have risen to
the position of president of their alma mater, and their names
have been carved along the cornice of Copley Hall.

Among Georgetown's alumni unrecorded in the North Bay
Window of Copley Hall because of lack of space are some distinguished Georgetown graduates who well deserve mention.
Condé Pallen, whose commentary on the "Idylls of the King"
drew a commendatory letter from Tennyson, is a striking
instance. He was for many years an editor of Catholic journals
and his service as managing editor of the Catholic Encyclopedia

was an important factor to the success of that work which has proved so valuable to non-Catholics as well as Catholics. Then there was Andrew J. Shipman, New York lawyer, who developed a marvelous facility for Oriental languages, and used his precious gift to help the Orientals of different rites of the Roman Catholic Church to secure opportunities for themselves in a strange land. He was close to the pastors, an adviser in the purchase of property and the erection of churches, as well as in the matter of naturalization of the members of their congregations as American citizens. Another distinguished Georgetown graduate was Thomas Walsh, a special student of Spanish literature and history, whose poetry gave him a place in the American Parnassus, and whose Catholic Anthology proved an admirable collection of poetry by Catholics, surprising even many Catholics themselves by the genuine poetic value of its contents.[4]

The Doctors Keyes, father and son, graduates of Georgetown, reached distinction in medicine in New York. Some of the members of the medical faculty have been very well and favorably known by their colleagues in medicine. Dr. John A. Foote was one of these, and Dr. William Gerry Morgan, some time president of the American Medical Association, another.

Among the living graduates of Georgetown Medical School who have attained deserved distinction are Dr. Bailey K. Ashford of Puerto Rico, who has done so much for public health in that island possession of the United States, and who in the performance of his duties has solved certain medical and pathological problems relating to our own states in the South, and Dr. Fielding H. Garrison, the author of a "History of Medicine," a book which has deservedly gone through a number of editions because of its scholarly character. He was for a number of years assistant librarian at the Surgeon General's library in Washington where he generously put his bibliographic knowledge of medicine at the command of those intent on writing on medical subjects. He is now one of the librarians of the William H.

---

[4] For the intimacies of the college history for three hundred years, see "Miniatures of Georgetown, 1634-1934," by Coleman Nevils, S.J., President of Georgetown University (Washington, D. C., 1934).

Welch Memorial Library of Johns Hopkins, Baltimore, and contributing editor to the Bulletin of the New York Academy of Medicine.

Georgetown College in its early days was controlled by American ex-Jesuits deprived of their membership in the Order by the brief of Pope Clement XIV suppressing the Society of Jesus. Upon the reorganization of the Jesuits in Maryland in 1805, the college was transferred to the Fathers of that Society under whose control and direction the university remains. By the act of March 1, 1815, Congress granted the power of conferring degrees and on March 30, 1823, the Holy See empowered Georgetown College to confer in the name of the pope degrees in philosophy and theology. By the act of June 10, 1844, Congress authorized the formal incorporation of the institution. Under this authority the school of medicine was opened in 1851 and the school of law in 1870. The university hospital was opened in 1898 and the training school for nurses in 1903. In 1901 the first session of the dental school was held, in 1909 the seismic station was erected and in February, 1919, the school of foreign service was opened.

CHAPTER VIII

FORDHAM UNIVERSITY

THE institution known since 1905 as Fordham University, before that for some sixty years as St. John's College, Fordham, was originally founded at St. Mary's in Kentucky in 1831. The university might well have assumed the privilege of celebrating its centenary in 1931. Several of the early colleges in this country, notably Yale and Princeton, celebrated their centenaries of foundations in towns more or less distant from the subsequent permanent home of the institution. The Jesuits would probably have remained permanently in Kentucky but for the fact that a misadventure in their establishment there made the development of the college ever so much more difficult than it would otherwise have been, so that when an offer was made to them to take up college work on the Atlantic seaboard, they were glad to accept it.

Bishop Flaget of Bardstown, Kentucky, had written to France in 1830 asking the French Jesuits, somewhat more than a dozen of years after the restoration of the Society of Jesus by the Pope, to found a college in his diocese. Postal communication across the Atlantic was slow and precarious. It took some time, besides, for the Jesuits to consult superiors and to make up their minds whether they could afford to send out of France, where their growing work was making ever larger demands on their resources of man power, the number of men who would be necessary to make a foundation of this kind successful. It was not until nearly six months after the bishop's letter was sent that the Jesuits in France were in a position to reply, accepting his invitation. They announced at the same time that they were busily engaged in making definite preparations to go to Kentucky. They started without hearing further on the subject from the bishop, as it would take at least three months, and probably longer, before a reply might come. Unfortunately this letter of the Jesuits was lost in the mail and so after many months, the bishop had recourse to other sources to secure the establishment of a college at Bardstown, the special work which the good bishop had originally called upon the French Jesuits for.

When a little later, all unexpected, the Jesuits arrived, the bishop was in a quandary what to do. The president of St. Mary's College, situated some twenty miles from Bardstown, which had been carried on with difficulty by secular priests for some years, offered to turn over that institution to the Jesuits. The bishop gladly consented to this arrangement which solved the problem that had arisen, and the president of St. Mary's, Father Byrne, agreed to stay at the college to act as president until the incoming teachers should have learned English.

The Jesuits began their college work at St. Mary's in 1831. Pupils were few, progress in building up the college was slow, the competition for students with the college at Bardstown added to the difficulties of the situation. Kentucky was still scarcely developed beyond pioneer conditions, and it is a never-ending source of surprise to see under the circumstances how much interest there was in education and how willing parents were to make even extreme sacrifices in order to secure opportunities for education for their children. Buildings and equipment were very limited, but men came out of the schools and colleges of that day who could think for themselves.

The Jesuits gradually increased in number. One of the additions to the faculty from France in 1836 was Father William Stack Murphy, who became famous as a writer and preacher, and in 1837 was made president of the college. Under his presidency the fathers made application to the Kentucky legislature for a charter of incorporation with all the powers of a university. That was a day when oratory was appreciated and according to tradition the legislature invited the president of the Jesuit college to appear before the legislators and they listened spellbound to his eloquence. The application of the fathers was favorably received, the charter asked for was promptly granted, and on January 21, 1837, St. Mary's took its place among the universities of this country. The first annual Commencement at which degrees were conferred was held in the summer of 1838.

It was not long before the fathers were brought to the realization that a college in Kentucky would have nothing like the same influence or opportunity for growth that it would have if it were situated on the eastern seaboard. When after some fifteen years at St. Mary's, Archbishop Hughes of New York City offered them the opportunity to take charge of the diocesan college and seminary at Fordham which he had founded with secular priests as the chief members of the faculty, the Jesuits gladly accepted the offer and began their college work there in September, 1848.

According to well authenticated tradition Archbishop Hughes himself once declared that he applied to the Jesuits of Kentucky rather than Georgetown to supply members of the Order for his college in New York because he feared that the eastern Jesuits might subordinate St. John's at Fordham to their older established institution so near the nation's capital. Bishop Hughes wanted to have full and free opportunity for the college in his diocese to develop to the highest degree with every incentive to that purpose. He wanted the Jesuits to have charge of it but perferred to have them without previous obligations that might interfere with their efficiency.

Bishop Hughes' desire that his college in New York should be second to none in the country had one fortunate effect. It brought to the development of Catholic higher education on the eastern seaboard, in addition to the Jesuits trained almost entirely under English influences, the French Jesuits also. While Jesuits are often said to be the same all over the world their training, though so rigorous, does not take away their individuality. Personally they differ very much. Certain national characteristics almost inevitably remain and are sure to make themselves felt in their work. This combination of French and English influences brought to the United States two strains of Jesuit scholarship which proved to be very valuable in bringing out the best factors in education.[1]

The curriculum at St. Mary's College, Kentucky, at the beginning of its history consisted of the classics, the physical sciences and mathematics, as these were taught in the French Jesuit colleges at that time. During the first half of the nineteenth century France had been particularly active in the study of science and possessed a number of distinguished scientists. It was in France too that mathematics had developed most deeply during that time, so that a strong incentive to good teaching in these departments existed. After some five years a class of philosophy in Latin was introduced and lectures on general ethics and special metaphysics and logic were added. This was within a quarter century of the time when the colonial colleges were giving up the *trivium* and *quadrivium* which had constituted the basis of their last two years of college work, so that the Jesuits came just in time to carry on the traditional teaching of the old medieval universities. They have continued ever since to make use in their curriculum of the Neo-Scholasticism which adapts the medieval scholastic teaching to modern advances in physical science and modern developments in the social sciences.

When the Jesuits came to Fordham they bought from Bishop Hughes the property (160 acres) on which the college and the seminary stood. The principal building on the grounds was the Rose Hill Mansion, for this had been the Rose Hill estate, and

---

[1] To these elements in Jesuit life in this country others were added as time went on. Both among the French and English Jesuits here in America there were a number of Irish accretions. Indeed John Carroll himself was quite proud of the Irish blood in his veins. A little later various missions were established in the United States staffed by Jesuits who came from various countries in Europe. The Italian province of Turin sent over a number of its members for the purpose of taking up missions in the distant West where they were the pioneers in education, founded the Rocky Mountain missions among the Indians and laid the foundations of what are now called the universities of Santa Clara and San Francisco. The German provinces likewise sent members of the Order to take up missionary and educational work among the Germans in the Middle West and at Buffalo. As a result of this there was a combination of national elements which serve to make the American Jesuits appropriately fitted to the task of influencing both in missions and education our heterogeneous American population.

the name was preserved for many years as the title of the college baseball team. The Rose Hills came to be widely known as one of the best of the college teams of its day and there are records of victories over Harvard and Yale, but never, I believe, over Princeton. For some seventy years, that is almost from the origin of the game, they have given a good course in baseball at Fordham. The fact that they took up the game very shortly after its origin, years before most of the colleges and a generation before sectarian institutions of learning generally in this country organized it, may be taken as an index of the definite purpose of the Jesuits to encourage among their students interest in athletics for the sake of the moral and physical values associated with them.

The Rose Hill Mansion which still stands is built of stone four square, fortress-like in character, three stories high, with a cupola that was added for the accommodation of the astronomical observatory. From very early days in Fordham special attention was given to astronomy and the Seniors met on certain nights in winter for the study of the heavens by means of a four-inch telescope. A practical introduction to astronomy was thus made one of the features of the course.

Associated with their studies in astronomy was a special course of physics and another in chemistry for which instruments of various kinds and experimental apparatus were imported from France which was the leader in the teaching of these sciences at that time. The early and progressive interest in physical science constitutes the answer to educators who suggest that the Jesuits confined their curriculum to the classics and did not afford opportunities for education in science.

The best known and most influential of the members of the faculty at Fordham in its early years was Father William Stack Murphy, a nephew of Bishop Murphy of Cork, Ireland, a distinguished scholar who had already attracted attention down in Kentucky and who now came to be very well known in New York. He was admired as much for his preaching as for his power of winning the hearts of young men in the classroom. After him in distinction was Father Augustus

Thebaud, the fourth president of the college. Toward the end of his life he wrote a series of books which attracted wide attention. Almost needless to say, there was little writing by Catholics at that time in this country and the old Jesuit who was a graduate of the Sorbonne in Paris and was a broadly educated scholar busied himself to supply something of the large lacuna that existed in American Catholic literature. Father Thebaud's volumes on "The Church and the Moral World"; "The Church and the Gentile World"; "The Irish Race, Past and Present," as well as others, came to find a place in most Catholic libraries and to be in the hands of many priests who it was said collected books rather more liberally then than they do now considering all the circumstances.

It is easy to understand that progress in the building up of the institution and increase in the number of students in the new location was not rapid. New York was only just beginning to become the Catholic city it later became. Many Irish Catholics were already emigrating from Ireland to America in the early '40's but most of them were very poor. The great immigration of the famine years in the later '40's brought even poorer people from whom expenditure for education could not be expected. The surprise was how soon they proved ready to make great sacrifices to afford their children educational advantages in spite of their own utter lack of education due to the English penal laws and the policy of the British rulers so deeply calculated to crush all Irish aspirations.

The outlook was much better, however, than it had been in Kentucky, and there was an encouraging gradual increase in the number of students until in the early '50's there were over one hundred, though only about one-third of them were college students. The remainder were in the preparatory and high school departments. If it is recalled that not long before the middle of the nineteenth century Columbia College (University) which now has perhaps the largest attendance of students in the world had less than one hundred and fifty on its rolls, it will not be surprising that the number of students at Fordham was not large.

The college drew students from many different states in the Union and especially from the South because southern Catholic families had learned to appreciate the value of Jesuit education while the Fathers were in Kentucky. On the whole the college was progressing quite satisfactorily and becoming more and more favorably known. Just before the beginning of the Civil War, old St. John's had an attendance of some two hundred boarders with a negligible number of day students, always less than a dozen.

The Civil War proved a serious setback to the college as it at once cut off the attendance of students from all southern states. Besides, economic conditions were disturbed, many young men were called away to military duties, and all the colleges reported fewer students. There were trying times for the college during the war and just afterwards, and then it was seriously disturbed by the panic of '73 which made it impossible for a number of parents to continue to send their sons to college.[2]

In the later '70's the number of students at Fordham had run down so that when I went there (1878), there were only 128 students, about 45 of whom were in the college classes, 40 in the high school and somewhat more than 40 in the preparatory department. These last were boys, as a rule, under fourteen. By 1882 the number had grown so that we were able to welcome the 200th boy and were given a holiday in celebration of the occasion. His name was Robert Emmet, son of the distinguished New York physician, Thomas Addis Emmet, and grandnephew of his namesake, Robert Emmet, the Irish martyr patriot.

In the early '90's the number of students rose to 300 and in the early years of the present century to 400. The proportion of college men in the house increased, so that the average number of graduates rose from ten in the '80's to more than forty twenty years later.

----

[2] The inclusive charges at Fordham for board and tuition at this time were $300, with $30 additional for laundry and certain other charges up to $350. St. John's was the most expensive Catholic college in the United States at that time. Many of the others charged $200 for board and tuition and a few, $250. The Canadian colleges offered board and tuition for $125, some of them even less, down to $110.

Under Father John Collins, S.J., as president—he has since been Bishop Collins of Jamaica in the West Indies—it was decided to enter the university field by the establishment of law and medical departments in connection with St. John's College as the Department of the Arts and Sciences. New York City had bought some three acres of the college property fronting on the Southern Boulevard and had erected thereon Fordham Hospital, a city hospital which has since come under the Hospital Board, and which promised to afford clinical facilities for the proposed medical school. The Board of Regents of the University of New York accorded the privilege of expansion.

The medical school entered upon its first year with 6 students, the first of whom was named Rosenberg. The property used to be known as Rose Hill Manor and the coincidence of the names seemed to be a happy omen. The father of the first student said that the reason why he wanted his son to enter the medical school at Fordham was that he himself had been a student of the Jesuits in Vienna and he knew that wherever they had jurisdiction there would be no taking away of the faith of the students as regards belief in God and a hereafter. The second year of the medical school there were 14 students. The numbers in the medical school doubled each year for the next seven years until there were nearly 300.

Some of the features of the medical curriculum are worth noting because they represented pioneer work in certain fields of medical education. From the beginning the professor of the history of medicine gave regular lectures with the purpose of providing a background of knowledge in the minds of students as to things medical in the older time, so as to enable them to appreciate particularly how much of supposed progress in medicine from generation to generation proved to be delusions. The course proved to be of special interest to the students. Alongside it a course was given in functional nervous diseases in the third and fourth year combined, so as to emphasize the place that the psychoneuroses occupied in life. The many strange remedies and modes of treatment employed for various affections which proved curative, yet after a while turned out to have no physical effect at all, were dwelt upon as one of the most important chapters in the history of medicine but also as one of the most important warnings with regard to the acceptance of new remedies until they had been thoroughly tested. In connection with these subjects, a textbook of "Psychotherapy" (New York, 1912), and a volume on "Cures,—the Story of the Cures that Fail" (New York, 1923) were published.

At the beginning of the medical course, the nearness of the New York Zoölogical Park and the Botanical Gardens suggested the advisability of having brief semester courses given to the students in botany and zoölogy under the tutoring of members of the staffs of those institutions. These courses took the students out into the open for an hour of work and were very much appreciated by those who were interested in their medical work not only from its practical side but with the idea that the greater the breadth of knowledge, the better was likely to be the success of the practitioner of medicine in later life.

For a while Professor Von Oefele, the distinguished Egyptologist, gave a series of lessons at the medical school with regard to Egyptian medicine and its relationship to our own. During the early years Dr. Thomas Darlington, commissioner of health of New York City, lectured to the students on public health problems and Dr. William T. Shanahan came down from Craig Colony to give practical points with regard to epilepsy; while Dr. Lawrence F. Flick, the distinguished tuberculosis expert to whom so many things in the modern crusade against tuberculosis are due, also lectured at the college. Professor Thomas Dwight head of the anatomical department of Harvard University was to have come to Fordham for a Commencement Address but for his untimely death.

Brief as was the existence of Fordham Medical School, several of its graduates and faculty made brilliant records. Colonel John Ryan devoted himself to the suffering people of the Balkans and went through a series of epidemics of typhus and cholera with them, saving a great many lives. On one occasion by running up an American flag over his hospital, he succeeded in diverting the fire of the enemy concentrated for a moment on that quarter of the town. After the Armistice, following a brief rest in this country, he took up once more the task of struggling with the epidemics in central Europe, only to succumb himself at last to typhus fever. One of the best known members of the faculty, William J. M. A. Maloney, offered his services at once at the beginning of the war to the British government, for he had not as yet become a citizen of the United States. He was among those who took part in the unfortunate episode at Gallipoli. The Turkish defense proved so obstinate that at one time he was, himself severely wounded, the ranking surviving officer, in the attack on one part of the peninsula. He had been the organizer of the graduate work at Fordham which brought Professor Head and a group of distinguished foreign physicians to Fordham.

The medical school continued to advance in numbers up to nearly four hundred, though even this number proved not to be sufficient to provide through the fees the funds necessary to carry out the program outlined for the teaching of medicine according to regulations adopted by the American Medical Association. An effort was made to secure an endowment that would pay the salaries of the six full-time professors required, but in vain. With the failure of that movement, the school was closed not long after the war, but with the definite idea that it would be opened once more in case there was sufficient patronage to enable the university to continue its support of it.

The history of the law school was more fortunate, doubling in number practically every year for about a dozen years, until there were well above a thousand students. The success of the school was soon assured. The graduates gave a good account of themselves in the bar examinations and in the practice of law, until it came to be recognized very generally that Fordham was giving a very practical preparation for the successful pursuit of the legal profession. The law school has continued for nearly thirty years to be one of the well-appreciated institutions of the metropolis whose graduates are proud of their alma mater and her success in educating lawyers of distinction.

Fordham was as fortunate as Georgetown in the distinction of her early graduates. One of those graduated at the first Commencement, July 15, 1847, was Sylvester Horton Rosecrans, who afterwards became the first bishop of Columbus. He was a brother of General Rosecrans, of Civil War fame, who was a teacher at West Point, and while there became a convert to the Catholic Church. He came down to Fordham in order to be received into the Church by the Jesuits. Of the first four graduates, three, including Rosecrans, became priests, and the fourth, Andrew Smith, became a lawyer. Among the graduates in 1847 were William Keegan who afterwards became Vicar General of the diocese of Brooklyn and was looked upon as one of the most distinguished American churchmen of that day. Andrew Smith became prominent at the New York bar. Among the graduates of '48 was Reverend Daniel Fisher who was the first rector of Seton Hall College, South Orange, N. J., the college and seminary of the diocese of Newark, N. J. Another of the graduates that year was Henry H. Dodge of Perrysburg, Ohio, who studied law and was advanced to the bench and came to be very well known in Ohio. His son went to Fordham and was graduated there a quarter of a century later. A graduate of the class of '49 who attained national distinction was Michael O'Connor of Charleston, S. C., brother of Lawrence O'Connor, who was a graduate of St. Mary's, Kentucky. Michael O'Connor became a fiery secessionist in the after years while his brother, a well-known architect, chose to reside in New York and espouse the cause of the North.

The most distinguished graduate of the year 1850 was David Merrick who after graduation entered the Society of Jesus and in the course of time came to hold some very important positions in the Jesuit colleges of the second half of the nineteenth century and lived to be a very old man. In 1857 Henry A. Brann was graduated after having made his preliminary studies at St. Francis Xavier's downtown. He rose to be one of the most distinguished clergymen in New York. He was one of the early students in the North American College at Rome and wrote the history of that institution. In 1860 Winand M. Wigger graduated. He entered the seminary and became a priest and subsequently the bishop of Newark, N. J. under whose episcopate the diocese of New Jersey came to be one of the most important bishoprics in the country. He proved a worthy successor to Bishop James Roosevelt Bayley who was promoted to the archiepiscopal see of Baltimore in 1872, and to Most Reverend Michael Augustine Corrigan, who was promoted to the archiepiscopal see of Petra as coadjutor to the Archbishop of New York, in 1885.

Among the members of the faculty in the very early days at Fordham, John Gilmary Shea, then a young man, was to achieve distinction. He was on the teaching staff in 1848 and '49, and left to become an editor and what we would call in our time a free lance writer. He devoted himself to the study of the early Indian missions in this country, and published a "History of the Catholic Missions among the Indian Tribes of the United States 1529-1854." One of his books, "Perils of the Ocean and Wilderness," telling the story of missionary adventure came to be the favorite reading of boys for whom it supplied the adventure stories of the modern time. Gilmary Shea came to be such an authoritative writer on Indian affairs that he was asked to contribute a series of articles on Indians to the Encyclopædia Britannica, then engaged in the preparation of its ninth edition. His great work, however, for which he was already preparing himself while at Fordham was his "History of the Catholic Church in the United States" which is very well known and has remained the authority on that subject ever since. Shea's life written by Reverend Dr. Guilday of the Catholic University (New York, 1926) enables us to understand the long years of research which he devoted to this work and what a magnificent contribution he made to one phase of the history of the United States.

In 1850 the degree of LL.D. was conferred by Fordham on Orestes A. Brownson, the well-known American philosopher, essayist and editor. Brownson had run nearly the whole gamut of religions before becoming a convert to the Catholic Church. He was ordained a Universalist minister but later denied all divine revelation. For some twelve years he was associated with the Unitarians. He was just past forty when he became a Catholic and after that he devoted his pen to the defense of the Faith.

For many years he edited Brownson's "Quarterly Review," which came to be looked upon as one of the most thoughtful magazines in the country. Altogether he wrote some twenty-five volumes octavo. The best known of these is "The Convert or Leaves from My Experience." His work on "The American Republic, Its Constitution, Tendencies and Destiny," attracted wide attention. His volume, "The Spirit Rapper," was a critical contribution to the literature evoked by the spiritualistic movement which followed the supposed revelations made by the Fox sisters at Hydesville, New York. In granting Brownson the degree and inviting him to make the Commencement address in 1850, Fordham very properly recognized the work of a distinguished Catholic writer who deserved to be ever so much better known than he was.

One of the traditions at Fordham in the late '40's is that of the residence of Edgar Allan Poe in the village of Fordham and his occasional visits to the college. Father Edward Doucet, S.J., afterwards president of the College, who was there as a young Jesuit not yet ordained, and Father David Merrick who was there as a student and afterwards became a Jesuit, both used to tell of seeing Poe on a number of occasions passing through the college grounds on the way down to the banks of the Bronx River where the New York Zoölogical Garden is now located, but which in those days was on the college property. The trees were very thick, there was an old mill down there, and the dam and the water wheel and the rather gloomy forest surrounding them must have caught the poetic fancy of the ill-fated Poe. Besides, Poe used the library at Fordham, for the Fathers had quite a collection of books that they had brought with them from St. Mary's, and especially a number of French books. Many of these volumes are still in the library and it is probable that some of Poe's ideas for his poems were secured from these old books. Here is a possible chapter in Poe's life that has never been written and that very probably would prove of interest.

A number of Fordham students enlisted in the northern armies and not a few of them reached distinction. Among them were the three McMahon brothers, one of whom, Colonel McMahon, fell bravely leading his men in that awful charge at Chancellorsville. His brother, afterwards General Martin McMahon, was very badly wounded in the same battle, indeed barely escaped with his life, and yet lived to a round old age looked upon as one of New York's heroes of the war. Another Fordham man to reach distinction in the Civil War was General James O'Beirne who went through many campaigns, was wounded several times, and lived on to be one of the oldest of Fordham's alumni toward the end of the nineteenth century.

The decade after 1850 presented some brilliant students. Besides the McMahons there were John R. G. Hassard and Arthur Francis who founded and edited "The Goose Quill," the first journal published at Fordham. Hassard became one of the most distinguished journalists in New York City. Not long after his graduation he became one of the staff of the "American Encyclopedia" and soon received the recognition of Ripley and Dana, the editors, because of his talents. After a few years young Hassard became the managing editor and was largely responsible for the work. He was later private secretary to Mr. Dana and associated with him in his work on various newspapers. In his later years Hassard was the musical and dramatic critic of the "New York Tribune" and was looked up to as one of the leading lights in whatever culture New York was trying to develop and absorb at that time.

Many graduates of Fordham have, as might be expected, become priests and have reached prominence and achieved distinction in the ministry. Fordham's most distinguished alumnus is John Cardinal Farley, Archbishop of New York. His predecessor, John Cardinal McCloskey, had been the first president of Fordham before the Jesuits took charge of it. After these in importance came Monsignor Mooney for many years Vicar General of the diocese of New York. The pastor of the New York orphans, Monsignor Mallick J. Fitzpatrick, the successor to Father Drumgoole of beloved memory, a Jesuit student who organized care of the orphans of New York City, was another Fordham graduate. Many other prominent Catholic clergymen are Fordham alumni, among them in recent years, Right Reverend Francis J. Spellman, Auxiliary Bishop of Boston.

Fordham has always been well represented on the bench in New York, the most notable exemplification of this being Honorable Morgan J. O'Brien, for many years Justice of the Supreme Court of New York and Presiding Justice of the Court of Appeals, still happily with us. Among his brother alumni of Fordham who were colleagues on the bench were Ellsworth J. Healy, Edward J. Glennon, Thomas F. Connelly of Portchester, N. Y., James M. Barrett and John J. Sullivan. Fordham has nearly always been represented in the House of Representatives in Washington and well represented in the Senate and Assembly in Albany.

Another of the very well known graduates at Fordham of the '50's was Mr. Thomas B. Connery ('53), who was for many years editor-in-chief of the "New York Herald." He was looked up to by the newspaper men of New York generally as one of the most distinguished of their guild and he was on terms of intimacy with most of the men engaged in literary and journalistic work in New York during the fourth quarter of the nineteenth century. He was afterwards secretary to the American Legation in Mexico.

Among the students and members of the faculty of Fordham who by pen and tongue attracted attention in the twentieth century are Austin O'Malley, author of works on pastoral medicine that made him known all over the world and have given his works a place in the libraries of theological seminaries where they are often referred to; Reverend Cornelius J. Clifford, professor of Scholastic philosophy at Columbia University, New York; Dr. James J. Walsh, medical director of the Fordham University School of Sociology, author of some forty books; Reverend John J. O'Rourke, S.J., former head of the Biblical Institute at Rome which took up the archæological investigations that have meant so much in Palestine in recent years; Honorable Martin H. Glynn, former Governor of New York, and for many years editor of an Albany newspaper whose expressions attracted attention throughout the country, he was chosen to make the nominating speech for Woodrow Wilson when he was placed in nomination for the Presidency of the United States; Michael J.

Mahony, S.J., author of a series of textbooks on logic and other phases of philosophy that are widely used in educational institutions throughout the country.

In 1925-26 the attendance at Fordham was almost exactly 6,000 in the University with about 550 in the prep school. The number on registration grew every year by more than ten per cent and reached a peak in 1930-31 when there were altogethr 9,578 students in attendance on university courses and 543 in the preparatory school.

CHAPTER IX

THE JESUIT "RATIO STUDIORUM" IN OUR COLONIAL COLLEGES

As we have said, papal approval was followed almost immediately by widespread Jesuit activity, noticeably the opening of schools. Before Ignatius' death fifteen years later a large number of colleges had been opened in the Catholic countries of Europe. There were colleges in Rome, at Naples, and a number of other towns in Italy, at Messina and Palermo in Sicily. Besides there were Jesuit colleges at Gandia, Spain, founded through the influence of Francis Borgia, Duke of Gandia, afterwards the third General of the Order, at Salamanca, Valencia, Alcalá, Burgos, Valladolid and Saragossa in Spain; at Lisbon in Portugal, at Vienna in Austria, and at Billom in France.

The very year of the founder's death saw the establishment of colleges at Ingolstadt, Cologne, Prague, Tyrnau (Hungary), and within a few years afterwards colleges were opened in most of the important cities of Europe, at Munich in 1559; at Treves in 1560; at Innsbruck and Mainz in 1561; in Belgium at Audenarde in 1566; at Douai in 1568; at Bruges in 1571; Antwerp 1575; Liège 1582, and even so far away—and the distance was ever so much greater comparatively in those times than it is in ours—as Mexico City where a college was founded in 1573. Before the close of the sixteenth century Jesuit colleges had been founded also at Lima in Peru, and as an offshoot from Mexico a college was founded in the Philippines which is still represented in the Ateneo de Manila. That institution as I write is rising phoenix-like from its ashes, for its principal building was destroyed by a fire in the fall of 1932. Undiscouraged, the Jesuits have taken up the work of replacing the old wooden structure by a fireproof college building. The former students have rallied generously to their support and it seems as though, in spite of the commercial depression, they would surely accomplish their purpose. Meantime by shifting their own residence quarters, taking on personal discomforts at which they never balk, the Jesuits were able to accommodate their students and continue their college work.

This list of Jesuit colleges opened down to the beginning of the last quarter of the sixteenth century might very easily be made much longer. Paulsen, professor of philosophy and education at the University of Berlin, supplies in his "History of Higher Education in Germany" (Leipzig, 1885) a much longer list to those who may wish it. Only the more important foundations are mentioned here but this affords an excellent notion of how widely diffused the educational work of the Jesuits was in the course of a single generation.

At first there was, as is easy to understand, no little variety in the teaching of the Jesuit colleges in the different European countries conducted as it was under the auspices of men of many different nationalities and varied educational experiences. Gradually efforts were made to systematize Jesuit education. Father Nadal, often referred to by the Latin form of his name, Natalis, was a close friend of Ignatius and succeeded him as the second general of the Order. One of the seven founders in Paris and a distinguished student of the University of Paris, noted not only for his talent as a teacher but also for his prudence and executive ability, Father Nadal was appointed rector of the new college at Messina in 1548. There he wrote his treatise, *De studiis Societatis Jesu,* the first plan of studies of the Society. Father Nadal's plan was, after trial at Messina, sent to the Roman College to be tested and there certain modifications of it were made. After some years of trial, a system was gradually evolved by Father Ledesma who taught for some years at the Roman College, the principal college of the Jesuits in Rome.

Father Ledesma's *Ratio Studiorum* continued to be the basis of Jesuit studies, though never slavishly followed, until the last decade of the sixteenth century when Father Claudius Aquaviva, the fifth General of the Order, considered to be one of the greatest of the Jesuit Generals, called to Rome a group of six experienced teachers chosen from different countries and provinces to draft a scheme of studies so that opinions from all over the world of scholarship might be available for the systematization of the Jesuit curriculum. The plan drawn up by them was sent to the various provinces of the Society and the provincials, that is the heads of the various provinces, who came to Rome for the fifth general congregation (1593-94) reported the results of the plan as practised during the years since its issuance and asked for some modifications. "At length in 1599 when every possible effort had been made, when theory and practice alike had been consulted and every advisable modification had been made, the final plan of studies appeared under the title: *Ratio atque Institutio Studiorum Societatis Jesu* (Naples, 1599), usually quoted under the abbreviated title *Ratio Studiorum*." [1]

This has continued ever since to be the groundwork of Jesuit teaching though there has never been any formal demand or command to follow it absolutely. Father Roothaan, one of the greatest Generals of the Jesuits in the modern times, that is since the restoration of the Society (1814), suggested certain modifications of the *Ratio* to suit modern times. It is supposed to be modified by the experience of teachers in such a way as will adapt it to the special interests of various countries and regions and above all will introduce such educational elements into it as will make it accord with modern advances in knowledge especially as regards mathematics and the sciences. The *Ratio Studiorum* is not at all the ironclad, hide-bound system of education that it is often declared to be by those who know little about Jesuit teaching but who often seem to think that they know a great deal. The *Ratio* may at any time be changed to bring it more closely in line with modern progress in knowledge but as it represents the fruit of educational thought and practice for some 350 years it is not surprising that the Jesuits are conservatively intent on maintaining the value of this educational treasure which they possess.

[1] Schwickerath, "Jesuit Education," B. Herder, St. Louis, 1903.

Jesuit colleges as organized under the *Ratio Studiorum* comprised seven classes. Three of these were in what we would call high school or preparatory school, and at least four corresponded to our college classes. In the five lower classes the classics constituted the basis of education. There were Third or Lower Grammar, Second or Middle Grammar, First or Upper Grammar. These were followed by Humanities, called also Classics, with intensive study of Greek and Latin prose writers. This corresponded nearly to our modern Freshman class. Then came Poetry class corresponding to our Sophomore, devoted to the classic poets and orators; and then the two Philosophy classes in which were studied natural, mental and moral philosophy, that is metaphysics, ethics and physics, as well as mathematics. After completing the grammar classes the students were expected to talk Latin in class and the teaching in the philosophy classes was all in Latin and the disputations which constituted a prominent feature of philosophy teaching were also in Latin.

In the Grammar classes and Humanities and Rhetoric there was teaching of geography and history as well as such other subjects as would illustrate classical authors. Many of the Jesuits were interested in archæology. Special attention was paid to mathematics and young members of the Order with special mathematical talent were in accord with the *Ratio* to be given particular training so that they might be able to teach the subject. From the very beginning the Jesuits were interested in astronomy and Father Clavius, in the first generation of the Order, was called to Rome by the pope to make the correction of the calendar (1583).

The Vatican observatory founded at Rome under the patronage of the popes was placed under the direction of the Jesuits. It is often said that the Jesuits were not interested in anything except the classics and especially the teaching of Latin with Scholastic philosophy. Any such expression as that can come only from someone who does not know the Jesuits and their educational ways and history, and above all is not familiar with the many books on scientific subjects written by Jesuits. About

five hundred Jesuits have the distinction of a place in Poggendorff's "Biographical Lexicon of the Outstanding Scientists of
All Time."

Before the end of the sixteenth century, that is about the time
when the *Ratio Studiorum* was being moulded into shape, the
Jesuits had some of the most distinguished teachers of Europe in
their schools, men whose names were known all over the continent. Among them were such men as Bellarmine, considered
one of the deepest thinkers of his time, around whose name a
whole library of controversial works were issued; Suarez, the
great Spanish philosopher recognized as a founder of international law by Grotius. He comes just after Thomas Aquinas,
in Jesuit estimation as an authority in philosophy. Then there
were Toletus and de Lugo with Vasquez and Molina, the great
Spanish theologians, Lessius and á Lapide from the Netherlands,
Peter Canisius, "the schoolmaster of Germany," and many others
of scarcely less prestige.

In the next generation, Father Athanasius Kircher, S.J., taught
the sciences in the Roman College and wrote a series of illustrated
textbooks of science that are still considered precious bibliographic treasures in many libraries. These were all in the hands
of Jesuit teachers of science all over the world and were the volumes most consulted by scholars everywhere who wanted to keep
in touch with progress in science. Many of the Jesuits were
deeply interested in science and have continued to be so down to
our time.

In spite of the success of their teaching and its eminent suit-
ability to the times, so that wherever they opened a college,
students flocked to them, the Jesuits are often blamed, as I have
said, for having devoted so much attention to Latin to the exclusion or at least to the neglect of the vernacular languages. It
must not be forgotten, however, that at this time Latin was the
universal language of scholars. They had the advantage of us in
this regard. To keep abreast with progress in the arts and
sciences, history and biography now, it is necessary for a scholar
or university professor in our time to know half a dozen languages. Three centuries ago all that was needed by the scientist

was to know one other language besides his mother tongue—Latin. This would prove the open sesame to all the books published anywhere in Europe that would be worth while except for vernacular literature.

The emphasis on Latin was not due to the Jesuits. It had come down from the Middle Ages and was quite satisfactory for the times in which they were teaching. They were merely fulfilling a need of the period in emphasizing Latin. Scientific books of nearly all kinds even those relating to medicine and mathematics continued to be published in Latin until the latter half of the eighteenth century.

It was soon recognized that the Jesuits could teach very well and that their pupils advanced more solidly and more thoroughly than those of other schools. As a result it came to be an accolade in the world of scholarship to have graduated from a Jesuit school. Many non-Catholics came to Jesuit schools as well as Catholics, as we shall see, and this led to aspersion on the part of Protestant educators of parents who did so un-Protestant a thing.

There has been much argumentation as to priority in features of the Jesuit teaching. One thing is perfectly sure that the Jesuits adopted and adapted the education which the founders had received at the University of Paris and, after half a century of experience with that, proceeded to systematize education in the way that they thought would be at once the most thorough and the most formative for their pupils.

The surest index of the success of Jesuit teaching was the large number of pupils who came to them in all the cities where they had colleges and they even attracted students from long distances. Demands were made on them to establish colleges in practically all the important cities of the continent. Even their enemies were ready to acknowledge that they were very successful teachers. The testimony of Lord Bacon, the English philosopher and Lord Chancellor, is very interesting in this regard. He said: "Of the Jesuit colleges . . . I may say as Agesilaus said to his enemy Pharnabaces, *talis cum sis, utinam noster esses.*" [2]

[2] "Advancement of Learning, Book I." "Since you are what you are, would that you were ours."

Ranke, the well-known German historian, whose history of the lives of the popes created such a sensation, has some very strong words of commendation for the Jesuits as teachers. Ranke was himself a man of deep originality of intellect who is often spoken of as a pioneer in modern historical writing with accurate documentation, so that his opinion on the subject is well worth while. Moreover his profound knowledge of the history of the Church and of Christian education, secured in connection with his studies in the lives of the popes, makes what he has to say carry special significance. He says: "It was found that young people gained more with them in six months than with other teachers in two years. Even Protestants removed their children from distant gymnasia to confide them to the care of the Jesuits." [3] Almost needless to say Ranke was a Protestant and was not likely to be partial in his judgment of the Jesuits, but he emphasizes the fact that many Protestants lamented the fact that the Jesuit schools had such an attraction for their Protestant brethren.

There were many others who called attention to this attraction that the Jesuit schools had for parents not of the Catholic faith. Wilhelm Roding, professor in Heidelberg, in a book bearing the significant title, "Against the Impious Schools of the Jesuits," complains in the preface; "Very many who want to be counted as Christians send their children to the schools of the Jesuits. This is a most dangerous thing, as the Jesuits are excellent and subtle philosophers, above everything intent on applying all their learning to the education of youth. They are the finest and most dextrous of teachers and know how to accommodate themselves to the natural gift of every pupil."

A whole sheaf of similar expressions might be gathered and indeed have been gathered in histories of the Jesuits emanating from Protestants who were forced to confess what wonderful teachers these Jesuits were. For instance, Andrew Dudith of Breslau quoted by Janssen, the historian of the German people, wrote: "I am not surprised if I hear that one goes to the Jesuits to school. They possess varied learning, teach, preach, write, dispute, instruct youth, without taking money, and all this they

[3] "History of the Papacy," Vol. I, Book 5, Section 3, p. 416, London, 1896.

do with indefatigable zeal; moreover they are distinguished for moral integrity and modest behavior." [4]

The systematization of their teaching meant very much for the success of their work. Our American historian of education, Quick, in his volume, "Educational Reformers," (p. 508) said: "The Jesuit system stands out in the history of education as a remarkable instance of a school system elaborately thought out and worked as a whole. . . . The system grew and was, and I may say is, a mighty organism. The single Jesuit teacher might not be the superior of the average teacher in good Protestant schools, but by their unity of action, the Jesuits triumphed over their rivals as easily as a regiment of soldiers scatters a mob. . . . For each class was prescribed not only the work to be done but also the end to be kept in view. . . . In this particular the Jesuit schools contrasted strongly with their rivals of old as indeed with the ordinary school of the present day."

None of these historical and educational writers whom I have quoted is a Catholic so that their testimony carries all the more weight under the circumstances. Only that there was absolutely no doubt about the superiority of the Jesuit schools these men would not have made such very definite declarations as to Jesuit education.

This Jesuit curriculum with its combination of classics and Scholastic philosophy would seem to many educators in our day, trained under modern conditions, as very out of date, not at all calculated to bring out the talents or cultivate the thinking power of the students. Above all the study of metaphysics and moral philosophy with the coordinate studies in logic, grammar and rhetoric would smack too much of the Middle Ages and of the medieval universities to be held of any great value for the modern time. It was of this old medieval curriculum, however, that Huxley, surely not at all medievally minded, said in his inaugural address as Lord Rector of Aberdeen University:

[4] There are further quotations of similar import in Janssen, Volume iv, pp. 473-476; Vol. vii, pp. 80-82. Many of them are cited in Schwickerath's "Jesuit Education." For further information see McGucken, S.J., "The Jesuits and Education" (1933) and "The Catholic Way in Education" (Milwaukee, 1934).

"The scholars of the medieval universities seem to have studied grammar, logic and rhetoric; arithmetic and geometry; astronomy, theology and music. Thus their work, however imperfect and faulty, judged by modern lights, it may have been, brought them face to face with all the leading aspects of the many sided mind of man. For these studies did really contain at any rate in embryo, sometimes it may be in caricature, what we now call philosophy, mathematical and physical science, and art. *And I doubt if the curriculum of any modern university shows so clear and generous a comprehension of what is meant by culture as this old trivium and quadrivium does.*" (Italics ours.)

As a matter of fact the curriculum of the Jesuit colleges came to be adopted to a great extent as the basis of the curricula in the European colleges generally but also in our American colonial colleges. This continued to be the case not only down to but after the Revolution and indeed until well on in the nineteenth century.

The Founding Fathers of our American Republic, that is to say the groups of men who drew up and signed the Declaration of Independence, who were the leaders in the American Revolution, and who formulated the Constitution of the United States which Gladstone declared to be the greatest document that has ever come from the mind of man, were, the majority of them, educated in the colonial colleges or in corresponding colleges abroad. The culmination of their educational training as definitely outlined in these college theses followed, as I have said, almost exactly the Jesuit *Ratio Studiorum*. The fact has been missed to a great extent in our histories of American education because of the failure to comprehend the significance of the lists of theses which were handed around among those who cared to take part in the Public Act or disputation on Commencement morning. Any old graduate who had the impulse to challenge any of the prospective Bachelors of Arts could put them to the test of "defending manfully" any of the theses on the sheet and the candidates were supposed to be ready to answer any objections made to the propositions laid down on the Commencement broadside.

Unfortunately for their preservation, these theses were published on large sheets of paper, hence the name broadsides, and only very few of them are extant. None of the colleges has a complete set of its own printed theses and some of them have none at all. Harvard succeeded in rounding out a reasonably complete collection through photostats from the Hunter collection in Edinburgh, and four of the other colleges have succeeded in gathering varying numbers of their theses. Those extant reveal exactly what the curriculum for the last two years at college was. The various accounts of colonial college work that have come down to us supply rather definite information as to the studies of the first two years. The last two years they studied moral, mental and natural philosophy, physics, metaphysics and astronomy and mathematics. During the preceding two years they finished the classics and gave a good deal of time to logic, rhetoric and grammar, the old medieval *trivium*. The method of teaching philosophy was by lectures and disputations, the students having in turn to defend theses each week during the year, and this defense was by the syllogistic method. The objections were always urged in Latin. The Jesuit textbooks on these subjects for the past three hundred years are still extant and demonstrate very clearly the method and content of their teaching.

All the theses are Scholastic in character and resemble closely those which are defended in the Jesuit colleges at the present time, many of them being identical in word and meaning. Indeed what made me recognize the significance of the Harvard theses when I came across them while looking up early printing in Massachusetts was the fact that the theses at Harvard in 1642 were so like those which we had defended in Fordham in the Public Act held by our class in 1884. When I submitted copies of the theses that had been published on Commencement day for what was called the Public Act to Jesuit teachers of philosophy who had themselves been occupied for many years with the teaching of Scholastic philosophy, they were all in accord in the declaration that these were Scholastic theses and that indeed they were so little affected by whatever sectarian influences were at work in the colonial colleges that they were practically identical with the theses that were still defended in the Jesuit colleges not only throughout this country but in various countries of Europe. It was not only the Jesuits who recognized this fact but also teachers at various Catholic universities especially at Ottawa, where they make a specialty of the study of medieval philosophy and where the director assured me that these colonial college theses were all "pure Scholastic formulas." It is well known that the supreme aim of the Jesuit colleges is to maintain the purity of their Scholastic philosophy as completely as possible.

The more these colonial college theses are studied in comparison with the theses published at the Jesuit colleges in our generation, the clearer it becomes that they both represent the heritage from the old Scholastic philosophy of the Middle Ages. The origin of that has been traced to the Schoolmen of the earlier Middle Ages and to Boethius. Some of the colonial theses can be traced back very far in the history of education. For instance, at Brown just before the Revolution, they had to defend the thesis, *Deus potest esse, ergo est,* "God can be, therefore He is." This is the old so-called ontological argument for the existence of God elaborated by St. Anselm in the tenth century. This argument Thomas Aquinas rejected but Duns Scotus, I believe, continued to hold it very firmly. The argument has had an appeal to a number of distinguished thinkers and scholars in the modern time. What interests us here is that while it finds a place among the colonial colleges over one hundred and fifty years ago and was still discussed very seriously during the nineteenth century, its origin dates back for some nine hundred years. Before a pronouncement on the part of the Church with regard to it, this mode of argumentation had been taught in the Jesuit colleges in many parts of the world.

The great difference between Jesuit education and secular education, that is education without ethics, comes out very clearly when comparison is made between the purpose of Jesuit education and that of our modern colleges and universities generally. The main purpose of education in the Jesuit colleges is exactly the same as it was in our colonial colleges. As is easy to see from their charters and especially the announcements made by their executives when the colonial colleges were first opened or when in successive years parents were invited to send their boys to these institutions, religion and ethics were the fundamental subjects for education. They declared very succinctly and emphatically that their principal aim was to make the students better Christians and in this way better citizens. The colonial colleges were without exception founded in order to supply an educated ministry but a correspondingly educated magistracy so that holders of political office might be so trained in character through their education that they would devote themselves to the benefit of the community.

Education was not organized for the purpose of enabling a man to make a living for himself but in order that he might make something out of life for himself and above all for others. The supremely successful men were considered to be those who in one way or another gave of their time and energy to the benefit of the whole community. The whole character of secular education has changed in that regard. Comparatively little attention is now paid to making students better men and better citizens. Religion has become to a very great extent a dead letter in college life, and moral education is waning to such an extent in its influence that very little positive advantage is expected of it.

Still the Jesuit schools labor to maintain as their chief purpose the making of better men as individuals and better citizens in their social relations to the community. Jesuit educators are still quite ready to declare that an education which does not aim to make men better men and better citizens is likely to do much more harm than good, for it is turning out educated conscienceless individuals than whom none could be more dangerous to organized society. Their supreme educational principle is that training the will is more important, as a factor in education, than training the intellect.

Ethics continues to be in the Jesuit colleges, as it was in the colonial colleges, the most important subject in the curriculum and one in which every student is expected to be deeply grounded. Ethics is not merely a theoretic but a very practical subject to be applied to life and conduct. In pre-Revolutionary days in this country ethics was usually taught by the president of the college under the most impressive circumstances. The students had thoroughly brought home to them the impression that the moral principles in which they were drilled and which they had to defend against all sorts of objections in their weekly disputations and their Commencement theses represented the condensed wisdom of the ages as regards human conduct and were founded upon the natural and the divine law, to be observed with the most faithful attention. Men might fail to keep these principles and observe these laws on occasions, but they knew what was right and wrong and their consciences had been trained to regulate life appropriately. In the modern Jesuit colleges one of the most distinguished of the members of the faculty is chosen as the teacher of ethics. It is felt that the real crux of education and its value for mankind lies in this department.

CHAPTER X

A MODERN BLACK-ROBE: FATHER DE SMET

WHAT may well be termed a romantic incident in American Jesuit history occurred in St. Louis in 1831 when a group of Rocky Mountain Indians, influenced by the traditions which had come down from their forefathers who had been converts to Christianity some hundred and fifty years before in New York and Canada, made a fifteen-hundred-mile journey to St. Louis begging for a "black-robe" to go back with them, to be to them what the "black-robes" had been to their ancestors of long ago. The tribal memories recounted that many generations before, men dressed in black robes had come to them while they were still in the East and had baptized them and their children and taught them how to pray to the Great Spirit. Their traditions declared that life had been happier for them than ever before as the result of the black-robes' ministrations. The Indians had been moved farther and farther westward with the advance of the frontiers, but they were quite convinced that with the black-robe as a counsellor and guide such as their fathers had had, a true friend on whom they could depend with the most absolute confidence for the solution of the problems that were always cropping up in their relations with the whites and also among themselves, tribal concerns would go much more smoothly. They were sure that they would find such a man among the whites and the sign that they had found him was to be that he wore a "black robe," that is the long soutane of the Jesuits.

Unfortunately at that time their request could not be complied with. The Jesuits were few in numbers and all of them were burdened with duties. They had taken charge of St. Louis Academy some five years before, the number of students had

grown and every Jesuit had more than he could do. The Indians
were tireless in their persistence. In the course of ten years four
Indian delegations in succession were despatched from the Rocky
Mountains to St. Louis to beg that black-robes be sent them. The
last one composed of some Iroquois who dwelt among the Flat-
heads and Nez Percés was successful. Father Pierre-Jean De
Smet was assigned to the task of complying with the Indians'
demands and in 1840 he accompanied them to their Rocky
Mountain home. He was a man of just about forty and he had
found his life work. For the next thirty-two years—for he lived
well beyond three score and ten—he labored among and for the
Indians and came to be looked upon as their dearest friend and
most dependable counsellor by many different tribes of different
character. He was their beloved father in God.

Ordinarily there would be the feeling that the missionary
"black-robes" of the seventeenth century, the Jesuit martyrs of
the Iroquois, Huron, Algonquin country, represented a very
different set of men from those to be found among the Jesuits of
the nineteenth century. The progress of civilization had made
men different. Cultivated college professors could no longer be
expected to give up their chairs in colleges to spend their lives
among savages. That was a thing of the past. The progress of
humanity had changed that.

Anyone who reads the life of Father De Smet, however, will
be quite persuaded that the spirit which animated the Jesuits of
the seventeenth century was just as characteristically developed in
the heart of Father De Smet and his companions of the nineteenth
century. The descendants of the Iroquois had found their "black-
robes." The Jesuits of this modern time are just exactly the same
as the Jesuits of two hundred years ago or, for that matter, four
hundred years ago. Their "spiritual exercises" still form them
to the same spirit of self-sacrifice as of yore. Many deeply educated men are still ready to give up all that culture has meant
for them and devote themselves to a life of hardship and trial
among the pagan savages where they meet with very little appreciation, and expect less, for their unselfish work. Their one consolation is that they are following in the footsteps of their Lord

and Master and that they are making the Gospel known to
those who are without the pale of the Church—and all of it
Ad Majorem Dei Gloriam, to God's greater glory.

Father De Smet was born at Termonde in Belgium, January
30, 1801, just at the beginning of the new nineteenth century.
When he was past twenty he emigrated to the United States,
having already developed a desire for missionary work among
the Indians. For the accomplishment of his purpose he entered
the Jesuits whose novitiate was then at White Marsh in Maryland. Only seven years had passed since the restoration of the
Order after their suppression, but he recognized the old spirit
of the Jesuits and he wanted to share in their missionary labors.
In 1823 at the suggestion of the United States Government a
new Jesuit establishment was determined on and located at
Florissant not far from St. Louis for work on the reservation of
the Pottawottomies and other Indians in that neighborhood. Here
was the beginning of Father De Smet's labors among the Indians.
Like so many Belgians he had a genius for language and he soon
knew several Indian tongues. Above all, it came to be very clear
before long that he had a special talent for understanding the
character of the Indians. He inspired them with confidence and
they came to him gladly with their troubles. He was now ready
for further service among the Indians and this proved to be his
career.

He set out for the Rocky Mountain country in 1840 and
received a most cordial reception from the Flat Heads and Pend
d'Oreilles. This reception itself must have been a source of great
encouragement after his long journey of some two thousand
miles through that wild and absolutely unsettled country and
he took it as a happy augury for the future of his missionary
work. During this very first year of his missionary labor Father
De Smet displayed that marvelous power over the red men which
was to characterize his future career and make him such an
immensely valuable bearer of conciliatory messages between the
Indians and the white men.

Almost needless to say he had to be satisfied with the life that
the Indians themselves led; he had to eat what was prepared by

the Indians and this often consisted of animal food to which he was unaccustomed and for some of which the habits of civilization had created a positive deterrence; he had to make long journeys on foot and still longer on horseback, but in Indian fashion without saddle; he had to put up with Indian inconsiderateness but that was all as nothing to him since he felt that he was doing them good not only for this life but above all for the life to come.

He began his missionary labors at once, imparting instruction to the Indians wherever he was brought in contact with them, baptizing some of them, especially their children, and gradually imparting the truths of Christianity. Having surveyed the missionary possibilities of the Indian country and realized how ripe for the harvest was the field of labor assigned him he promised the Indians to establish a permanent mission on his return from St. Louis. He took advantage of the journey back to St. Louis to visit a series of Indian tribes, the Crows, the Gros Ventres, and others. In all, during this missionary journey, he traveled nearly five thousand miles through that as yet almost utterly unexplored region. On his return to St. Louis he was more anxious than ever to continue his missionary labors and he did not hesitate to express his conviction that there was a most promising opportunity for missionary work among these Indians. They had a traditional background that was most favorable for the exertion of the influence of their beloved black-robes, and all that was needed was men who would be ready to carry on the work.

In the following year he returned to the Flat Heads, living up in what is now Montana, and with Father Nicholas Point he established St. Mary's Mission on the Bitter Root River some thirty miles north of Missoula. During the course of this year he visited the Cœur d'Alènes and realized that here too was an inviting field for missionary labors. An immense task was opening out before him and De Smet appreciated very thoroughly that he needed help of every kind, so he went to Europe in 1843 to solicit funds and to invite workers interested in spreading Christianity and civilization to take up the work. In 1844 he returned with new laborers for the missions, among them being six Sisters of Notre Dame de Namur. In order to avoid—particularly for the sake of the Sisters—the long journey through unbroken country overland from St. Louis to the missions, he returned in a vessel that made the trip around Cape Horn. This ship cast anchor in the mouth of the Columbia River at Astoria, so well known at that time because of Astor's commercial enterprise and above all because of Washington Irving's account of it.

From here Father De Smet made the journey by canoe to Fort Vancouver to confer with Bishop Blanchet. Arrangements were soon made for a series of missions and the good Sisters who had so bravely left their comfortable houses in Europe now found themselves occupied with the care and instruction of the Indian squaws and above all the children. They accomplished their task so successfully as to make family life among the Indians something quite different from what it had been before. The Indian braves took much more interest in their wives and children than they had done before Christianity came to give a new meaning to marriage, and civilization developed to soften manners and customs.

In the course of a very few years in spite of the slowness of the spread of information and the rude means for the diffusion of news among the Indians, Father De Smet's name came to be known among all the tribes of the Northwest and the missionary came to be held in the highest respect. The Indians became thoroughly persuaded that the black-robes with their old traditions were among them once more, quite as willing as ever to help their Indian children in the solution of the problems of life and protect them as far as possible from the impositions of the white men. As a consequence of this confidence Father De Smet was able to do an immense amount of good not only to keep the Indians from hostilities with the white settlers, though the treatment of the Indians by the whites was, almost needless to say, often extremely arrogant and cruel, but he was able also to prevent the hostilities among various tribes of Indians which were occurring so frequently.

The Black Feet Indians of the Northwest, a very warlike and quarrelsome tribe, were a constant menace to other tribes of

Indians in their neighborhood and especially to some of those in whom Father De Smet was particularly interested. He determined, then, to make a journey among these hostiles in the hope of influencing them by his personal persuasion. It was a very risky adventure that might readily end in death but his dauntless courage won the hearts and the confidence of the Indians who promised him a safe conduct. He found them very stubborn. Indeed it was not until after a battle with the Crows in the Yellowstone Valley in which the Black Feet were defeated that they consented to listen attentively and respectfully to the blackrobe. He accompanied them to Fort Louis in their own country and while there he was able to induce them to conclude peace with the other Indians with whom they were in almost a perpetual state of warfare. He left them in a much better state of mind and left Father Point, S.J., one of his companions, to found a mission among this formidable tribe.

He had now spent nearly four years among the Indians and he was destined to enter upon a new phase of his career. His wonderful power over the Indians, as his biographer in the "Catholic Encyclopedia" says, "his almost inexplicable and seemingly instantaneous ascendancy over every tribe with which he came in contact and his writings with regard to the missions which made him famous in both hemispheres caused the United States government to look to him for help in its difficulties with the red man." He had been an humble missioner, now he became a public character. His work for the Indians henceforth was to consist in pleading their cause before Europeans and becoming their intermediary at Washington whenever Indian patience would be exhausted by the inroads and injustice of the white men and hostilities would break out.

His power over the Indians was strikingly exemplified in certain events that took place on the Pacific coast after the discovery of gold in California. In 1851, owing to the inflow into California and Oregon of the vast numbers of whites caught by the gold fever, the Indians of that region became restless and manifested tendencies of hostility to the whites. The more we know of what actually happened as the result of the encroaching

of the white settlers on Indian land, above all the more we consult Helen Hunt Jackson's book, "A Century of Dishonor,"
which shows so clearly how many insults and tantalizing impositions the proud Indians had to suffer, the more we can appreciate the fact that the whites were very much more to blame
than the Indians.

A general congress of Indian tribes in this region was determined on by the United States authorities and was held in what
was known as Horse Creek Valley near Fort Laramie not far
from where Denver now is. The United States Government
requested Father De Smet to attend the congress, confident that
he would have a deep and favorable influence over the Indians
and that his very presence would be a pacifying influence during
the discussions. He made the long journey—in those days an
extremely trying experience—not without avail, for his presence
soothed the ten thousand Indians who had assembled for the
congress and in spite of the lamentable grievances they had
suffered he brought about a satisfactory understanding.

This was only the beginning of his work as a diplomatic
go-between for the government and the Indians. In 1858 he
accompanied General Harney as a chaplain in his expedition
against the Utah Mormons, and, at the close of this campaign,
the government requested him to accompany the same officer to
what were then Oregon and Washington territories where it was
feared that an uprising of the Indians would soon take place.
This was the territory in which Father De Smet was best known
and the presence of the beloved black-robe had the desired effect,
for the Indians loved and trusted him implicitly.

When the Civil War broke out soldiers were recalled from the
frontier country, or at least their numbers were very much
reduced and the Indians smarting under insults and injuries of
many kinds threatened to take advantage of this opportunity to
begin hostilities with the whites. Fortunately Father De Smet
had visited the Sioux country where there was most disaffection
and his experience convinced him that a serious situation confronted the government and his warning had the effect of
saving many lives. The Indians rose in rebellion in August, 1862,

and at the request of the government De Smet made a tour of the Northwest. When word was brought to him that a punitive expedition had been determined on to teach the Indians a lesson as it were, he refused to lend it the sanction of his presence. He knew that the Indians were more sinned against than sinning.

In the course of years the condition of affairs among the Indians became more critical and further outbreaks were threatened. The United States government appealed to Father De Smet again in 1867 and asked him to go among the red men as an organizer of peace. He knew that they were enraged by the white men's perfidy and cruelty but he was asked by the government officials "to endeavor to bring them back to peace and submission and prevent as far as possible the destruction of property and the murder of the whites." Without any delay Father De Smet accepted this invitation from the government and set out for the upper Missouri interviewing thousands of Indians on his way and receiving delegations from the most hostile tribes. Before the Peace Commission that had been organized could deal with the situation that had developed Father De Smet fell ill and was obliged to return to St. Louis.

The following year, however, he was ready once more for his work among the Indians. In 1868 he again started on what Chittenden calls in his biography of Father De Smet [1] "the most important mission of his whole career." For some time he traveled with the Peace Commissioners. He knew how distrustful the Indians were and knew that they had been aroused to dangerous irritability. He determined therefore to make his way alone into the very camp of the hostile Sioux. His biographer says of him: "Father De Smet alone of the entire white race could penetrate to these cruel savages and return safe and sound. The missionary crossed the Bad Lands of what is now South Dakota and reached the main camp of the Sioux in which were sheltered some 5,000 warriors under the leadership of Sitting Bull."

He was received with extraordinary enthusiasm. What is more

[1] "Life, Letters and Travels of Pierre Jean De Smet," p. 92, New York, 1905.

his counsels were at once agreed to, for the Indians had absolute confidence in him. Representatives of the tribe were sent to the Peace Commission. A treaty of peace was signed July 2, 1868, by all the chiefs. This result has been looked on as the most remarkable event in the history of the Indian wars. Two years later, in 1870, he visited the Indian country to arrange for a mission among the Sioux.

He was occupied in many other ways, however, in the interests of the Indians. On their behalf he crossed the ocean nineteen times, visiting popes, kings and presidents, and finding his way into almost every European country. By actual calculation he traveled nearly two hundred thousand miles on his errands of charity and what that would mean of trial and hardship in those frontier days and with nothing but Indian trails to follow and stormy Atlantic crossings to endure is easy to understand.

Father De Smet was a worthy Jesuit not only because of his missionary labors but above all because of his writings and his scientific observations. His biographer in the Catholic Encyclopedia says: "His writings were numerous and vivid in descriptive power, rich in anecdote, and form an important contribution to our knowledge of Indian manners, customs, superstitions and traditions." It was marvelous that he was able to make the many geographical observations that enabled him and his fellow missionaries to find their way over the trackless country of the early days. Some of his letters serve to show his power of scientific observation and they would deserve to be placed beside the "Jesuit Relations" of the centuries before in this regard. He had frequent narrow escapes from death in his travels through these unknown territories and he often took his life in his hands when penetrating among hostile tribes. He was a bringer of peace; he knew how uncertain were Indian tempers yet he never faltered.

His personal character was charming and his disposition made him beloved among his brother Jesuits. He was almost childlike in the cheerful buoyancy of his disposition and he preserved this characteristic to the end of his life though he had spent many years among savages and been received by many of the kings and distinguished statesmen of that time and been honored by them. He was made Chevalier of the Order of Leopold by the King of the Belgians.

His main title to fame accrues from his extraordinary power over the Indians, a power which no other man of his generation is said to have possessed in anything like an equal degree. To give a list of the Indian tribes with which he came in intimate contact and over which he acquired an astounding ascendancy would be to enumerate almost all of the tribes west of the Mississippi in his time. All his contemporaries who were in touch with the Indian situation recognized his marvelous control resembling something like fascination over the minds of the Indians. This was largely due to his open-hearted sincerity. Protestant missionaries are united in declaring that Father De Smet was the sincerest friend the Indians ever had. The effects of his work for them were not permanent to the degree which he had planned, but that was because the Indians were swept ahead by the white invasion along the frontiers and gradually became engulfed by the white settlers of the Northwest. He had planned that there should be for the Indians of the Northwest of the United States something like the peace and happiness which his brother Jesuits nearly two hundred years before had secured for the Indians of South America. No one knew better than he that the so-called Reductions were really great colonies in which the Indians were protected from the injustice of the whites and brought under the influence of Christian civilization.

Father De Smet would like to have done for the Indians of the Northwest what Father Kino, S.J., somewhat more than a century before, had succeeded in accomplishing for the Indians of the Southwest, or what Father Rasle had done two centuries before for the Abnakis in Maine. Father Kino organized ranches and fruit colonies, what might well have been called agricultural stations, and even planned and executed a certain amount of irrigation, so that no wonder what had sometimes been spoken of as the American desert blossomed like the rose. Father Kino succeeded in making the Indians care for work, and the tribes with which he had to deal were of very much the same character as those among which Father De Smet was doing his missionary work throughout the Northwest. The discovery of gold, which rapidly advanced the frontier and which tempted a great many people to make their way to the West, made Father De Smet's plans impossible of accomplishment. The Franciscans succeeded for a time in exemplifying in the missions of California what could be accomplished with some of the lowest Indians of the country but their missions were overrun and their Indians driven out and bitterly imposed upon so that all that we have is the memory of their wonderful work in the ruins of their beautiful mission buildings.

Like the good Jesuit that he was, Father De Smet wrote out "Relations" of his missionary experiences. The first one of these was "Letters and Sketches with a Narrative of a Year's Residence Among the Indian Tribes of the Rocky Mountains" (Philadelphia, 1843). This work was translated into French, German, Dutch and Italian, and was one of the best sellers in its day. It told a story of adventure which caught the attention of those who like to have their adventures at least at second hand and it attracted the notice of those who like to think of the freedom of life in the great open spaces. His book thus anticipated, but in very different spirit, many books and stories that have become popular since. The first venture into print was so successful and proved so helpful to his beloved Indians that Father De Smet wrote "Oregon Missions and Travel over the Rocky Mountains" (New York, 1847). This, like its predecessor, was translated into a number of foreign languages. Nearly twenty years later in the midst of the Civil War he published "Western Missions and Missionaries" (New York, 1863) and some two years later when the war was over, "New Indian Sketches" (New York, 1865).

Father De Smet's biography has been written very sympathetically by Chittenden and Richardson, already referred to. This book contains a number of Father De Smet's hitherto unpublished letters but is most valuable because it contains a map of his travels which shows how far this modern apostle of the Indians went in the course of his work among these savage tribes. He had proved himself the "black-robe" that they had come seeking over and over again through several thousand miles. He was utterly devoted to their interests, nothing was too much for him to do for them, and his rugged health and strength were constantly used for their advantage. He is a great American hero, unknown except to those who have been particularly interested in the Indians or in the Jesuits.

He planned to make the Indians happy by wooing them gradually from their roving life and having them settle down in simple village conditions that would have required only a modicum of work and would have permitted and encouraged hunting and fishing, which the Indians enjoyed so much, thus gradually weaning them from their barbaric condition. The effects of his work for them were not enduring in the way or to the extent which he had planned because the Indians were swept away before the oncoming rush of the white settlers who broke into the Northwest. He planned to make for them a counterpart of the Reductions of Paraguay of which Cunningham Grahame wrote so alluringly in his story of "A Vanished Arcadia." That Father De Smet's plan was not a mere idle dream can be best appreciated from all that the Franciscans had been able to do for Indians of much inferior mental caliber down in California only some two generations before De Smet began his work. Circumstances made this impossible and one of Father De Smet's trials was to see his plans gradually being swept away before his eyes by the advance of the frontier ever westward, an advance accompanied by impositions of various kinds practised upon his beloved Indians, irritating them into outbreaks of hostilities costly in lives and property to both white man and red.

Father De Smet was only one of a group of Jesuits, altogether there were several score of them, who took up this work among the Indians of the Rocky Mountains and the Northwest. He happened to be the one picked out to be the pioneer and leader of his brethren manifestly by a superior thoroughly observant of human nature who realized that this Belgian Jesuit was eminently fitted by character and makeup for this work among the Indians. Long ago Cæsar after very definite personal experiences among these Teutonic people declared *horum omnium fortissimi sunt Belgae* "the bravest of all are the Belgians." Such they have proved to be in the missionary field all over the world, and Father De Smet was a striking example.

We are passing over in silence the work done by the other Jesuits in the same Rocky Mountain field but that is only because their lives were passed in the monotonous round of missionary duties from day to day for many years. They are the obscure heroes of whom sometimes we have the feeling that it takes more real courage and constancy of character to carry out their humdrum daily life of duty than to take the startling risks of more adventurous life. These men, like the good Sisters of Notre Dame and the Ursulines, who came to share their work, were deeply heroic. They represent those who are entered in the book of life who are known only to Him for Whom their work was done.

One of Father De Smet's companions on one of his journeys to the Indians in the Northwest was Father Christian Hoecken, S. J., who was the founder of the mission among the Pottawottomies at St. Mary's in Kansas. He furnished a striking example of the fact that Father De Smet's unmentioned Jesuit colleagues on the missions—unmentioned because there is not room for an account of their good work—had all of his courage and readiness to make sacrifices for the benefit of others. Part of their journey to the Northwest was to be accomplished by steamer up the Missouri in 1851. An extremely contagious disease—probably the Rocky Mountain fever in severe form which has been studied so assiduously in recent years and has cost the lives of some of the pathologists who gave themselves to the study—broke out among the passengers on the steamer. Father Hoecken for the sake of his Indian protegés had devoted himself to the study of first aid and accumulated simple medical information to an extent that would enable him to be helpful to his Indian converts in ailments or after injuries and he now gave himself to the care of the ailing passengers aboard the steamer though he realized the perilous danger which he was incurring by doing so.

He made himself all to all and became at once nurse, doctor

and spiritual father to the sick and dying until he himself fell a victim to the disease. Like his Jesuit brothers in France who during the Great War gave themselves wholeheartedly to the care of sufferers from epidemics, Father Hoecken eminently deserved to receive the Cross for Epidemics for his utterly self-forgetful services to others. His body was at first buried on the deserted shore of the river in the wilderness, but the place of his burial was faithfully marked by his Jesuit colleagues and his remains were afterwards transferred to the little historic mound at Florissant near St. Louis close to the remains of his companions who had given themselves so unselfishly to the noble work of civilizing and Christianizing the Indians in the great Northwest. They little recked whether their names should be known or not. They had given themselves to what they considered a divine work and they cared not what men might think of them or whether they should be forgotten. They had done their duty, hard though it often was, as they saw it. Father Hoecken was well worthy of a place among them for his forgetfulness of self and thoughtfulness of others.

The Jesuits have continued their work among these Indians of the Northwest down to the present time and some of those who have been attracted by work among the Indians have found satisfaction for their desires from missionary labors under the most difficult circumstances among the Eskimos in Alaska. Their story will be dealt with in the chapter on Alaska Missions. Many of them deserve a chapter by themselves because of their heroic unselfishness, but there is not room for that. Certain prizes have been established in France to be awarded by the French Academy to those who in humble circumstances and without any recognition on the part of others and without any thought that they are doing wonderful things, go on humbly year after year working wholeheartedly for the benefit of others. Surely these Jesuits and the devoted Sisters of the missions would well deserve to be the recipients of prizes of this kind and perhaps some time there will be foundations to supply them, though probably those who deserve them the most would be the first to deprecate the diversion of the monies necessary for this purpose from funds that might be used, as they are convinced, to much better advantage in the missions. Meantime it is the names of such men and women that are surely written in the book of life because they followed the Master and carried their cross of daily existence and forgot about themselves and cared for others who were in need of care through long years of patient labor and self-effacement.

CHAPTER XI

A JESUIT SOLUTION OF THE INDIAN PROBLEM

THE most disgraceful chapter in the history of the United States is undoubtedly that which concerns our governmental and social relations with the Indians. Treaty after treaty was broken with them, their lands were taken away from them, their hunting grounds were violated, their rights were scouted, their wrongs made little of, and when they reacted offensively and defensively against these outrages they were massacred and the scattered remnants driven out—before advancing civilization! The Indians simply had no rights that the white man was bound to respect. Helen Hunt Jackson told the story of all that in her book "A Century of Dishonor" when the first hundred years of our United States history had elapsed. In the fifty years that have passed since her book was issued others have written the story of subsequent events and instead of improvement as might be expected conditions were worse and our relations with the Indians continued to be the greatest dishonor of our civilization.

The worst stigma on the history of our republic is the treatment of the Indians. Bad as conditions were since the United States became a republic, they were worse during the colonial period. No wonder that the distinguished American lawyer, William M. Evarts, himself a descendant of the early settlers in New England, declared, much more in earnest than in jest, that when the Pilgrims landed they fell first on their knees in thanksgiving for their preservation, and then the next day they fell on the aborigines, and this became their policy until the Indians had practically disappeared. Beneath the witticism there is a bitter denunciation of the lamentable treatment of the Indians which has continued all down the centuries since the landing of the whites.

As a contrast to this there was in New England during the late seventeenth and early eighteenth centuries a striking example of how the Indians might have been treated and what tractable mortals they proved to be when they were given a square deal and looked upon as brother human beings and not merely savage redskins of a lower order of nature who must yield at the behest of the whites whatever rights they had to land and living in the region that had been theirs and their ancestors' for many generations.

A Jesuit priest, Father Sebastian Rasle, who came to live as a missionary for some thirty-five years among the Abnakis, that is the "Indians of the East," in their home country along the Kennebec River in central Maine, taught this precious lesson of the way the Indians might be treated as brother human beings and how well they responded to such treatment. He even made it clear what good Christians they came to be when dealt with honorably and humanely as brother Christians. Father Rasle has been the subject of much intolerant misunderstanding and abuse and his motives have been impugned and his conduct mis-represented but as religious intolerance has gradually faded away, historians more and more have come to recognize the beauty of his character and the charm of his personality as well as the tireless patience and unselfish devotion which enabled him to accomplish so much for the genuine civilization and Christiani-zation of the Indians among whom he was placed. Few men of our colonial history deserve more commendation for the way they devoted themselves so successfully to the difficult task of making the Indians over into something better and nobler, than this worthy Jesuit. His life is of the greatest possible interest because it reveals so characteristically what the Jesuits were trying to do for the Indians in these missions among the Indian tribes of New York, New England and Canada, of which we have heard so much in recent years because the development of our history has brought ever more and more details of knowledge with regard to that time.

Fortunately these Abnakis of Maine were of milder disposi-tion, less prone to go on the warpath, and readier to take instruc-

tion than the fierce tribes of the Iroquois. As a result Father
Rasle succeeded in making such headway as regards their civilization and Christianization, that he created for them almost a
veritable social settlement in their home among the mountains
and lakes of Maine. Luckily a certain number of his letters have
been preserved which enable us to understand just exactly how
he was occupied and what an intensely busy man he was for
these thirty years of his life among the Indians. A great change
has come over the estimate held of him as the result of careful
historical investigation of the conditions surrounding his life as
a missionary and his death as the result of an attack of the New
Englanders on the Indian village in which the Abnakis had had
their home for as long as the memory of the men of the tribe ran.

The work that Father Rasle accomplished, some of it under
the most discouraging circumstances, makes his career of surpass-
ing interest. He is one of the personalities that stand out during
the colonial period.

Father Sebastian Rasle was born January 4, 1657, at Pontalier
in the diocese of Besançon in eastern France. He made his
studies, including two years of philosophy as well as the classics,
at the Jesuit college which is still in existence there though interrupted for many years by the expulsion of the Order from
France. He had finished his undergraduate studies at the age of
eighteen and he entered the Jesuit novitiate in 1675. After some
further studies he became a teacher of grammar and humanities
with great success. Even before his ordination to the priesthood
he had, while still only a scholastic, displayed great missionary
zeal and devoted himself to the spiritual needs of the working
people of the neighborhood where he was stationed. As a result
when he was sent to make his theological studies at Lyons he
was given the position of director of the Sodality of Laborers
and Porters. He was ordained to the priesthood in 1688 at the
age of thirty-one.

His missionary zeal as a young man made it a matter of little
surprise to those who knew him well that he should offer himself as a candidate for missionary work among the American
Indians. He was well aware from the "Jesuit Relations" which

he had read and heard read in the refectory, that he was risking his life, for there were already Jesuit martyrs at the hands of the Iroquois in New York and Canada, but that, so far from deterring him, had the opposite effect. The fact that a number of brother Jesuits in the Indian missions to which he aspired had suffered almost intolerable hardships and even tortures and some of them had lost their lives, made him all the more anxious to devote himself to the Christianization of these Indians. For men like him life was a great adventure to be lived for the highest purpose and if crowned by martyrdom all was well indeed.

Something of the placidity of his disposition and his readiness to take the best with the worst as it came in life will be appreciated from the fact that the vessel on which he sailed was three months in crossing the ocean because of the storms and the contrary winds it encountered, yet the young missionary priest described it as "a sufficiently happy voyage." He had evidently put himself in the mood to stand bravely and uncomplainingly anything that came his way. He landed at Quebec but remained there for only a short time. He wanted above all to get in direct touch with the Indians and his zealous wish in the matter was responded to by his superiors without delay.

Father Rasle had shown himself to be a thoroughly intelligent man before being sent on the missions. Indeed as was true of so many other of the missionaries he was looked upon as one of the especially talented Jesuits of his generation with a particular talent for acquiring new languages. It so happened that there was a little Indian settlement some ten miles from Quebec near the mouth of the Chaudière River which had been made by Abnaki Indians whose principal tribe was settled farther south on the Kennebec River about the center of Maine. He was sent down there to become acquainted with the language of these Indians so that a little later he might be brought in touch with the main body of the tribe in Maine.

He succeeded very well in learning the language and took up the task of compiling a grammar and dictionary of it for the benefit of his brother missionaries. In the meantime his letters to his friends and relatives in France tell of the difficulties

encountered in the study of this first Indian language to which
he was introduced and also how amused the Indians were at the
mistakes that he made. It might easily be thought that a missionary spirit of this kind intent on the conversion of the Indians
would live on a plane of high seriousness and would be lacking
to a great extent in a sense of humor. There was none of that
over-seriousness in Father Rasle, however. On the contrary, he
could even see and appreciate a joke when it was on himself.
We have a number of examples of that in his letters. He won
the hearts of the Indians by his cordial, happy-hearted ways, and
by his manifest desire to create conditions that would make his
contacts with his Indian friends as intimate as possible. His
early years of missionary experiences must have given his
superiors ample evidence of his readiness to be all things to all
men at no matter what the cost to himself, so long as he was
able to win them to Christ.

Something of his ability and his positive genius for languages
will be understood from the fact that in the course of four
months he had learned so much about Abnaki that with the help
of some of the more intelligent members of the tribe he was able
to prepare a grammar and a catechism which were of great
service, not only in enabling the Indians to understand their faith
ever so much better, but which also greatly simplified the matter
of further conversions so far as his brother Jesuits were concerned.
He had done the drudgery which made the work of others ever
so much easier than it would otherwise have been.

The Abnakis among whom his mission was situated had all
been converted to Christianity some time before, so that residence
among them was a comparatively simple matter and his position
as their pastor did not involve any special hardships and involved
no dangers. It was not without its trials, however, for the pastor
was supposed to live and eat with the Indians and this was
sometimes a very trying thing. Father Rasle had been brought
up in good circumstances and he had all a Frenchman's appreciation of delicacy in eating, so that some of the habits and table
customs of the Indians required a good deal of self-repression to
bear with placidly. Father Rasle tells in one of his letters how

a lump of meat almost raw would be extracted from a pot and passed along the line that every diner might taste a bit out of it. At first the delicately reared Jesuit refused to join in this eating but this qualminess was noted by his hosts and met with deserved rebuke. The chief said to him, "You are a religious man and you pray. You must overcome yourself." Father Rasle took the admonition very simply to heart and thereafter took his bite in turn when the meat came around and kept his stomach from rejecting it though not without considerable effort.

After two years of missionary work among the Abnakis, he was assigned by his superiors to take up the mission among the Illinois Indians. He devoted himself earnestly for some time to securing knowledge of the language of that tribe for there were Jesuits in Quebec who had been among them. This preparation once over, he set out on the long canoe trip of nearly a thousand miles. It was a lengthy and difficult journey, not without its dangers, and with many almost appalling hardships. He encountered storms on the lakes and his party almost perished in them and they nearly starved. Often he and his companions had nothing but lichens gathered from the trees to enable them to support themselves and avoid absolute starvation. Finally they reached brother Jesuits at Mackinac with whom he stayed over the winter and then took up the mission among the Illinois.

He stayed only two years among the Illinois and then was transferred by his superiors back to his mission among the Abnaki whom he had learned to appreciate so highly. This time he went not to the little Indian village on the Chaudière but to the tribal center on the Kennebec. Here he spent the next thirty years and succeeded in bringing his Indian friends to a condition of happiness and civilization that seems almost incredible. The Abnakis had been begging for missionaries for some time before Father Gabriel Druillettes was sent, shortly before the middle of the seventeenth century, to found the mission among them. He made many conversions and indeed the Abnakis became so attached to the faith that when they feared that they would not be able to attend services regularly a number of them migrated to the settlement at Sillery not far from Quebec.

Father Rasle found a flourishing mission already in existence and was able to give the strength and vigor of his young manhood to developing it in such a way as would bring happiness to the Indians themselves and prove a model of what could be accomplished by missionary work among the Indians.

What Father Rasle accomplished among the Indians will be best appreciated from the letters to his relatives which describe the details of his daily life. This picture which Father Rasle gives of his work among the Indians, confirmed as it is by testimony from other sources, demonstrates how much these Jesuits were taken up with the idea of making life have a meaning for these savages, not only for this world but for the next. It has often been said that the good missionaries concentrated the attention of their Indian converts too much on other worldliness to the neglect of life here, but these letters of Father Rasle reveal very strikingly how much missionary efforts made for terrestrial happiness for these Indians in the highest sense of that expression.

Many people would very probably have the feeling that life among the Indians to a man of education and culture like Father Rasle must have been after a time intensely monotonous and time must have hung rather heavily on the missionary's hands. The usual persuasion would be that after Sunday services, morning and evening, were over, there would be almost a week or at least until the following Saturday evening before the missionary would be called upon again, unless perhaps there was some dying patient to confess or some injured or ailing person to comfort. So far from anything like this being the case, what we learn from Father Rasle's letters is that he was so busy that it was hard for him to find the time to write and that his days were crowded from early morning until nightfall with many and various duties undertaken for the benefit of the Indians.

Father Rasle begins the letters to his nephew by saying, "During the more than thirty years that I have lived in the heart of these forests with the savages I have been so occupied with instructing them and forming them to Christian virtues that I have but little leisure to write many letters even to those who are most dear to me." He gives some idea of what makes him so busy by his description of the church which he has built for the Indians "neat and very ornamental." He felt that nothing was too good for the service of the Lord and as he knew how much Indians were taken by decorations and ornaments and by ceremonies, he tried to make all these as effective as possible. As he said in his letter to his nephew,

"I thought nothing ought to be spared either for the decoration of the church or for the ornaments which are used at our holy ceremonies, the vestments, chasubles, copes, sacred vessels. I have secured everything appropriate and what I have secured would be so esteemed in our churches in Europe." He tried to carry out the ceremonies as much in conformity with the rubrics as possible for he knew that the spectacle thus afforded touched the hearts of his Indians deeply. Besides in this he was following the old-time tradition of the Church. He had the Indians themselves assist in the ceremonies so far as that was in accord with the custom in Christian countries, and it is easy to understand that relatives of the Indians who were chosen to take part in the church ceremonials were sure to be affected deeply by the sight of the participation of those dear to them in the religious ceremonies which they had come to reverence so highly.

Father Rasle tells his nephew: "I have formed a little brotherhood of about forty young savages who assist at divine service in their classics and surplices. They have their special duties. A certain number of them are servers on the altar of the Holy Sacrifice of the Mass. Others chant the divine offices and sing the hymns at Benediction of the Blessed Sacrament. Still others take part in the processions which they organize with a great crowd of savages taking part in them who often come from long distances to attend them. I am sure that you would be edified at the fine order which they keep and the piety which they show."

The Indians were ready to labor in the construction of church buildings and rejoiced at the opportunity afforded them thus to do something in the service of the Lord. Father Rasle tells the story of their building chapels quite apart from the church and village: "They have built two chapels about three hundred paces from the village. One of these is dedicated to the most holy

Virgin and is situated above the river so that her image may be seen by those who pass by (the river was the principal avenue of travel in those days). The other chapel, dedicated to the guardian angel (probably meant more particularly for the younger folk in the congregation) is at the lower end of the settlement along the same river." Father Rasle adds: "Since both of these chapels are on the roads which lead either to the woods or the open country many people pass them but the savages never pass without offering a prayer. There is a holy emulation among the women of the village as to who shall the better decorate the chapel of which they have the care when the procession repairs to the church. All that they have, jewels, pieces of silk or calico and other things of that kind, are used to adorn it."

Father Rasle was evidently very proud of the organization of religious life among the Indians and what he had been able to accomplish in developing the spirit of religion among them. He said: "None of my neophytes fails to appear twice a day at the church; in the early morning to attend Mass and in the evening to assist at the prayers which I offer at sunset. As it is necessary to fix the imagination of these savages which is only too easily distracted, I have composed suitable prayers to make them enter into the spirit of the August Sacrifice of the altar. They chant them or properly recite them out loud in unison during Mass. Besides the sermons that I give them on Sundays and holydays, I scarcely allow a week to pass without giving a short exhortation to inspire horror of the vices to which they are most inclined or to strengthen them in the practice of some virtue."

Father Rasle's daily round of duties as he has arranged them makes it very clear how little time was likely to hang heavy on his hands and how scanty was the leisure he had for writing letters or anything else not directly connected with his work for the Indians. He wrote: "After Mass I teach the catechism to the children and young people. A large number of old persons assist at this catechism class and reply with docility to the questions which I ask them. The rest of the morning until noon is devoted to hearing all who wish to speak to me. They come in crowds to share with me their troubles and disturbances of mind and they air whatever complaints they have against their country-men or they consult me about all sorts of problems, their marriages, their ailments and other particular affairs. I find it necessary to instruct some, to console others, to reestablish peace in families at variance, to settle problems of various kinds, to calm troubled consciences, to correct others by reproofs always given with gentleness and charity, in short my daily duty after Mass is as far as possible to render them all contented." These duties filled up the morning and it would seem as though surely the rest of the day Father Rasle must have had a good deal of time on his hands. That is not the impression to be gained from his letters, however. He said, "Afternoon I visit the sick and go around among the cabins of those who have need of particular instruction. If they hold a council, and this is a frequent occur-rence among the savages, they depute one of the principal men of the assembly to beg me to assist with the decision of their delib-erations. I go as soon as possible to the place where the council is being held. If I judge that they are taking a wise course I approve of it. If on the contrary I find anything to say against their decision, I do not hesitate to set forth my opinion in the matter which I support by as solid reasons as I can find and they conform to it. My advice always fixes their resolutions."

Among the Indians many had the feeling that they could not do anything of importance for the tribe without the assistance at the council of their good pastor. Father Rasle tells how respectful to him they are in this matter so that "they do not even hold their feasts without inviting me. Those who are invited bring each a dish of wood or bark. I give the blessing over the food. They put in each dish the portion prepared. The distribution being made and the food consumed I say grace and each retires. This is the order and custom of their feasts."

No wonder, then, that Father Rasle reverts to the crowded character of his occupations and how the routine of life has become filled with duties of all kinds as regards the Indians. He wrote: "In the midst of these occupations, you will not find it difficult to understand how rapidly the days slip by."

Indeed Father Rasle was so much occupied in his care of the Indians that he came to realize after a while that for the sake of his own interior life and spiritual cultivation he must secure time for recollection and for the recital of his office. He confesses: "There was a time when I found only with difficulty an opportunity to recite my office and to secure regular repose at night. Discretion is not the virtue of savages." They would come to him like children at any hour of the day or night and he was anxious to find some hours each day for his own spiritual development. In accordance with this resolution he says: "For some years I have made it a rule to speak to no one from evening prayer, which came some time between eight and nine o'clock, until after Mass the next morning. I have forbidden them to come to me during this time unless it is for some important reason, as for example to give the sacraments to a dying person or some other duty which cannot be put off. I employ the time that is thus afforded me in prayer and in repose from the duties of the day." He was a man of prayer for whom anything less than several hours of prayer each day seemed too little to devote to communication with the Lord.

His thoughts were never far from his church and the special duties connected with it. Morning Mass and evening services were conducted every day. In the winter both of these were conducted in the darkness and they needed lights in the church. Father Rasle was very much pleased to find that he could secure in the neighborhood an abundance of material for making wax candles. He wrote to his brother:

"The abundance of light adds not a little to the beauty of the church and the chapels; I have no need to be saving of wax, as this country furnishes it to me in abundance. The islands of the sea are bordered with laurels which in autumn bear berries a little like those of the juniper. They fill their kettles with them and boil them with water. As soon as the water boils, the green wax rises and remains on the surface of the water. From a measure of three bushels of this berry one obtains nearly four pounds of wax; it is very pure and very good, but neither soft nor manageable. After several attempts I have found that by mixing as much tallow, either of beef, mutton or moose, as of the wax, fine, hard and serviceable candles may be made. With twenty-four pounds of wax and as much tallow one can make two hundred long candles of more than a foot in length. One finds an infinity of these laurels on the islands and along the sea coast; a single person will easily pick four measures in a day. The berry hangs like grapes from the branches of the tree. I have sent a branch to Quebec with a cake of wax; it has been found excellent."

The redskins—*les peaux rouges,* as the French were accustomed to call them,—so far from finding the presence of their pastor a source of embarrassment when they were at work or play, on the contrary were glad to have him with them even during their time of special diversion in summer when they moved on to the seashore and stayed there for several months. The Indians were glad to erect a little chapel for Father Rasle in order that he might be close to them during their hunting and fishing. He writes with regard to this to his nephew: "When the savages go to the seashore to pass some months hunting ducks, bustards and other birds which are found there in great quantities, they build on an island a chapel which they cover with bark near which they prepare a little hut for my dwelling. I take care to carry there part of the ornaments from their little chapel at home in the village and the altar furniture, and the service is performed there with the same propriety and the bringing together of the same crowds of men and women as at their village."

Not only his days but his months and his seasons were filled up so that it is easy to understand that he was quite sincere and serious when he assured his relatives that he was so occupied that the days follow one another quickly and time passes without any of that monotony that one might think would be inevitable under the circumstances. He wrote in one of his letters:

"You see, my dear nephew, what are my occupations. For as to what regards me personally, I will tell you that I only see, only

hear, only speak to savages. My food is simple and light. I was
never able to adapt my taste to the meat and to the fish smoked
by the savages; my only nourishment is maize, which they
pound and of which every day I make a kind of pudding which
I cook with water. The only sweetening which I have here, is
to mix it with a little sugar to correct the insipidity. This is not
wanting in these forests. In the springtime the maples hold
in store a liquid similar to that which the sugar cane of the
Islands contains. The women occupy themselves in collecting
it in bark dishes, when the trees distil it; they boil it and
obtain from it a fairly good sugar. The first distilled is always
the best.

"The whole mission of the Abnakis is Christian, and very
zealous to preserve their religion. This attachment to the Catholic faith has induced them even to this time to prefer our alliance (that of the French) to advantages which might be derived
from the English who are their neighbors. These advantages
would be of very great importance to our Indians. The facility
of trading with the English, from whom they are distant but
one or two days' journey, the ease with which the journey can
be made, the admirable market they would find there for the
purchase of the merchandise which suits them; these things
certainly hold out very great inducements. In place of which,
in going to Quebec—it takes more than a fortnight to reach
there—they have to furnish themselves with provisions for the
journey. They have different rivers to pass and frequent portages to make. They are aware of these inconveniences and are
by no means indifferent to their own interest, but their faith is
infinitely more to them, and they believe that if they detach
themselves from our alliance they will shortly find themselves
without a missionary and without the sacrifice of the Mass, with
scarcely any exercise of their religion and in manifest danger of
being replunged into their former heathenism. This is the bond
which unites them to the French. Attempts have been made to
break it, sometimes by wiles which were held out to their simplicity, and sometimes by acts of violence, which could not fail

to irritate a nation exceedingly jealous of its rights and liberties."

It is not surprising to find that the American historians who have looked most carefully into the details of Father Rasle's career have high words of praise for him. Abbott in his "History of Maine" (second edition, p. 171) says that Father Rasle "was a gentleman by birth, education and culture. Religious zeal incited him also to leave the endearments of a home of opulence and congenial companionship and spend thirty-five years in the then unbroken wilderness of Maine." No wonder under the circumstances that the historian of Maine speaks of him as a remarkable character who deserves particular attention.

Bancroft has some words of high appreciation for the "venerable Father Rasle" and what he accomplished for the savages to whom he ministered under conditions that would seem almost impossible for a civilized and cultured gentleman who had spent some years in teaching in the colleges of France when France was the most highly cultivated country in the world and who preached the gospel of Christianity but first fulfilled it himself. Bancroft said:

"At Norridgewock, on the banks of the Kennebec, the venerable Sebastian Rasle, for more than a quarter of a century the companion and instructor of savages, had gathered a flourishing village, founded a church, which, rising in the desert, made some pretensions to magnificence. Severely ascetic—using no wine, little food except pounded maize—a rigorous observer of the days of Lent—he built his own cabin, tilled his own garden, drew himself wood and water, prepared his own hominy, and, distributing all he received, gave an example of religious poverty." [1]

Charlevoix in his "History of New France" tells the story of how Father Rasle suffered from a broken leg and thigh bone and then afterwards endured agonies in the treatment of his deformity in order to be able to go on with his missionary work. His holy father Ignatius, as he spoke of him, had after the battle of Pampeluna gone through the tortures of an operation in

[1] Bancroft, "History of the United States," Vol. 3, p. 333.

order that he might not be deformed for appearance at court. Father Rasle felt that he might emulate that example in order to be able to go on with his missionary work. Father Charlevoix who was present at that operation has spoken highly of Father Rasle's courage and his endless patience. Father Rasle feared that his deformity might lead his superiors to think that he was no longer able to go on with his work as a missionary and so they might summon him back to civilization. He preferred to stay with his children of the forest confident of how much his presence meant in bringing them to an ever-greater recognition and understanding of the truths of Christianity and the practice of their religion.

Williamson in his "History of Maine" (vol. 2, p. 191) though he takes the side of the English colonists very strongly against Father Rasle and the Indians and sets the Jesuit missionary down as the principal instigator of the unhappy relations between the Indians and the English, cannot help but recognize the lofty character of the man and the endearing place which he secured for himself in the affections of the Indians because he had shown them so clearly that he was intent on just one thing, their good here and hereafter. Williamson said: "He was a man of talents and learning, and by his condescending manner, religious zeal and untiring perseverance had greatly endeared himself to his tribe. He had resided with them and had been their tutelar father thirty years; and many of them he had taught to read and write." Even those who by their religious intolerance found it easy to say the bitterest kind of things with regard to Father Rasle cannot help but appreciate his thoroughgoing devotion to the Indians and his readiness to do everything in the world for them, as of course he had been doing for over thirty years. Here is one of the Indian lovers of whom if there had only been a few more the story of conditions among the Indians would be very different from the centuries of disgrace that it has been.

All of his biographers are agreed in declaring that Father Rasle won the hearts of the Indians by his tender care for them. When they were ailing he was their physician but often also their nurse. He stayed with them for long hours and sometimes during the whole night when they were suffering from fever. He prepared special dishes for them so that they might be tempted to eat when they were recovering. He loved and was beloved by the children who gathered around him whenever he made his appearance in public; he was evidently considered by all the tribe as a dear father in God who was ready to do anything that he possibly could to make life more livable and happier for them no matter what it might cost of personal sacrifice on his part. Father Rasle gave a striking example of what a Christian gentleman can be though living under the circumstances that would seem to indicate that there could be only room for barbarism. He made it easy to understand that the word savage which means only a man who lives in the forest may readily be applied to human beings who are interested in the simplicities of life and are intent on not allowing *things* to occupy so much of their attention that thoughts have not the place in life they should have.

Whittier has put into the mouths of the English soldiers who put Father Rasle to death the words which show the animus of their attack upon the missionary:

> *Death to the Babylonish dog,*
> *Down with the beast of Rome.*

At that time the Church of Rome was considered even by educated ecclesiastics of the Anglican Church and learned bishops of that communion the Scarlet Woman of Babylon and the Beast of the Apocalypse. About the time of Father Rasle's death Sir Isaac Newton, the great English mathematician, was explaining the meaning of the Apocalypse for the benefit of his brethren of the Anglican faith in England in terms of the Pope as Anti-Christ and Rome as the Scarlet Woman of Babylon.

The Church was declared idolatrous to the last degree because of her worship of images. Pictures and statues were considered to be so many idols. The destructive instincts of the New England soldiery were aroused by such declarations from their ministers and the Cross was above all a hated symbol. Whittier [2] has well depicted this in his lines descriptive of the scene immediately after Father Rasle's death:

> *Spurn—for he sees ye not—in wrath*
> *The symbol of your Savior's death,*
> *Tear from his death grasp in your zeal*
> *And trample—as a thing accursed*
> *The cross he cherished—in the dust,*
> *The dead man cannot feel.*

Some idea of Father Rasle's influence over Indians will perhaps be best secured from an incident in his career which brought about the conversion of a neighboring tribe of Indians. These Indians were distantly related to the Abnakis so that when one of their chieftains died they sent a delegation of the principal men

[2] Whittier, in "Mogg Megone," has also given a vivid description of Father Rasle's little church in the wilderness and of the Indians making their way from their birch canoes and the forest paths to hear Mass for the living and to pray for the dead, while the Jesuit missionary stretches his arms over them in blessing and in prayer:

> On the brow of a hill, which slopes to meet
> The flowing river, and bathe its feet—
> The bare-washed rock, and the drooping grass,
> And the creeping vine, as the waters pass—
> A rude and unshapely chapel stands
> Built up in that wild by unskilled hands;
> Yet the traveller knows it a place of prayer
> For the holy sign of the cross is there,
> And should he chance at that place to be,
> Of a Sabbath morn, or some hallowed day,
> When prayers are made and masses said,
> Some for the living and some for the dead—
> Well might the traveller start to see
> The tall dark forms, that take their way
> From the birch canoe on the river shore,
> And the forest paths, to that chapel door;
> And marvel to mark the naked knees
> And the dusky foreheads bending there—
> And, stretching his long, thin arms over these
> In blessing and in prayer,
> Like a shrouded spectre, pale and tall,
> In his coarse white vesture, Father Ralle!

of their tribe to convey the information of the death to the Indians at Norridgewock in order to have them join in their sorrow for their chieftain. They arrived at Norridgewock on a special festival day when the Indians, under the direction of Father Rasle, were taking part in a procession which was conducted with as much pomp as possible by the priest himself, his choir and altar boys and by the Indians of the town. The visitors were very much taken by the pageant and asked to be told the meaning of it. Father Rasle, familiar with Indian languages, was able to tell them very simply and yet satisfactorily, and assured them that he would be quite willing to instruct them further, so that they might become Christians themselves. They asked to be permitted to communicate with their wise men at home and appointed a day on which Father Rasle should come to set forth the claims of Christianity and, as a result of his instruction, they asked to be baptized and to become Christians, for they found their brother Indians of Norridgewock very well satisfied with this new doctrine and that, while looking forward to happiness hereafter, they were finding happiness here too in their new-found faith.

Unfortunately the lands of Father Rasle's Indians were situated in disputed territory. They occupied a region that represented a sort of buffer state between the British colonies and the French Canadian possessions. The New England colonists were definitely committed to making the eastern boundary of New England not the Kennebec but the St. Croix River. The good pastor knew the hostility aroused against him and realized that his life was in danger and that the bitterest kind of feelings against him had been aroused among the English, so that a price was put on his head. His superior in Montreal some three years before his death pointed out to him the serious dangers that were crowding around him and suggested that it was time for him to take steps to withdraw from the enmity of the English who had sworn to destroy him. Father Rasle pleaded to be allowed to remain with his beloved Indians among whom he had been for more than thirty years. He replied to his superior that his mind was made up and he was ready to face any danger that might come. He added, "God has confided this flock to me, I will follow its lot only too happy to lay down my life for it."

Rasle as a Jesuit fell heir to all that bigoted hatred that was bound up in the word Jesuit for the English. The penal laws in England were still in effect and the General Court of Massachusetts issued a proclamation July 13, 1720, "Resolved that a premium of one hundred pounds be allowed and paid out of the public treasury to any person that shall apprehend the said Jesuit within any part of this province and bring him to Boston and render him to justice." This proclamation was made to the Indians, demanding that they surrender Rasle and every other Jesuit priest. No wonder that the Indians were bitter not only on account of these attacks upon their priests and also upon their faith, but above all for the same cause which was at the bottom of all their trouble with the colonists, the stealing of their lands. Even when Rasle, though not fearing at all for himself, advised the Indians to leave their lands and go to Canada where they could live in peace, the chief of the Abnakis said, "I have my land where the Great Spirit has placed me and while there remains one child of my tribe I shall fight to preserve it."

It has been the custom to misrepresent Rasle and to characterize him as much more interested in the preservation of French territory and the submission of his Abnakis to the French government than in the spread of Christianity. Men like Parkman, Bancroft and Whittier were carried away by the old English traditions that gathered around the name of Jesuit but in recent years a revulsion of feeling has come about and it has been recognized that Rasle did no more with regard to the political situation and the loyalty of the Abnakis to the French than did the Puritan ministers with regard to the English cause, and that besides, Rasle during his long years among the Indians had accomplished wonders for their Christianization and civilization as can be so readily seen from his description of their daily life and above all their religious practices and the happiness that went with them. The old Puritan tradition of utter hostility to his name has given way and the world is beginning to know that

Father Rasle, scholarly to an extent that put the Puritan ministers to shame, humble, loyal, self-sacrificing Jesuit missionary, must be considered as one of the great glories of our country.

Rev. Convers Francis, D.D., a Protestant clergyman who devoted considerable attention to New England history, in his life of Sebastian Rasle—published in the Library of American Biography (Second Series, vol. 7) under the editorship of Jared Sparks, well-known professor of history at Harvard and afterwards president of that university—described some of the conditions under which Rasle had to do his work. The good priest lived almost exclusively on Indian corn which he himself ground up to make into a form of hominy. The only condiment there was with this was maple sugar and not much of it. He shared the meat of the Indians but as the stock of food in the tribe sometimes ran low he shared also their periods of famine so that he was sometimes reduced to living on nuts and acorns. Whenever special food was sent him by friends in Canada, particularly at times of scanty provision among the Indians, he always shared it with those around him and told his friends he could not think of any better food than his flock. All of those who touch on Father Rasle's life emphasize his voluntary poverty and the very simple life with none of the superfluities of existence that he led. His work and his prayer proved enough for him. He lived a life of devotion to these two occupations.

Sprague in his life of Rasle says: "So far as the patient toils of missionary life and love for the darkened soul of the Indians are concerned we may place the names Eliot [3] and Rasle in a friendship which they indeed would both have rejected but which we may regard as hallowed and true."

A New England expedition sent out in August, 1724, surprised the village of Norridgewock when all but fifty of the warriors were away. They were powerless in the surprise attack. Rasle was in his hut and when he heard the sounds of the attack he

---

[3] Eliot was the apostle of the Indians from the Puritans who gathered the Indians about him in Massachusetts and made a dictionary of their language, the sort of work that the Jesuits had been doing wherever they established themselves among the Indians.

knew that it was for him the English had come. To save his people he rushed into the street to offer himself up. On his appearance a shriek of satisfaction went up from the English. A hundred muskets were levelled at him and he fell riddled with bullets at the foot of the cross which he himself had erected in the center of his little parish. Seven Indians who tried to shield him died with him. When after the departure of the troops the Indians were able to return to the village to bury their dead and attend to the wounded, they found the body of their dearly beloved pastor pierced by numberless wounds, scalped, the skull split by blows of a hatchet, mouth and eyes filled with mud, the bones of the legs broken and all the limbs mutilated. Savages as they were accounted, they must have wondered how any human beings could have been animated with such fiendish cruelty.

When the Bostonians returned, the scalp of the Jesuit was immediately auctioned off as a very precious trophy of the victory.

As Reverend Convers Francis says, the Puritan militia thought it a meritorious act to destroy what they called the "idols" of the Church and carry off the sacred vessels. After staying for some days in the neighborhood, they fired the wigwams and the church feeling that they had accomplished a condignly religious duty. Thus ended the proud Norridgewock tribe, and the work of the old Jesuit, who was now approaching seventy and more than half of whose life had been spent with the Indians, was at an end. But it lived on to be a stimulus for the Catholics of Maine over a century later, and Father Rasle's fame as one of those who tried to understand and help the natives and not to impose selfishly upon them and take advantage of them, will probably keep his memory alive for as long as there are Catholics in that region of New England.

Rev. Mr. Francis has gone into his history very faithfully in its sources and discusses all that has been said pro and con. He thus summed up his recognition of the character of the good missionary for whom he had acquired manifestly a deep respect and admiration:

"I cannot review his history without receiving a deep impression that he was a pious, devoted and extraordinary man. Here was a scholar, nurtured amidst European learning and accustomed to all the refinements of one of the most intelligent nations of the old world, who banished himself from the pleasures of home and from the attractions of his native land and passed thirty-five years of his life in the forests of an unbroken wilderness, on a distant shore, amidst the squalid rudeness of savage life, and with no companions during these long years but the wild men of the woods. With these he lived as a benefactor, as a brother, sharing their coarse fare, their disgusting modes of life, their wants, their perils, their experiences under the stern inclemencies of a hard climate, always holding his life cheap in the toil of duty, and at last yielding himself a victim to dangers which he disdained to escape. And all this that he might gather these rude men as he believed into the fold of the Church, that he might bring them to what he sincerely held to be the truth of God and the light of heaven."

Here is a glorious tribute forced from the writer in spite of his feelings with regard to the Roman Catholic Church and its missionaries. He cannot help but see how unselfishly this Jesuit missionary against whom the prejudices of a lifetime were accumulated, proved a brother indeed to these savage men of the wilderness, and how it would be utterly impossible for him to have spent these long years in the circumstances in which he did only that he was led by the highest motives and heroic readiness to follow in the footsteps of Christ Himself in bringing the poor ignorant Indians into the fold of Christ.

Father Rasle was destined to be a focus for bigotry even long after his death. A wooden cross was raised over his grave near the village where he had spent his thirty years among the Abnakis but this was cut down by New England bigots. In 1833 Bishop Fenwick of Boston purchased the site of the ancient village where for so many years Father Rasle's little church, sacristy and residence had stood, and on August 23, 1833, about one hundred and ten years after his death, the Bishop dedicated a granite monument to the memory of the martyred priest.

Some five thousand people had gathered for the Mass celebrated on this spot and the eloquent bishop spoke for an hour. The inscription on the monument was as follows: "The Reverend Sebastian Rasle, Frenchman by birth and a missionary of the Society of Jesus, who after evangelizing the Hurons and Illinois became the apostle of the Abnakis, keeping them for thirty-four years in the faith and love of Christ. Unterrified by the perils of war and often testifying his readiness to give his life for his flock, he died the best of shepherds on this very spot amid the slaughter of his people of Narantsouac on the 23rd of August, 1724. To him and to his children in Christ who died along with him, Benedict Joseph Fenwick, Bishop of Boston, built and dedicated this monument, August 3, 1833. A.M.D.G."

The monument to Father Rasle had been erected through the cooperation of Catholics and Protestants, one of the most ardent of these being Kavanagh, afterwards the great governor of Maine, and the well-known friend of Longfellow to whom the American poet dedicated one of his books. The monument, however, was thrown down at the time of the Know-Nothing movement not very far from the time when a brother Jesuit was tarred and feathered by bigoted zealots. But some seventy-five years later, in 1907, Catholics and Protestants again, Church dignitaries and State officials, united at his grave to pay him the tribute which civilization so long denied him.

CHARTER XII

A BROTHER JESUIT IN MAINE IN THE
NINETEENTH CENTURY

PROBABLY the easiest and surest way to understand what happened to Father Rasle, S.J., at Norridgewock in Maine in 1724 is to read the account of what happened to Father John Bapst, S.J., just one hundred and thirty years later in the same state, in 1854. Father Bapst, a Swiss by birth, after a preliminary stage of education, became a Jesuit at the age of twenty. Ordained to the priesthood some fifteen years later he asked to be sent on the Indian missions to America. Like Father Rasle he knew well the story of what the Jesuits had done among the Indians two centuries before and what they had to suffer even unto martyrdom. There was no doubt that he looked forward to the chance to emulate them in their work and if necessary also in their sufferings. He was sent as a missionary to the Indians in the neighborhood of Old Town, Maine, but soon found that there were a number of white Catholics in that region who had been for years without the service of a priest and who were very glad indeed to welcome one. He continued his ministrations to the Indians but his heart was deeply touched by the religious conditions among the whites.

After a while he established himself at Eastport, Maine, and made this his headquarters for the whole state. At first he knew almost no English and no Indian, but during his years at college he had shown himself talented in languages and it was not long before he overcame the language handicap so far as both whites and Indians were concerned.

He made a number of converts to the Church but found even

greater satisfaction in bringing back lapsed Catholics to the practice of their religion. They had not lost their faith through any fault of theirs but from lack of opportunity to practise it and because they had been deprived of the grace of the sacraments. In the course of a few years, under Father Bapst's kindly ministrations, so many of these had come back to the observance of their duties as Catholics that they made a congregation large enough to disturb the feelings of their Protestant neighbors. At that time there was a very definite conviction in many non-Catholic minds—a conviction that carried over in country places and small towns into the second half of the nineteenth century— that Catholics, as soon as their number made it possible, were preparing to bring about the destruction of their neighbors of other beliefs. They were supposed to be secreting guns and ammunition for this purpose in the basements of their churches and also in the rectories. Thoughts of this kind continued to occupy the minds of many Protestants in the Middle West and in the Southern States until almost the beginning of the twentieth century.

Father Bapst came to be very well known throughout the state of Maine and his work was thoroughly appreciated by all fair-minded people. It was recognized by those who were acquainted with him personally that he was deeply interested in the dissemination of religious truth and that he was as far as possible from being a zealot or a fanatic. One thing that was manifest was that he was utterly negligent of his own ease or comfort. He spent himself in long journeys, often on foot, going from place to place throughout the wide state of Maine. Even the severe winters did not deter him from his missionary labors. Above all he was preaching the Gospel to the poor and he was trying to help their temporal as well as their spiritual welfare. He found that drinking to excess was one of the worst evils for his flock, so he organized temperance societies in a number of places and these accomplished an immense amount of good. He was interested in making men temperate and not regulating their lives by law, but his work was an important factor in the movement that for many years after the middle of the nineteenth century made

Maine a place where there was less drinking of strong liquor than almost anywhere else in the country.

Father Bapst's strikingly successful work among Catholics and the impressive force of his personality gained him many friends among the better classes, but this only served to arouse more poignantly intolerant bigotry in the minds particularly of people in small towns and in the rural districts. Nowhere is intolerance so bitter nor bigotry so deep as among the residents of backward country localities. After all, the words "pagan" and "heathen" mean only dwellers in the country and on the heath. In the early Christian days it was particularly the country bumpkins who maintained their old-fashioned beliefs in the face of Christianity as it continued to make progress in the cities. Father Bapst was destined to be the object of the utterly intolerant hatred of these country folk.

During the decade from 1850 to 1860 when Father Bapst's work was attracting attention, a movement in American politics known as Know Nothingism (so called because when members of the party were asked questions about it they were instructed by their officials to say that they knew nothing) attracted many adherents. Their numbers increased to such an extent that at one time it seemed almost inevitable that they would elect a president of the United States. The policy of this party was a revival of the old Native American Movement of early in the century. This in turn was only a natural inheritance of the partisan politics of post-Revolution days which though supported by some of the best minds in the country was founded on very bitter bigotry. Federalism grafted upon the constitution of the State of New York a provision denying the privilege of citizenship to any foreign-born Catholic unless he should first abjure an allegiance to the pope in matters ecclesiastical.[1]

[1] Organizations of bigotry like Know Nothingism make themselves manifest every generation at least in the history of the United States. In spite of vaunted progress in education and advance in culture we in the twentieth century still are treated to the sight of manifestations of it in various unmistakable forms. After Know Nothingism we had experience with the organization known as the Patriotic Order of the Sons of America, which during the hard times due to the depression that occurred in the early part of the last decade of the nineteenth

The bitter feelings aroused with regard to Father Bapst were no mere incidental set of circumstances and not in the least due to any personal fault of his but to the intolerant political and religious movement in the midst of which he became the scapegoat for the passions of a mob. He was not unconscious of the perils which surrounded him but went on with his work because of the call of duty, and though he was a man extremely sensitive in feeling, he did not allow his shrinking sensitiveness to take him out of the sphere of danger in which circumstances had placed him.

The name Jesuit was enough to evoke the bigotry of ignorant Protestants around him and it was not long before this put Father Bapst in serious personal danger. He realized more and more as time went on the bitter feelings which had been aroused and the personal peril that might result from it. Friends warned him of possible evil consequences, but he was a Jesuit who had volunteered for the Indian missions and was quite ready to take the chance of any personal risk that went with his priestly ministrations.

The Know Nothings resolved to put an end to Father Bapst's activities in Maine. Under their influence violence had been the order of the day in a number of cities throughout the country. In 1851 a large Know Nothing element in Providence, R. I., was deeply disturbed by the establishment there of the Sisters of Mercy and the foundation of a Catholic school. The convent was threatened and also the bishop's house. One or more of

century threw so many Catholic workmen out of their jobs and aroused feelings of bitterest intolerance among ignorant people who knew no better.

In our own time, a generation later, we had the Ku Klux Klan to help us understand just what preceding movements of this kind were like. Somewhere in this country there has always been a group of men organizing opposition to the Catholic Church partly because of bigoted intolerance which they drank in in their childhood almost unconsciously, but mainly because of utter selfishness and disregard for the rights of others on the part of the organizers. Cunning men have learned that it is comparatively easy to capitalize intolerance among men who know no better and that it is possible to make a handsome living out of it. The surprise is what a large number of presumably intelligent Americans they succeed in duping. It is true that these are mainly people without education but it is astonishing how many of the members plume themselves on their mental development.

the churches were marked for destruction. The mob actually
marched up to the convent prepared to put it to the flames, but
finding it guarded by a number of Catholic Irishmen and, recall-
ing Bishop O'Reilly's declaration that the Sisters and their convent were to be protected at whatever cost, the Know Nothing
leaders decided not to molest the Catholic property and the mob
dispersed. During the preceding decade a riotous mob in Philadelphia dealt with less firmly had burned the convent and St.
Augustine's Church and put the lives of the Sisters and priests
in serious jeopardy. In the '50's similar hostile demonstrations
and threats of violence occurred in many cities. In Cincinnati
in December, 1853, there were serious outbreaks and the cathedral was threatened. In 1854 Know Nothings and Orangemen
from New York invaded St. Mary's Church, Newark, smashed
the windows and demolished the statues,—they were engaged
as they said in getting rid of the worship of idols. Unfortunately
one unoffending bystander, an Irish Catholic, was shot and
killed.

When in 1854 Father Bapst proposed to establish a Catholic
school at Ellsworth in Maine it was felt that this was the climax
of Romish presumption. His case was actually brought before
the Common Council and an order was issued for him to be run
out of town. On June 5, 1854, he was dragged out of the residence of one of his flock, tarred and feathered and ridden on a
rail to the woods outside the town and ordered to leave the
neighborhood for good. Some of the mob proposed to burn him
to death but better counsel prevailed, though it was a wonder
that Father Bapst was not seriously injured. The shock to which
he was subjected affected him very deeply and was considered
to be one of the reasons for a premature senile degeneration of
mind which fortunately did not develop for some years until he
had actually accomplished a memorable life's work. The reaction
throughout the state against the rioters—and there were reper-
cussions of it throughout the country—was so strong that Father
Bapst felt that he could come back and continue his work without adding fuel to the flame of bigotry. Some of the most prominent citizens of Ellsworth held a meeting to extend to him their

sincere sympathies and deep regret for the insults and injuries that had been inflicted on him. A citizen's committee of expiation, organized for the purpose, presented him with a gold watch, appropriately engraved, expressing their feelings of regret and their sincere desire to repair the injury done to him as far as they could. Jesuits are not as a rule allowed to wear gold watches, as not in accordance with their vow of poverty, but special permission was given by the General of the Jesuits at Rome to wear this watch and so for many years he continued to be distinguished by the fact that he was the only Jesuit wearer of a gold watch anywhere in the world. He himself did not like the distinction and I remember how difficult it was at Fordham on one of his visits there to get him to show it to students who had heard the story and pleaded to be allowed this intimate touch with an historical incident so memorable as this seemed to them to be.

Before his death Father Bapst was destined to do some magnificent work for education. Just at the beginning of the Civil War he was chosen rector (president) of the Jesuit college in Boston, which at that time was the institution where the young American Jesuits were educated. This was one of the most important positions that a Jesuit could then hold in their educational institutions in this country. Later he was selected as the provincial, that is the regional superior of all the houses of the Jesuits, in New York and Canada. He was looked up to by his brother Jesuits as one of the most learned and valuable members of the Order in this country. He was a scholarly man, with broad cultural sympathies, great executive ability, yet of tender sympathetic character, an extremely hard worker, utterly thoughtless of himself and his personal comfort, and supremely thoughtful of others. His life and ways were taken as a model by many of the young Jesuits of his time and he himself was looked up to as an exemplary Jesuit.

He and his distinguished predecessor of some two centuries before in Maine—Father Rasle—became the victims of the religious intolerance of Protestant neighbors, so often aroused by the name Jesuit and the connotation given it by English bigotry in the days of Catholic persecution. Both of these men in spite of severe hardships and trials during many years lived on almost to the psalmist's limit and beyond it, noted for the intensity of their devotion to the duties around them. They were of gentle retiring personal character who made many friends among those who knew them personally and whose enemies were only those who were not personally acquainted with them but whose enmity was aroused by what they heard from people who knew no more in reality about them than they did themselves. At a distance of two centuries these two Jesuits demonstrated their readiness to face fearlessly whatever might come to them in the cause which they had vowed to serve just as faithfully as possible. Their lives help us to understand the reason for the dangers to which they were subjected.

CHAPTER XIII

UNITED STATES CHIEF JUSTICES AND JESUIT FRIENDS

CHIEF JUSTICES of the United States Supreme Court are regarded as highly representative of what is best in American life so far as intellectual ability, devoted citizenship and patriotic love of country are concerned. Without exception they were men who gave up the opportunity to earn a large income in the practice of law to accept the moderate salary of a Justice of the Supreme Court because this office represented opportunity for patriotic service. They were distinguished lawyers, ready and willing to make very definite sacrifices not only for themselves but for their families, in order that they might through their life work in the judiciary, the third of the coordinate departments of the United States Government, interpret legislation in such a way as to maintain the Constitution of the United States and through that government of the people, by the people and for the people as it had been organized for us by the Fathers of the republic.

Our Chief Justices probably represent the highest minded citizens of our history. To have been their confidential friends and enjoyed the privilege of special intimacy with such men is a guarantee of uprightness of life and straightforwardness of character. No hint of devious ways in life nor of guidance by hypocritical principles is compatible with such relations. The ermine of the judgeship is so easily soiled that only the most careful selection of close friends can be permitted to those who would retain their characters unsmirched by contact with anything but the best citizenship.

It so happens that two of the Chief Justices of the Supreme Court of the United States have been very faithful Catholics and their Catholicity has brought them intimately in association with the Jesuits during many years of their lives and especially while they were holding the position of Chief Justice. Both of these men enjoyed very long terms of service as Supreme Court Justices so that they represent altogether some sixty years out of the one hundred and forty years that the Court has been in existence. These two men, Roger Brooke Taney, and Edward Douglas White, were looked up to by their colleagues as well as the members of the bar of this country as among the most distinguished lawyers in this country. They were men of marvelously balanced minds who could make the nice distinctions often so necessary in the interpretation of law and who could be depended on to reason more closely than any others about difficult questions of human relations.

Most of the Justices of our Supreme Court have demonstrated their ability as lawyers in the practice of their profession and have won the admiration of their professional colleagues before there was any thought of their selection as the highest representatives of the law in this country. They have all of them been much more than formalist lawyers, they have been men who knew and sympathized with their fellow men and who were among the best judges of character and personality in the country. The roll of the Chief Justices is a roll of honor indeed and these two men are looked up to as among the most distinguished to occupy this seat of high honor.

CHIEF JUSTICE TANEY

More and more in recent years it has come to be recognized that the great fourth of the Chief Justices of the Supreme Court of the United States, John Marshall, had a worthy successor in Roger Brooke Taney whom President Jackson nominated for the Chief Justiceship in 1836 and who served until his death nearly thirty years later. Chief Justice Taney was for many years sadly misunderstood by a great many of his fellow citizens as the result of his decision in the famous Dred Scott case. Dred Scott, a Missouri slave, taken to the territory covered by the Missouri

Compromise which forbade slavery in the territory, brought suit for his freedom. The case came by appeal to the United States Supreme Court. The decision of the Supreme Court (1857) written by Chief Justice Taney, put Scott out of court on the grounds that a slave could not be a citizen of the United States or have any standing in the Federal courts. It took four years of bitter civil war and cost over a million of lives as well as the expenditure of two billions of treasure to reverse that decision handed down by Chief Justice Taney after a lifetime devoted to the study of Constitutional Law.

As a southerner born in Maryland south of the Mason and Dixon Line, Taney might be expected to have had prejudices with regard to slavery that were imbibed almost with his mother's milk, but he had certainly done everything in the world to throw off any prejudice he might have had on the subject. As early as 1819, at the age of forty-two, he was a courageous opponent of slavery. As a comparatively young man he set free the slaves whom he had inherited from his father. He went much farther than that, however, for he recognized that he owed duties to the slaves that his family had owned and he continued to feel his responsibility toward them long after their manumission. So long as they lived, he provided for the older ones among his former slaves when, with advancing years, they became unable to support themselves. He allowed them a monthly pension and considered the payment of this as one of the most sacred obligations by which he was bound.[1]

Chief Justice Taney had a thoroughgoing sense of duty which was exemplified on many occasions and he had a character that fairly won the hearts of those brought in intimate contact with him and that drew to him the respect of political opponents and the trust of all those who knew him. We shall see that over and over again in the course of a long career at the bar political

---

[1] The judicious character of the man and above all his thoughtfulness for others is well illustrated by the fact that "the allowances were always in small silver pieces—none exceeding fifty cents—as more convenient and not so liable to be taken from them improperly by those with whom they might deal. Each of them had a separate wallet for the amount which was brought monthly to the member of the Chief Justice's family who attended to the matter.

opponents selected him for official positions, and participants in lawsuits, aware of the existence of disfavor in his mind with regard to their cause, yet were willing to trust their cases to him because they knew of his high conscientiousness and his lofty sense of honor that gave them assurance that their interests would be safe in his hands, all the safer, very probably, because he may have harbored some prejudices against them at the beginning of the suit.

In connection with his attitude toward the colored race there is a very interesting tradition with regard to him in Frederick, Maryland, the town in which he lived for many years. He was a devout Catholic and went to Confession regularly, even as Chief Justice. He always insisted on taking his place in the line of penitents outside the confessional and making his way by due order of succession in to Confession. A good many of those who stood in line with him were Negroes, for there was a notable proportion of Negroes among the Catholics in Frederick. Some of these, recognizing the Chief Justice, would insist on offering the distinguished jurist, of whom everybody in Frederick was so proud, their places in the line of penitents, in order that he might not have to spend any more time than was absolutely necessary waiting for his turn at the confessional. He always refused to take advantage of these good-natured and well-meant offers, and though he always thanked his colored brother Catholics for their consideration of him, he insisted on holding his due place and taking his regular turn with the rest of those who were going to Confession.

Quite needless to say he was well known by the Jesuits who were in charge of the church and the pastor suggested that he should come to Confession apart from the others so that he might not have to waste any time. He offered to make special arrangements to hear him at Taney's own convenience but the distinguished lawyer refused to consider any such amelioration of ordinary conditions just for his convenience. He had the feeling that since his Confession was to God through the person of the priest he was no better than any other individual and ought to take his turn with the others. While he was Chief Justice of the United States Supreme Court he declared to his confessor who wished to save him time in the fulfilment of his duty of Confession that the Supreme Court heard the various cases in regular succession and that no amount of influence or respect for persons could bring about any distinction as to the order in which cases would be heard.

Chief Justice Taney had been under the influence of the Jesuits most of his long life. He was born at the beginning of the Revolution (March 17, 1777) in Calvert County, one of the Lower Counties of Maryland, where the Jesuits were in charge of the parish work. His father, Michael Taney, was of Catholic ancestry and education, and his mother, Monica Brooke was also a Catholic. He was educated at private school and by private tutors until he was fifteen and then Georgetown College not yet being open he entered Dickinson College, Carlisle, Pa. Here he obtained his B.A., in 1795, and then he began the reading of law in the offices of Judge Chase one of the Chief Justices of the General Court of Maryland. For a time after his admission to the bar he returned to his father's home in Calvert County to practise his profession and was elected to the House of Delegates when he was scarcely twenty-three years of age and was the youngest member of the Assembly. In 1801 he established himself in Frederick and this put an end to his political career, for Frederick County was strongly Republican and Taney belonged to the opposite party. He soon came to be recognized as one of the most distinguished members of the bar in Maryland, and then, as he measured his intellectual acumen with men of other states in arguments before the United States Supreme Court, he came to be looked upon as one of the great lawyers of the United States.

Some of the cases in which he took part, as for instance the Wilkinson case in which General Wilkinson was tried before a court martial at Frederick for having conspired to treasonable purpose with Aaron Burr, gave him a national reputation. The cause was very unpopular. As Van Santvoord says in his "Sketches of the Lives and Judicial Services of the Chief Justices of the Supreme Court of the United States" (New York, 1854), "Wilkinson had aroused the jealousies of the people when he suspended the habeas corpus act in 1806. . . . The manners of Wilkinson were haughty and unprepossessing. He scorned instead of attempting to conciliate popular favor; and besides he was in peculiar odium with a large portion of the people of Frederick by reason of his having on a former occasion successfully prosecuted before a court martial in that town a gallant and veteran revolutionary officer."

Notwithstanding all this, Taney consented, when selected by Wilkinson, to become one of his legal advisers. He undertook the defense of the accused and fearlessly and without hesitation braved the public opprobrium. For several months he labored loyally, faithfully, zealously and, it must be added, successfully for his client. Wilkinson was acquitted, his sword was restored. The only fee that Judge Taney would receive was the satisfaction of having helped to free a man and show his lack of guilt though so many of the people of Frederick, including Taney himself, had been deeply prejudiced against him. General Wilkinson is said to have known that Taney shared the feelings of a great majority of the people of Frederick but he regarded Taney so highly, not only for his abilities but above all for his integrity and honor, that he was willing to commit his cause to him.

There were other cases, notably one in which he defended a Methodist preacher known as Father Gruber who had been indicted for preaching insurrection among the slaves at a camp meeting of Negroes. The case excited great feeling for many of the inhabitants of that neighborhood were slaveholders and their feelings could not but pervade the court. In this case once more the fact that Taney was a Catholic would seem almost to preclude the possibility of the Methodists entrusting their cause to him, but in this, as in the case of General Wilkinson, there was so much confidence in Taney's rectitude and probity, his thoroughgoing integrity of character, that even those with bitter prejudices were quite willing to trust him.

Toward the end of the first quarter of the nineteenth century Taney removed to Baltimore and very soon came to be looked upon as the leading lawyer of the city. He came to be not only confessedly at the head of the Baltimore bar but would have been almost without a rival except that William Wirt removed to that city in 1829 to dispute with him the scepter of professional eminence. While in practice in Baltimore he entered upon that more enlarged sphere of practice that took him before the Supreme Court of the United States and he was frequently engaged in argument there. His name came to be found upon the record as counsel in almost every case of importance arising from the Maryland district. Among his colleagues, often his opponents in trials, were such men as Webster, Clay and Calhoun, and before long Taney came to be looked upon as one of the most distinguished lawyers in the United States. Many of these cases were important and created precedents that were to be cited forever after.

In 1827 Mr. Taney received the appointment of Attorney General of Maryland. His appointment was made by the Governor and Council, and, to quote Van Santvoord, "It is a fact worthy of mention as it is equally honorable to both parties that Mr. Taney was at that time politically opposed to the body which conferred upon him the honor." Governor and Council were a unit as ardent supporters of Mr. John Quincy Adams who was then president of the United States while Taney himself was equally decided and open in his preference for General Jackson. Despite the fact that party feelings ran high in those days the Maryland Council did not hesitate to confer the appointment upon Taney, thus evincing in the most marked manner their high appreciation of his personal character as well as of his distinguished professional abilities.

Taney occupied the Attorney Generalship of Maryland for some four years and resigned it to accept the appointment as Attorney General of the United States. This office had during the preceding twenty years been "adorned with the most splendid talent which the country produced," such men as Pinckney and Richard Rush who, on his appointment as minister to England, was succeeded by William Wirt, "whose classic intellect and genius during a period of twelve years threw a new lustre around this dignified and responsible position." Taney's record as Attorney General shows a great number and variety of cases argued by Taney and furnishes ample testimony of his professional ability, industry and success.

Some six years later when the question of the United States bank came up, President Jackson made Taney the Secretary of the Treasury in order to carry out his policy of controlling the Bank of the United States. The Senate refused to confirm the appointment, the first time that that had ever happened in the history of the country, so Taney's name was withdrawn and, on the death of Chief Justice Marshall, Taney was appointed by Jackson to replace him. The complexion of the Senate having changed politically in the meantime, Taney's appointment was confirmed and at the age of fifty-eight he entered upon this very honorable position. He was destined to occupy it for nearly thirty years and to be of immense influence in shaping the destinies of the country by the interpretations of the Constitution which were made as the result of his faithful study of that document and his profound knowledge of the fundamental principles of law and his familiarity with English law.

During that time he filled with honor and ability what has come to be looked upon as probably the most honorable position in the United States. He is noted for having completed some of Chief Justice Marshall's work. For instance, Justice Marshall was strongly of the opinion that the admiralty jurisdiction of the Federal courts ought to be held to extend over the lakes as well as over our great rivers as far as they are navigable beyond the flow of the tide. No convenient opportunity, however, ever occurred to permit Marshall to express these views in a judicial decision. "The task passed into the hands of his successor on the bench by whom it was performed in precisely the same manner that it would have been done by Marshall himself" (Van Santvoord).

Many other important cases were tried. For instance the judgment in the case of Kennett et al. vs. Chambers, a case arising in the Texas district, was to furnish an opportunity for a decision affecting our relations with foreign countries. Justice Taney's decision reaffirmed the safe and wisely conservative principle that it belongs exclusively to the political department of the government to recognize a new government in a foreign country, which claims to have displaced an old and established one, and until such recognition the judiciary are bound to consider the old order of things as having continued. Justice Taney's interpretation of the Constitution of the United States as regards the relation between the States and the general government established firmly state rights and at the same time provided for sufficient power in the general government to make the nation secure. Taney's greatest colleague on the bench of the Supreme Court during many of these years was Justice Story. Story thoroughly appreciated Taney and spoke with high admiration of his abilities and attainments even before the latter came on the bench. Further acquaintance, especially after Taney's appointment to the Supreme Court, ripened into reciprocal esteem. The intercourse between this eminent colleague and the Chief Justice was always of the most cordial character, and though at times the two, as might have been expected from their very different environment and education, differed in opinion *toto cælo* especially upon questions of Constitutional construction, yet they habitually cherished for each other feelings of mutual admiration and personal esteem. When after ten years of intimate association on the bench Justice Story passed on, Chief Justice Taney was called upon to perform the sad duty of responding to the announcement of the death of his eminent associate. Justice Taney dwelt upon the fact that Mr. Justice Story's contributions to legal interpretation brought him respect and honor not only in this country but beyond the seas and his works upon various branches of jurisprudence had made him known to eminent men wherever judicial knowledge is esteemed and cultivated. "Wherever he is known his opinions are quoted with respect and he is justly regarded as one of the brightest ornaments of the age in which he lived."

Justice Taney himself came to be looked upon as one of our greatest jurists. It has been said that as Chief Justice "Taney did much toward the building up of the system of practice in the Supreme Court, framing it after that of the English courts yet so modified as to be adaptable to the changed conditions existing in the United States. His opinions were arrived at rather by deep reflection and application of established legal principles to the questions presented to him than to exhaustive research of authorities. While giving due respect to formal decisions he did not rely slavishly upon precedents. By his dignified though kindly bearing he always commanded the utmost respect of his Court. He had few if any personal enemies and the purity of his private life was never questioned even by his political opponents" (Van Santvoord). He counted some of the most distinguished men of the country among his friends and politicians of distinction were proud to claim his acquaintance and looked upon him as a man to whom the nation owed honor and respect for a life devoted to the benefit of his country at a very modest salary when he might have been earning very large sums of money in the private practice of law in some of the most distinguished cases being argued at that time.

When he came to die he asked that he should be buried beside his mother in the little old Catholic churchyard in Frederick. This was an enclosed plot of ground on one portion of which there was for many years the Jesuit novitiate and Junior House of Studies. A more obscure place for burial could scarcely be found since practically the only ones who ever entered that enclosure, where beneath the trees reposed the bodies of the Chief Justice of the United States and his mother, were the young Jesuits and on rare occasions some of their friends. The faithfulness of his affection may be judged from the fact that his mother had been buried more than fifty years before and yet he wanted to be buried beside her.

He had been close to the Jesuits all his life and especially during the first half of his career while he was at Frederick. He is said to have remarked that buried there he would surely have the prayers of some of the young men who were entering upon their lives as Jesuits, making the sacrifice of everything for the sake of their intention to do all for the glory of God. He could not think of any place where his body might rest more peacefully than beside that of his mother and amid the friends with whom he had been so closely associated in life. Of course his burial there precluded the possibility of a splendid tomb being erected in his honor but that was one of the things that he wanted particularly to avoid. There is a handsome statue of him in Monument Park in Baltimore, for the State of Maryland wanted to honor him as one of her most distinguished sons.

Justice Taney had a deep and abiding reverence for the Jesuits and, as he had known them personally and intimately and was a man who knew men and their ways, his judgment with regard to them must surely be considered as implying the highest compliment to their character and citizenship. It is always the men who know the Jesuits best who think the most of them. Their enemies and those who are most ready to speak in deprecation of them are often utterly unacquainted with them but have acquired prejudices against them at second hand. To have been high in the esteem of Judge Taney is surely to be considered as of sterling worth, upright, honorable, conscientious, without hypocrisy, in a word as representing contradictions of all the traits that are so often attributed to the Jesuits by those who know little about them.

Tyler in his biographical sketch of Chief Justice Taney [2] says that as religion was so prominent in the life of Chief Justice Taney he feels it a duty to give due prominence in his biography to this subject. For that purpose he publishes a letter from Father McElroy, S.J., the pastor of the parish church in Frederick, who was a close friend of the Chief Justice for most of his life. The biographer had known Father McElroy personally from his boyhood as one of the most estimable of men. He became pastor of the Frederick Catholic Church November 29, 1832, and from that date an intimacy and sincere friendship commenced between him and Chief Justice Taney. Both of them lived to be old men but when Tyler wrote Father McElroy was still living in the maturity

[2] "Memoir of Roger Brooke Taney, LL.D., Chief Justice of the Supreme Court of the United States," by Samuel Tyler, LL.D., of the Maryland Bar, Baltimore, 1872.

of his faculties at the age of ninety. He publishes the letter, then, which he had received from Father McElroy:

"Frederick, March 2, 1871.

"My dear Sir:

"In answer to yours of the 28th ultimo, I have to state, at your request, the few particulars of which I am cognizant concerning Judge Taney's *practical religion.*

"An essential precept (as we think) of the Catholic Church is confession for the remission of sins—very humiliating to the pride of human nature; but the well-known humility of Mr. Taney made the practice of confession easy to him. Often have I seen him stand at the outer door leading to the confessional, in a crowd of penitents, majority *colored,* waiting his *turn* for admission. I proposed to introduce him by another door to my confessional, but he would not accept of any deviation from the established custom.

"A few days after the death of his wife, I called on him in Baltimore. He was much crushed and broken in spirits after such a severe bereavement, as might be expected. He received me, however, with his usual kindness and courtesy. During my visit, a gentleman, with his carriage, sent to let Mr. Taney know that he came expressly to give him a little airing in a drive to the country for an hour or two. He (Mr. Taney) sent for answer that he must decline his kind offer; and then, turning to me, he said: 'The truth is, Father, that I have resolved that my first visit should be to the Cathedral, to invoke strength and grace from God, to be resigned to his holy will, by approaching the altar and receiving holy communion,'—preceded, of course, by confession.

"I must confess, this edified me very much. In Washington, he continued to practise all the duties prescribed by the Catholic Church."

Chief Justice Taney's biographer tells a little story of the Chief Justice's ways as regards prayer that is very interesting: "Mr. Justice Daniel of the Supreme Court (while all the Justices were boarding at the same house in Washington) just before the hour for going up to the Court opened the door of the room of the Chief Justice and found him on his knees in prayer. He withdrew instantly but mortified that he had forgotten to rap before he entered the room. He made an apology as soon as possible for the intrusion which the Chief Justice accepted with the remark that it was his custom before he began the duties of the day to seek divine guidance through prayer. Mr. Justice Daniel though a particular friend of the Justice had never before learned of this special religious practice. My information is from Justice Daniel himself and from a member of the Chief Justice's family as well as from other intimates of the household."

It may seem to some readers presumptuous to put Chief Justice Taney alongside of Chief Justice John Marshall, his great predecessor. I suppose that there are few men whose opinion in that matter would carry more weight than that of our own Charles O'Conor of New York who was for so long looked upon as one of the most brilliant and at the same time solidly intellectual of the pleaders before the Supreme Court of the United States during the period while both men were alive. Charles O'Conor was looked upon as very probably the most distinguished lawyer in New York and perhaps in the country. On the occasion of the death of Chief Justice Taney the members of the bar of the Supreme Court of the United States held a meeting in which due honor was paid to the lamented Chief Justice. A number of the most distinguished lawyers in the country took part in the proceedings and among them was Mr. O'Conor who did not hesitate to place Chief Justice Taney beside even Chief Justice John Marshall as one of our greatest American jurists. He said:

"I will speak only as a living witness, and of my own times. These bring into view the last two of our Chief Justices. Their acts have made their names immortal. They have left to us, and transmitted to posterity for their admiration and guidance, a series of judgments, not merely marked by profound learning and ability, but placing this august tribunal foremost amongst human authorities. The jurisconsult, of whatever clime or future age, cannot find a safer precedent than in these. They embody and enforce the cardinal virtues, Wisdom, Justice, Temperance, and Fortitude.

"Who shall hesitate to recognize the moral greatness of the Supreme Court under the presidency of John Marshall, and his most fit and worthy successor, Roger B. Taney? It secured justice to the humblest individual who appealed to it for the protection or enforcement of his rights; but, when occasion required, it also summoned to its Bar the greatest States in our united galaxy, and with mild dignity, but resistless power, executed justice upon them. It curbed their every attempt to transcend the just limits of their authority."

Before the end of his remarks Charles O'Conor could not repress his desire to pay a personal tribute to the dead Chief Justice though he confessed that it would be a very difficult, indeed his words were "a hopeless task" to express all that those who knew him felt for his loss. The great New York lawyer's words may well stand as a summary of what his contemporaries who knew him best thought of the great Chief Justice:

"I will not attempt the hopeless task of intensifying by mere words the strong emotions of affectionate and reverential regret for our great loss universally felt. Those who knew Chief Justice Taney, who witnessed in his administration of justice the gracious dignity of his bearing and the stern impartiality of his judgment, find in their own vivid recollections a voice with which mine cannot compete. Those who have not enjoyed that high privilege will gather from the perusal of his recorded decisions far better conceptions of his worth and intellectual greatness than any mere eulogium could inspire.

"I will only add my fervent prayer and express my anxious hope that He who determines the fate of nations, who has fostered this mighty Republic unto unsurpassed greatness—He, at whose footstool she now sits, though bereaved of her chief judicial magistrate, still radiant in the fulness of her power and majesty, may so direct the counsels of those who rule her destinies, that the future historian of our times may not be impelled to write, as he drops a tear upon the grave of Taney, *Ultimus Romanorum.*"

CHIEF JUSTICE WHITE

Another distinguished Chief Justice of the United States Supreme Court much nearer to us in time than Chief Justice Taney was, like him, a close friend of the Jesuits. This was Justice Edward Douglas White. During the early years of his college training he had been a student at St. Mary's, Emmitsburg, Md., where so many of the Catholic priests and bishops of this country were educated. He afterwards attended Loyola College under the Jesuits in New Orleans and later went to the Jesuit College, Georgetown, D. C. Before the time of his graduation arrived, he enlisted in the Confederate army and served during the Civil War with distinction. In 1868 he was admitted to the Louisiana bar, thus following in the footsteps of his father and grandfather who had been practising lawyers. His father, Edward White, was well known as the seventh governor of Louisiana.

Some six years after his admission to the bar White was elected State Senator, an office which he filled with prestige. Some twenty years later he was appointed to the Bench of the Supreme Court of Louisiana, a position which he occupied with distinction for some dozen years when he was elected United States Senator from Louisiana. In 1894 he was appointed Associate Justice of the United States Supreme Court by President Cleveland. Sixteen years later in 1910 he was named Chief Justice of the Supreme Court by President Taft. This was the first instance in the history of the Supreme Court of a president naming a Chief Justice who was of different political affiliation from himself. "Taft, a Republican, a Protestant, and of northern interests, appointed to the Chief Justiceship the ex-Confederate soldier, a Democrat and Roman Catholic, Edward Douglas White, who was to bring new prestige to the court."

Coming from Louisiana where owing to the original jurisdiction having been French, the law of France is the basis of legal procedure instead of the English common law, White introduced another very important element into the decisions of the Supreme Court. He is declared by those who were in the best position to judge to have been the greatest authority on the civil law who has graced the United States Supreme Court in its history. In cases involving the government, in spite of the fact that he had been so intensely southern in his sympathies he was a Federalist in his decisions and not, as might readily have been expected, an overweening states rights man.

Chief Justice White was highly admired by his colleagues in the Supreme Court and was looked up to as a very distinguished jurist whose all absorbing purpose in life was that of establishing justice and insuring civil rights for the benefit of the citizens of the United States. He was the recipient of many degrees from universities, and was honored by selection as the recipient of the Laetare Medal from the University of Notre Dame in 1914. This medal is conferred annually on some Catholic layman who has been an outstanding figure in Catholic circles during the years before the honor is conferred. At the time of his death Chief Justice White was chancellor of the Board of Regents of the Smithsonian Institution.

As his career drew to a close Chief Justice White came to be looked upon as one of the most learned jurists in the country, a man whose reasoning on points of law stamped him as possessed of an intellect of very high order, thoroughly capable not only of seeing the niceties of law but also of bringing out the distinctions which make for a sense of justice between men. His long years of service as Chief Justice of the Supreme Court of Louisiana and then as Associate Justice of the Supreme Court of the United States with a memorable legal career that culminated in the exalted position for more than a score of years of Chief Justice of the United States Supreme Court, gave him a prestige almost unrivalled in this country. All this judicial experience made him a man thoroughly capable of knowing the law of the land if anyone ever did and above all knowing men and their ways and their character. All during this long life of preoccupation with the judiciary that made him looked up to by all his colleagues in the legal profession, Chief Justice White continued to be a faithful Catholic and an intimate friend of the Jesuits. During his life in New Orleans he frequently visited the Jesuits and was on terms of the most intimate friendship with some of the old Fathers with whom he used to discuss the principles of jurisprudence and their application to concrete examples of human conduct.

As Chief Justice of the United States and during the years while he was on the Supreme Court Bench he was a constant attendant at Georgetown University Commencements and other university functions, for as an alumnus he was proud to acknowledge his obligations to his old teachers. It is the enduring friendship during a lifetime of such men as Taney and White that means more as a revelation of the genuine character of the Jesuits than anything else possibly could.

"By their friends ye shall know them," is probably the best criterion that we have as to the character of men. It would have been quite beyond the bounds of possibility for the Jesuits of New Orleans and of Washington to have maintained the friendship of such men as Taney and White if they had been in any sense of the word Jesuitic according to the meaning that became attached to that term because of religious bigotry in England during the period of bitter intolerance of the penal days. The ugliest of connotations still clings to the word in the minds of many people but only those who have never known the Jesuits as they are. To know them is not only to respect them thoroughly but to love them for what they have been and above all for what they are. They have always been the same and while it would have been quite impossible for so large a number of men not to have had some of them unworthy of their high vocation, the surprise is how few there were of the unworthy and how marvelously the spirit of St. Ignatius formed men into such high characters as are almost invariably found among the Jesuits.

These friendly relations of the Jesuits with men who were to occupy in later life the exalted position of Chief Justice of the United States, begun in early years and continued into old age, are the best possible testimony to their straightforward and sterling character. Youth might have been led into friendship without knowing more than the superficial aspects of men but that could not be true for mature middle age and above all not for the older years when men had developed thoroughgoing intellectual discrimination fostered by the judicial habits of years, continued throughout long life.

Neither of our great chief justices would for a moment have continued friendship with men with regard to whom there was the slightest suspicion of hypocrisy, or indeed of any policy in their conduct except that by which they exemplify in their lives the motto chosen for them by their founder, Ad Majorem Dei Gloriam, "For the Greater Glory of God." As faithful Catholics themselves, the Chief Justices could not have expected less than that from their old teachers. It is from the enduring friendship during long lives of such men, themselves examples of what is highest in intellectual life in America that we find the touchstone by which the character of our American Jesuits may be properly estimated.[3]

[3] Among the Associate Justices of the United States Supreme Court in recent years, the Honorable Joseph McKenna, who came to be looked upon as one of the distinguished jurists of the country as the result of his opinions as delivered before the Court, was a student of the Jesuits. He attended St. Joseph's in Philadelphia though he was appointed from California to which his family had migrated when he was a young man. He declared in later life that he was "proud of his connection with the little Jesuit college in Philadelphia" where he received his early training. During his years as Associate Justice he maintained rather intimate contact with the Jesuits both in Washington and at Georgetown.

CHAPTER XIV

JESUIT SCIENTISTS IN THE UNITED STATES

A VERY ready presumption would be that since the Jesuits were priests or the great majority of them students for the priesthood, there would be little question of their reaching distinction in science. Their preoccupation with their priestly duties would not permit of the time for scientific study and the persistent observation necessary for success in it. It would be expected then that a chapter on American Jesuit scientists would be rather meager in size. As a matter of fact, however, the Jesuits in connection with their school work have always devoted themselves to science, and their superiors among the Jesuits have always encouraged members of the Order in the study of science and afforded them the opportunity to do original work in the sciences whenever they demonstrated the possession of special talent for such work. What has been true in the past in this regard has been just as true in this generation and what Professor Foster said in the "Quarterly Journal of the German Astronomical Society" ("Vierteljahreschrift der Astronomische Gesellschaft," 1890, p. 60) is true for other sciences besides astronomy: "Among the members of the Society of Jesus in the past and in the present we find so many excellent astronomers and in general so many investigators of purest scientific devotion that it is of important interest to their colleagues in science to take note of them."

As a matter of fact the number of distinguished scientists who have been members of the Society of Jesus is simply astounding for those who are unfamiliar with them. Poggendorff's "Biographical Dictionary of the Exact Sciences" contains in its first two volumes the names of 8,847 scientists, according to Poggendorff's connotation of that term, from remote antiquity until the

year 1863. Among these nearly 9,000 names a little more than ten
per cent are those of Catholic clergymen. This number is mag-
nificently significant of the attitude of the Church to science if
we only reflect that clergymen took up science as a favorite avoca-
tion while for most scientific discoverers the pursuit of science was
in some form their vocation in life. Most of them belonged to
professions which obliged them to devote themselves to the exact
sciences and they were teachers of physics, mathematics, chem-
ists, engineers, nautical authorities and the like. Clergymen, however, as a rule took up science as a pleasure not a task that they
were bound to do. Nearly fifty per cent of these nine hundred
Catholic clergymen mentioned in Poggendorff as the outstanding
figures in the history of the exact sciences are Jesuits.

The interests of the Jesuits in science here on the American
continent was extremely well exhibited in the seventeenth century
in what have now come to be known as the "Jesuit Relations."
These, as we have said in the chapter on "The Jesuit Relations,"
were a collection of letters sent home to their brethren in Europe
by the missionaries in order that they might have details of information with regard to the labors and interests of the Jesuit
missions. The custom of writing such letters had been begun by
St. Francis Xavier whose immense success as a missionary in the
East had attracted so many others to the field of missionary labor.
These letters of Jesuit missionaries told not only the story of their
own personal experiences with the Indian and their missionary
work with its success or failure in the making of conversions, but
also told of curiosities of all kinds that they met with in their
missionary journeys, described the rivers and the islands and the
lakes, the waterfalls and mountains, as well as other natural
curiosities with which they were brought in contact. They described the various plants and flowers and trees and many kinds
of vegetables, and especially the herbs of different sorts which the
natives in America used in medicine often with interesting results.
Tobacco and maize as well as cotton and other plants indigenous
to this country received special attention. These were the first
contributions to the science of botany on this continent, but the
Jesuits also described the fauna as well as the flora and told of

the customs of the Indians and their habits of life and by so doing were making distinct contributions to anthropology and ethnology. Scientists of the modern time have recognized this and have given the missionaries due credit for all that they accomplished in fundamental science in this country.

While the Jesuits were laying the foundation of American ethnology and anthropology, they greatly added to the knowledge of geography, described the heavens together with the weather and climatic conditions and everything else that might be of any possible influence. They were close observers and trained writers and so they told the story of what they saw succinctly and understandingly. That is why several hundred years after these letters were written, the "Jesuit Relations" have become more and more interesting. Edition after edition of them has been published. Of these we have spoke in the chapter on "Jesuit Relations." Here we are interested only in the science contained in them but that is sufficient to make it very clear that far from being any inhibition on scientific studies among the Jesuits, on the contrary knowledge of science was cultivated and scientific study encouraged in striking fashion.

Here in America a group of Jesuits made distinguished contributions to science mainly in connection with Georgetown University Observatory. Their fields were meteorology and astronomy. The selection of this field of study is not surprising and is thoroughly in accordance with Jesuit traditions, for Father de Backer in his library of writers of the Society of Jesus demonstrates that over two hundred writers among the Jesuits have made valuable contributions to astronomical literature. The best known of these was Father Clavius to whom Pope Gregory XIII entrusted the correction of the calendar. The great Jesuit mathematician astronomer succeeded in reaching what may well be considered a final solution of the calendar for all human purposes. During the century after Clavius a whole series of Jesuit astronomers reached distinction. Among them were such men as Fathers Scheiner, Cesatus, Riccioli, Grimaldi, and a number of others of only less distinction.

With that example before them it is easy to understand that a great many Jesuits became interested in astronomy and some of them here in America did excellent original work. Owing to the exile of the Jesuits from Rome after the revolution of 1848 Father Secchi, who was later to do such distinguished work in astronomy at the Vatican Observatory, was in residence at Georgetown and began some of his great original investigations at the observatory there. After some years he was allowed to return to Italy and continued his work there.

His literary work in astronomy is almost incredible. He sent nearly seven hundred communications to some forty-two scientific journals, over three hundred of these appearing in the "Comptes Rendus" and in the "Astronomische Nachrichten," the French and German journals of astronomy which present the authoritative records of advancing original work in this department of science. Besides this Father Secchi wrote five books, one on the sun, a second on the stars, a third on cosmography, a fourth on the unity of the physical forces, and a fifth, a posthumous work, on the elements of terrestrial physics.

The titles of his productions in book form and in the shape of articles for scientific magazines without comment and without repetition cover the amazing number of nineteen large pages in double columns of Sommervogel's "Bibliothèque de la Compagnie de Jesus."

It was not for his writing, however, but for his observations that Father Secchi's name came to be irrevocably attached to certain departments of astronomy. He made observations of great value on every form of heavenly bodies and on almost every object that can be seen in the skies. He made frequent measurements of the heights of the mountains of the moon and called attention to many special features of its surface. He examined all the planets diligently and was one of the first to see the so-called canal on Mars and to observe Jupiter's third satellite as spotted.

Father Rigge, S.J., who for many years was the professor of astronomy at Creighton University in Omaha, Nebraska, wrote of him: "He made many metroscopic observations on the comets and examined carefully the spectra of nebulae, meteors and auroras. It was with regard to the fixed stars more than with any other class of heavenly bodies, possibly more even than to the sun itself, that Father Secchi has won for himself an undying name. Besides measuring innumerable positions of double stars (Gledhill's work on 'Double Stars' mentions his observations on almost every page), he was the founder of a new branch of astronomy (Stellar Spectroscopy) and his analysis was so comprehensive and so thorough that Secchi's types of stellar spectra will probably remain for years to come an essential illustration in astronomical textbooks."

Having accomplished all this in astronomy it would seem to be out of the question for Father Secchi to have made any serious studies in other departments. While at Georgetown, however, he occupied himself for a time with the study of electricity and his first book, "Researches on Electrical Rheometry" was accepted for publication by the Smithsonian Institution in September, 1850, and appeared as volume III, article 2, of "Smithsonian Contributions to Knowledge," (Washington, 1852). His observations on electricity naturally led him to magnetism and he was one of the first to build a magnetic observatory and record and investigate carefully the behavior of the magnetic elements of the earth. Whatever he touched he illuminated. He built a third observatory for meteorology. His ingenuity enabled him to invent a number of instruments for the automatic observation of the weather, and one of these, his meteorograph, was exhibited at the Paris Universal Exposition of 1867 and won for its inventor the grand prize of 100,000 francs and the Cross of the Legion of Honor. This distinction was conferred upon Father Secchi by the Emperor Napoleon III in person in the presence of the emperors of Russia and Austria and the kings of Prussia and Belgium.

The Emperor of Brazil sent him a golden rose as a token of his appreciation of the wonderful work that he had done for science.

It is not too much to say that Father Secchi as the head of the Roman Observatory was probably the greatest astronomer of the second half of the nineteenth century. He was the father, as we have said, of astronomical spectroscopy and one of the most in-

genious of men in the invention of instruments that would help
out scientists in the making of astronomical observations and he
achieved marvelous success in the application of his work to
science and teaching. At the beginning of the twentieth century
practically all of the modern textbooks in astronomy mentioned
his name with respect and continued to use his theories and illustrations for teaching purposes. Secchi's typical sun spot as well as
other figures still appear in every popular no less than in every
technical treatise on the sun.

It was with regard to the sun that Father Secchi's greatest
work was done. His textbook, "Le Soleil," written in French and
printed in Paris in 1870, is the fundamental treatise which demonstrates just what was astronomical knowledge of the sun during
the nineteenth century. For a generation after his time every
book written on the sun quotes this textbook of Father Secchi
and its illustrations were largely drawn from by other writers of
textbooks until well on in the twentieth century. It was translated
into most modern languages and became a standard work on the
subject.

Besides his work on sun spots in which Father Secchi is a
modern pioneer his observations on the corona of the sun during
eclipses and especially his photographs of this subject place him
among the distinguished original contributors to our knowledge
of astronomy in the nineteenth century. In his own time his observations were considered the best of their kind that had ever
been made, far ahead of anything that had been accomplished
before. He was a man of unceasing industry, interested only in
two things, in scientific work and especially astronomy, and his
religious duties as they were required by his Order. He was as
faithful in one of these as he was in the other.

His superiors encouraged his work in every way, gave him
opportunities for it, provided him with assistance, and his brother
Jesuits showed very clearly how proud they were of his achievements. Jesuit colleges all over the world took up his textbooks,
made the significance of his observations a matter of common
knowledge in their classes, and were proud indeed to make
known his original observations all over the world.

Another distinguished astronomer who was for a short time the head of the observatory at Georgetown was Francesco de Vico. He had a European reputation and was the assistant director of the Vatican Observatory at Rome for some years. He was known as the comet chaser for he had discovered eight of them and the well-known comet of five and a half year period bears his name. He afterwards became the director of the Vatican Observatory and was holding that office when the Revolution of 1848 drove the Jesuits from Italy. He was received with great enthusiasm in France and the English offered him the directorship of the observatory at Madras in India but he preferred to go to Georgetown to be with his brother Jesuits in the United States. Unfortunately he died at the early age of forty-three. The place that he occupied in the astronomy of the day can probably be best appreciated from the fact that Herschel, the royal astronomer of England, wrote Father de Vico's obituary in "Notices of the Astronomical Society."

Father Secchi had devoted himself to meteorology almost as successfully as to astronomy and above all had succeeded in inventing some very ingenious instruments for weather observations. Still another Jesuit, this time working within the boundaries of the United States, was destined to accomplish even more for the science of the weather. This was Father Algué of Manila who by means of comparisons of observations in various parts of the islands made by his brother Jesuits succeeded in working out a formula of weather signs which portend the coming of a cyclone or typhoon and especially storms that are of destructive character. He came to be looked upon as the world authority on the sudden storm of the equatorial region. He invented the baroclycometer which enabled him to prophesy the coming of a storm long before there was any serious disturbance in his own neighborhood. His observations enabled shipping to avoid the worst of the storms. When cyclone warnings were sent out shipping would delay putting out to sea for a day or more and shipping that was near port anywhere would make for safe harbor rather than proceed to its destination and run unnecessary risks. Not only a great many vessels but above all a great many lives were saved in this way.

This meteorological work was so successful and so thoroughly practical in its application to weather conditions out in the Philippines that when the Philippines passed under the dominion of the United States, the American government asked Father Algué to come over to this country for the purpose of applying his observations made in the East to the West Indies where so often on sea and land men suffer from destructive hurricanes. He succeeded in working out warnings of the approach of one of these storms in the West Indies as well as he had done in the Philippines. Further developments were made along this line and as a result of the work thus begun many cities in the West Indies have full warning of the possible approach of cyclones and not only can take precautions to save vessels but also to make all shipshape in town so that there will not be loose objects to be blown around bringing destruction in their train. In connection with the work Father Algué came to be looked upon as one of the most distinguished of meteorologists in the world about the beginning of the twentieth century. He was an extremely modest man, a hard persistent worker, deeply interested in science but also in missionary work and a fine teacher. He was a typical Jesuit and was beloved by all his brother Jesuits who knew him.

At the invitation of the United States Government he took up the issuance of a large work in two volumes with an atlas in addition on the Philippine archipelago. This was published some thirty-three years ago by the government printing office at Washington. The work was written in Spanish and contributions were made to it by a group of Jesuits who had spent many years in the Philippine archipelago and who had absorbed a large amount of information with regard to all sorts of scientific interests in the Philippines.[1]

After his return from the West Indies Father Algué was at

---

[1] The title of the book was "L'Archipielago Filipino, por Algunos Padres de la Mision de la Compañia de Jesus en estas islas." Two vols., Washington, Government Printing Office, 1900.

the astronomical observatory at Georgetown for some time and he worked successfully at the solution of a problem that has called for an immense amount of solicitous attention on the part of astronomers. This is the question of the exact moment of star transits and the difficulty that even the observations made by the same observer are subject to considerable variation as a result of what is known as the personal equation. Father Baum, S.J., a Hungarian observer, and Father George Fargis, S.J., of Georgetown University observatory, had each of them suggested methods of overcoming this difficulty by instrumental means. Father Fargis eliminated the personal equation in transit observations by a photographic process. His method was an improvement upon one with which Professors Pickering and Bigelow had been experimenting at Harvard and seemed to solve the difficulty. Father Algué during his time at Georgetown invented a modification of this which seemed to promise much.

There is a group of Jesuits in various parts of the world in astronomical observatories who are keeping in touch with each other in what concerns certain of the mechanical and observational problems of astronomy. They have with the inheritance of generations of Jesuits at various parts of the world behind them as a stimulus, accomplished good work the memory of which will be maintained for many generations yet. Father Braun, S.J., for instance, of Mariaschein, Bohemia, suggested the invention of the spectroheliograph for photographing the whole sun with its spots and prominences. Father Braun also has written books upon gravity and cosmogony which have received high praise from a number of those who about the beginning of the century were best fitted to judge of their significance. Sometimes Jesuits have been the severest critics of Jesuit observers, however, and there is no partiality in the matter of accepting astronomical or meteorological conclusions just because they happen to come from colleagues of the Order.

In 1888 Father Hagen, S.J., another Jesuit scientist who had already demonstrated that he could do surprisingly good work in astronomy under the most trying conditions, was selected as the head of the observatory at Georgetown. Father Hagen was a German Jesuit who had been teaching out in the little college of Prairie-du-Chien, Wisconsin, and was summoned home to take up teaching in Germany when the president of Georgetown University asked and obtained permission for him to stay and become the director of the observatory there. From here he went by special invitation to the Vatican observatory in Rome to become its director as a successor to Father Denza who had succeeded Father Secchi, S.J., who had also had experience at Georgetown.

Father Hagen was born in 1847 at Bregenz in the Tyrol and made his studies at Feldkirch in Austria. He entered the Society of Jesus at the age of sixteen and because he was a brilliant student was given the opportunity to make special studies at Munster and Bonn. It so happened that at both of these universities his professor was Edward Heis, the distinguished German astronomer, noted for his attachment to Catholicity, and whose work on the variable stars, on the milky way, on meteoric swarms and the zodiacal light deservedly brought him such wide recognition in the nineteenth century. His Jesuit pupil was destined to follow in his path in many of these subjects and add to what his distinguished master had taught him.

After his ordination to the priesthood Father Hagen was sent to the United States to take up teaching and was stationed for nearly ten years in the '80's at Prairie-du-Chien, Wis. His principal occupation was teaching mathematics and the physical sciences and he succeeded in rousing the interest of students in these subjects much better than it had ever been done before. None of those round him, however, had any idea of the genius of the man. In spite of many discouraging circumstances he took up the study of astronomy, and mounted a three-inch telescope on gas pipes, having secured though only with difficulty a small shed in which to house it. He had only a limited amount of time at his disposal for astronomical observations and he took up the study of the variable stars. It was not long before his observations began to attract attention in the astronomical world and notwithstanding the makeshift character of his astronomical equipment he did some excellent work. It was in the midst of this that the chance was afforded him of becoming the director of the observatory at Georgetown and almost needless to say this opportunity was welcomed very heartily and he soon began his work there. In the course of the next ten years Father Hagen's work made him known throughout the astronomical world.

Father Hagen's "Atlas of the Variable Stars" is highly appreciated by astronomers everywhere. His "Synopsis of the Higher Mathematics," some four volumes quarto, secured a noteworthy reception from the mathematical world and bore the mark of exact scholarship which characterizes all of the Jesuit work in science. Father Hagen continued for the next twenty-five years after his appointment as director of the Vatican observatory to attract attention by some of his observations and especially those which required long and careful assiduity to bring out astronomical results. He was another one of these tireless men of single-hearted interest who are ready to devote all their time and energy to the accomplishment of a great purpose.

Like his predecessor, Father Secchi, Father Hagen was helped in every way by his Jesuit superiors and by his Jesuit brothers in the Order. They were naturally very proud of his work and here in America his brother Jesuits were gratified to think that he had received the training here on this continent which enabled him to go on with his work. Personally he was one of those modest scholars ready on request to help others in their work as I had reason to know for myself on a number of occasions when he helped me in tracing out historical connections in the matter of the relations of science and religion that required the attention of someone on the spot in Rome.

In recent years many Jesuit colleges, especially in this country, have made a specialty of the science of seismology, that is of earthquakes, their occurrence, location and intensity. There is a chain of Jesuit seismological observatories extending all around the world, many of the most important of them situated here in the United States. For some years the seismological observatory at Georgetown University was the best equipped department of its kind on this continent and whenever there were earth tremors at a distance Georgetown was looked to to send out announcements with regard to the location of the quake and the intensity of the movement of the earth connected with it. Newspaper reporters consulted the director of the observatory for the data for their reports and Father Tondorf, in charge of the observatory, came to be very well known throughout the country. At the present time there are a number of such stations throughout the United States with Jesuit directors who are quite ready to announce the interpretation of the seismographic signs and the other records. The Jesuits have achieved distinction then that is recognized everywhere in the scientific world for what they have done for the three sciences of astronomy, meteorology and seismology.

These are of course three scientific subjects with regard to which there are few practical applications and practically no opportunity for money making. Jesuit studies have, however, in these three fields proved of value for humanity. The observations of Father Ricard, S.J., of Santa Clara University on sun spots seem to point to a connection between these and certain changes in the weather and particularly the long-range changes that are connected with the eleven-year period of meteorites and apparently with a similar period in the waxing and waning in intensity and in number of spots on the sun. Much more will have to be known about that before the significance of Father Ricard's observations can be determined but there are some very interesting fulfilments of weather prophecies that seem to demonstrate the parallelism of these meteoric phenomena.

So far as meteorology is concerned, the observations made for the typhoons of the East and the hurricanes of the West Indies have proved of great value. The instruments designed by the Jesuits are now to a great extent superseded by wireless communications so that the possibility of knowing weather conditions from many quarters has advanced meteorology beyond where it was. In the meantime many lives and a great deal of property have been saved by the Jesuit observations in the Philippines.

Seismology would seem to be a science that could have very little significance for the practical life of humanity and yet Dr. Reginald A. Daly, professor of geology at Harvard University, suggests that the geologists are now as it were x-raying the earth deriving their information through seismic disturbances and he explains the process as follows:

"Just as the chemist is studying the anatomy of the atom, the astronomer the structure of the star by the study of light and heat waves, just as the depth of the ocean can now be tested by measuring the echo of sound waves from the bottom of the sea, so the geologist can now infer something of the structure of the earth by analyzing the long waves set in motion by the mighty hammer of an earthquake."

Very few people realize that there is an earthquake shock of more or less intensity on the average every hour during the day, something about ten thousand of them in the year. An earthquake of the first magnitude occurs every twenty days or so but fortunately most of them originate under the ocean which covers by far the larger portion of the earth's surface, and so comparatively little damage is done. The geologist now records the waves set in motion by these earthquakings to add to our knowledge of the earth's invisible interior almost in the same way as a surgeon explores the interior of the human body with the x-rays. Jesuit seismological observations then go on record and others may reach ulterior conclusions with them.

CHAPTER XV

THE ALASKA MISSIONS

Probably the most difficult mission country in the world is in our own United States in the territory of Alaska. The intense cold of the winter time often forty degrees below zero but sometimes even more than fifty, reaching even sixty degrees below in the midst of the blizzards that occur every winter while the Arctic night adds to the cheerlessness of the situation—all this makes life as trying as it can be consistent with ultimate survival. By contrast there is a short hot summer with the sun almost constantly above the horizon to make refreshing sleep difficult indeed. The summer brings with it a plague of mosquitoes to add to the climatic trials. No wonder the white population of Alaska is reported as dwindling. The gold rush brought a substantial influx of inhabitants from all over the United States, but also from many other countries, but most of these have gone and many more would go only that now their all is centered in Alaska. Meantime the Eskimos continue to increase and prosper because their climate is not tempting to the white man and the Jesuits are occupied in caring for them and have found them a very manly intelligent race whose talents make the introduction of civilization and Christianity among them very well worth while.

It is now more than fifty years since the Jesuits, engaged in missions among the Indians of the Rocky Mountain region, took up the missions in Alaska. They have continued ever since to devote themselves to the religious care of the Eskimos and of such whites as penetrate beyond the cities and towns of southern Alaska. The early missionaries were men who had endured the

255

trials of missionary life among the Indians and who were thoroughly trained and finely equipped so far as thoroughgoing forgetfulness of self could go for this work among the Eskimos in Alaska. Their missionary letters with regard to their mission folk showed that they found them to be a simple kindly people in whose hearts they very soon found a welcome. They represented a great contrast with the rather difficult Indian tribes, above all the Sioux and the Blackfeet, with whom the Jesuits had been associated for some fifty years. The mission to the Eskimos gave great promise because the children especially were glad to gather around the Fathers and as the rising generation has come to adult years their affectionate respect for the missionaries has been one of the very kindly things of a world in which selfishness usually plays so large a rôle.

Several score of Jesuits have taken their share at one time or another in the work of the Alaska missions. Many of them have had individual experiences and missionary careers which give them a place in the history of the Order and of its missions comparable to those attained by the Jesuit missionaries who worked among the Indians in various parts of this country during the past three hundred years. Only a few of them can be mentioned but their careers serve to illustrate the fact that the Jesuits in our day continue to be what they were in older times. So far as readiness to take up the most difficult tasks is concerned—provided there was the promise in connection with them of the conversion of disbelievers to Christianity and the gradual development that made for happiness not only here but hereafter—the modern Jesuits are manifestly blood brothers of those who made the Jesuit missions of the long ago such striking examples of high ideals under the most trying conditions. The Rocky Mountain missions have a history of scarcely more than a generation in our time but they demonstrate very clearly that the spirit of the Jesuits is the same now as it was some ten generations ago and that the Jesuits continue to be what their founder made them by example and training and constitution four hundred years ago.

The founder of the Alaska missions was Father Cataldo, a Sicilian, exiled from his own country by a revolution in Italy,

who volunteered for the work of the Rocky Mountain missions
more than seventy-five years ago. He joined Father De Smet,
the founder of the Rocky Mountain missions, whose story I have
told in the chapter on the modern black-robe. Father Cataldo
caught the spirit of this great missionary among the Indians and
after years of service he himself proposed to go farther and take
up the difficult work among the Eskimos in Alaska. In spite of
the severe hardships through which his mission life led him and
the very delicate health he had at the beginning, he lived to be
well past ninety years of age. He came to be well known and to
exercise deep influence in the Northwest and in Alaska, and he
was one of the great pioneers of these territories. He was shy and
retiring in disposition, shunned publicity and above all notoriety
and devoted himself to whatever was found for him to do with
the most faithful attention. Those of us who had the privilege
of his friendship toward the end of his life learned to know his
charm and came to realize how his personality won the hearts of
young men particularly. Except that he had the Master's work
to do he would have welcomed the obscurity of some quiet out
of the way mission for himself. Only his missionary zeal
prompted him to go on with his work no matter what the cost
to his feelings might be.

Father Cataldo was born in Sicily March 17, 1837. He was
very delicate as a child and no one expected him to live to grow
up. At the age of two he was actually pronounced dead and
preparations for his funeral were made. He continued in delicate
health as a boy, he was frail as a young man, and as a result his
schooling was interrupted from time to time for his health's sake.
He was a brilliant student whenever he was able to work, but
his studies were often interrupted. When he was not quite sixteen, in spite of his delicate health he was received as a novice
among the Jesuits. The good fathers, who admired the purity
of his life and the brilliance of his talents, hoped that the absolute
regularity of his religious life would prove a stabilizer for his
health, as it did, but not without recurring spells of sickness.
Nothing daunted him. His intense preoccupation with whatever
was the duty of the moment was a noteworthy trait of his char-

acter. One of his superiors said of him that "he had not a frame of adamant but he had a soul of fire." He had the optimism that so often is noted in tuberculous patients and which is sometimes looked upon as a bad sign, but it has been said that "tuberculosis takes only the quitters." Quitting was the last thing in the world that anyone would attribute to good Father Cataldo. His motto if it had ever been consciously framed would undoubtedly have been, "never give up."

In the midst of his studies as a young Jesuit the Italian revolution of 1860 came to interrupt his quiet scholarly life—as revolutions have so often done before and since. The Jesuits are a shining mark for revolutionary aims. They are men of peace who present no resistance. As a rule they have magnificent school buildings that can be used to advantage by revolutionists and so banishment is accorded them. They are permitted to come back a little later but they understand very well that the new situation will not be any more permanent than the preceding one. Their founder, Ignatius of Loyola, asked as a sign of divine favor for his institute that they should suffer persecution, for that would surely maintain the spirit of the institute. His prayer has been answered. With ninety other members of the Order Father Cataldo had to take the road of exile from his native land.

He went to Rome where he met the General of the Order, Very Reverend Peter Beckx. He had but one request to make of him, that he be sent on foreign missions. The Father General sympathized with the undaunted spirit of the young man and sent him to Louvain in Belgium to prepare for the missions by gaining a thorough knowledge of English and French while making his studies in theology. After his ordination, anticipated because of his exile, when he was yet only twenty-five years of age, he wrote to the General of the Jesuits asking to be sent to the Indian missions in America.

About the time Father Cataldo's letter reached Rome, another letter arrived from America urgently asking for missionary priests. This seemed like an interposition of Providence, so Father Cataldo was directed to proceed at once to America to complete his theology in Boston and round out his knowledge of

English in the field of his future labors which was to be the Rocky Mountain mission among the Indians. The raw climate of the Atlantic seaboard worked havoc with Father Cataldo's always delicate health. An Italian physician had pronounced him an incurable consumptive. His American physician in Boston repeated that verdict. Providentially, as Father Cataldo used to say, his first assignment was not to the Rocky Mountains and the Indians but to sunny California. This promised to give him a renewed lease of life at least for some time. Here at Santa Clara College he had the opportunity to finish his theology and after a year he passed the crucial test of the Jesuit examination in philosophy and theology, manifestly with excellent success since the following year he was himself assigned to teach philosophy to the young Jesuits (1864). Almost needless to say only Jesuits who are recognized as of higher talent are chosen for this occupation.

Fortunately he was allowed to remain there for three years. The local superiors wanted to keep him as a teacher because he was a very valuable asset in the position of professor though he himself still cherished the idea of going on the missions among the Indians. He had made the offering of himself for the missions to Almighty God when his health threatened to cripple his usefulness for life. Since his health had improved so marvelously, that seemed to be an index that his sacrifice was acceptable to Providence. The whole question was referred to the General at Rome who declared that the decision must be made by Father Cataldo himself. With characteristic humility Father Cataldo turned for advice to the brother infirmarian of the college who was an experienced observer of the ailing. Father Cataldo wanted to know what were the chances of his being able to work successfully in the Rocky Mountains. The infirmarian quite frankly told him that in the high altitude with pure air and daily rides on horseback in the wide open spaces of the west, he might possibly live for years and even to a good round age. Horseback riding was one of the treatments for consumptives in those days. Altitude has always been one of the auxiliaries for the treatment of consumption since old Grecian times. Hippocrates is said to have

prescribed for a patient suffering from the affection "buy a cow
(for the sake of the milk) and go away into the mountains."

Father Cataldo reported this prognosis to the General at Rome
and the reply was that he should go to the mountains at once.
His Jesuit colleagues who thought they knew him well were
quite sure that he would not long survive the hardships of
service among the Indians. One said, "He may live three
months," another gave him a year or at most two; a third
declared that Father Cataldo was more tough and wiry than most
people thought and he might live for five years. More than sixty
years later, when Father Cataldo had been seventy-five years a
Jesuit and was well over ninety years of age, he said, "The last
of these prophets died long ago. I have prayed for their souls
and I have lived on these sixty and more years since."

He was one of the gentlest and kindliest of men. He was like
a father in his dealings with his brother Jesuits when he was
their superior and many a young Jesuit who was brought into
close contact with Father Cataldo felt in himself the stirring of
a vocation to take up missionary work among the North
American Indians or among the Eskimos in frozen Alaska. He
had accomplished so much in spite of all the handicaps of poor
health and utter unaccustomedness of climate—for his family had
been Sicilian for all their history—that others were bound to
feel that they might well hope to rival his achievement in bringing Christianity and civilization to these benighted people who
had not had the chance to see the brighter side of life.

Father Cataldo's first mission among the Indians was neither
encouraging nor satisfying. His missionary efforts had very little
effect upon them. Except for the baptisms of dying children
more than ten years passed almost without a conversion. Some
dying old folks permitted themselves to be baptized, some of the
squaws developed a vague interest in religion, but on the braves
of the tribe little influence was exerted. The situation would
surely have discouraged anyone of less zeal and persistence but
Father Cataldo continued to share in the life of the tribe though
he was still delicate in health and it very soon began to be evident
that the rude life among the savages lived mainly out of doors

though in the cold blizzard region of the Rockies, instead of being a detriment to his health, was proving to be a benefit. In the course of the year he became rugged and thoroughly capable of sharing the wanderings of the tribe.

When he had been more than a dozen of years with the tribe he met with an accident in which he suffered from a badly broken leg which was set in the rude way of the savages and had to be rebroken and set again at the cost of a great deal of pain. Father Cataldo bore his sufferings so patiently and without complaint that he quite won the hearts of the braves of the tribe for this virtue of patience in the midst of suffering was the one moral trait that they thoroughly appreciated. Above all the chief of the tribe became a close personal friend. Now that Father Cataldo had proven himself a man in their Indian sense of the word, they were ready to listen to his religious ministrations. In spite of the crippling incident, this brave Jesuit in the course of the next few years was able to found a series of most successful missions among the Indians in the Rocky Mountains. In the course of his travels undertaken in order to secure health and assistants for the mission, he discovered a number of young men in this country and in Europe who, after hearing the story of the chance there was to follow the Master by work among the Indians, were ready to share the trials and hardships of the missionary life. It is surprising what human nature is ready to do and how well it will devote itself to doing it in spite of the most serious difficulties, when an appeal is made to the idealistic side of humanity. When the heart is deeply touched a man takes up seriously a mode of life fervently devoted to the benefit of others and not himself. Under Father Cataldo's fostering care, the Rocky Mountain missions among the Indians gradually developed until many thousands of the Indians were under the care of the Jesuits. Also the Ursuline and Notre Dame Sisters whom the Jesuits had brought in to help them in their work of evangelization had founded schools which brought Christianity and civilization into the hearts of the Indians.

This fine achievement of Father Cataldo among the Rocky Mountain Indians brought with it no mood of complacent satisfaction and above all no feeling that he might settle down now to the oversight of his missions without further effort. He knew that there were a large number of Eskimos up in Alaska who, owing to the difficult climatic conditions, had never been approached by missionaries and he had the urge to "go and teach all nations." In the early '80's some Jesuits accompanied him into Alaska and mission foundations were made in various places. The Eskimos proved to be tractable, kindly folk who welcomed the missionaries and many of them soon became Christians. The one effort of the missionary was to bring to the Indians such knowledge of the meaning of life in terms of the hereafter as would enable them to make something more out of life than the mere living from day to day until the end came. As time has gone on, conditions have shown the possibility of a native clergy among the Eskimos and those who know them best declare that they are more suitable than any of the other American natives for the priesthood.

To make the missions a success the missionaries had to share the lives of the Eskimos and to bear the extremes of temperature which prevail in Alaska where it is almost as hot in summer as it is cold in winter. The missionaries had to take long journeys in the fulfilment of their sacramental duties even in the height of winter and sometimes they were caught in blizzards and storms, in the midst of which some of them lost their lives but always there were others ready and willing, yes, even anxious to take their places. They had to suffer as much as polar explorers but without intervals in the temperate zone and year after year they went on with their work but it was all in a lifetime and taken bravely as it came.

These missionaries were often widely separated from one another and would not see a white man for months at a time as a rule and under these circumstances they followed the custom of the Order and wrote letters describing their experiences for their brother Jesuits back home. Some of these letters I was asked to translate out of Italian into English for the "Woodstock Letters," the community journal of the Jesuits of the United States. They told simply and straightforwardly the story of their activities among the Eskimos, the trying conditions they had to endure from the intense cold but dwelling on the tractability of their mission folk, their kindliness and simplicity of heart, their interest in the missions.

These letters from Alaska were written just as the "Jesuit Relations" had been written centuries before with the idea of letting those who had known them as fellow students, some of whom had been classmates, know just what was happening in this corner of the Lord's vineyard. The letters were often read during meal time and would then be a subject for discussion during the recreation period which always followed the meals.

Two purposes were served,—edifying material was provided for discussion during recreation and the full power of the example set by these missionaries in distant parts was secured. The motives of young men who were devoted to their studies and who might easily have had very human incentives intrude on their spiritual life were thoroughly purified and the true inwardness of their vocation as Jesuits brought home to them. The atmosphere created by such reading was that these were the stories of Jesuits who were doing a Jesuit's work not for any self-glorification but *ad majorem Dei gloriam*. Vocations to the missions were thus fostered and it was felt that a special blessing came down on their houses of education whenever the spirit of vocation to the missions led young men to make the sacrifice required for this.

When his superiorship was concluded Father Cataldo continued as a simple missionary in the work among the Indians unto a very old age. When he was well above four score he was made the superior of a mission among the Indians in the Dakotas and his appeals for help came to many of us who had known and admired him in the middle years of his life and who each year were glad to note that he was still in the land of the living and still going on with his work among the Indians. His iron will enabled him to use all his powers to the best advantage and develop them to their fullest. Like a number of other of these missionaries of the early days he lived far beyond the psalmist's limit and, best of all for himself, was able to work and not prove a burden to others. His broken leg so rudely set and still more rudely mended made him somewhat lame and it continued to be a source of annoyance to him to the end of his life. His declining years saw him beloved by his brother Jesuits and also by the lay folk who had been brought in intimate contact with him and loved above all by his Indian charges who were drawn close to this black-robe who had spent his life among them and had been a father and brother to them all at all times.

Father Cataldo's experiences—and as is easy to understand they were many and various in his long life—were not exclusively with the Indians. One of them that he liked to tell because of the sequel to it, was the story of an encounter with a lynching party. A prospector from Oregon discovered galena, a combined lead and silver ore, in the northern Idaho mountains and reported his discovery to friends in Portland. A rush to the region of the discovery followed but the discoverer could not locate his find. Enraged by what they thought was a hoax practised on them, the participants in the rush decided to hang the prospector in the morning. Father Cataldo learned their intention and with the help of friendly Indians aided the man to escape during the night. The baffled mob decided to lynch Father Cataldo instead of the prospector but an Irishman in the crowd objected to hanging a priest and his influence proved enough to save Father Cataldo's life.

The sequel was that some years later Father Cataldo visited Portland to buy an altar lamp for his mission church. While there he met a man who inquired of him if he was the missionary from the Cœur d'Alène Indians. His answer was in the affirmative and then he was told that the man he had rescued was a prominent Mason and that his brother Masons wanted to do something for the courageous priest in return for his self-forgetting humanity. When they learned that he had come for the purchase of an altar lamp they insisted upon buying it for him and it hangs with an inscription containing the names of the donors in the church at Cœur d'Alène. It has been suggested that this is unique among all the altar lamps of the world.

RIGHT REV. JOSEPH RAPHAEL CRIMONT

Father Cataldo's very distinguished successor in the superiorship of the Alaska missions is Right Reverend Bishop Joseph Crimont. According to their rules Jesuits are not allowed to become bishops or higher ecclesiastics and it is only after special command from the Pope that they become members of the hierarchy. There are usually several cardinals at the Curia in Rome who were Jesuits in their younger years and who have been advanced to the dignity of cardinal because their services were particularly wanted at the Vatican on account of their scholarship in some special line which makes them extremely valuable as counsellors to the Holy See and the Roman Congregations. Besides these, Jesuits are appointed to bishoprics in missionary countries where the work is very difficult and where the Jesuits are exclusively occupied with the missions so that a member of the Order provides a hierarchical center as bishop which enables the Order to do its work with greater facility. There are American Jesuits who are bishops in Belize and Jamaica in the tropics, as well as in certain parts of the Philippine Islands almost under the equator on the other side of the globe. These Jesuit bishops are merely very zealous missionaries who are granted powers and dignity in connection with the administration of the sacraments which enable them and their brother Jesuits to carry on their work more successfully.

It is in this category of Jesuit bishops that Bishop Crimont of Alaska must be numbered. He is himself one of the most zealous and successful of the missionaries in that region. He is a man noted for his scholarship, who has demonstrated his attainments in philosophy and theology. He has, however, given himself whole-heartedly to the work among his flock in the diocese, and he has come to be looked upon as a model of what a Jesuit can be under such circumstances.

Altogether there are some 10,000 Catholics in Alaska, of whom something more than one-half are whites. The 4,500 natives are scattered in many parts of that vast territory and Bishop Crimont has devoted himself now for more than thirty years to organizing missions among them so that Christianity and civilization may be brought to them and that life may mean something more than the effort to secure food enough today that they may not be starving tomorrow. The relations during these fifty years now between the Jesuits and the Eskimos have been most cordial and the score of Fathers connected with the work there have accomplished an immense amount of good. Life has been hard indeed in that trying clime but it has been borne with the patient hardihood that has characterized the work of difficult Jesuit missions throughout the world.

FATHER WILLIAM JUDGE

Father Cataldo, S.J., was the hero of the Indian and Eskimo missions in our generation but Alaska was to have another Jesuit hero who drew all hearts to him because he was manifestly so little interested in himself and so much interested in others. This hero of the Alaska missions came in the person of a native-born American who had asked of his superiors over and over again with gentle persistence to be sent on the Indian missions in the Rocky Mountains and Alaska, and whose request to his great joy was at last granted. This was Father William Judge who had proved his capacity in executive positions in the Jesuit colleges in the eastern part of the United States, and whose destiny now seemed to be to devote himself to the Eskimos in Alaska. He had not been long in the territory, however, before the news that gold had been found in the Klondike caused a rush of gold seekers that fairly swamped all the accommodations that the Alaska towns could furnish. Juneau particularly was crowded with men and not a few women, all intent on making their fortunes at a single stroke by some lucky discovery or hopeful to secure a competency by gathering enough of the precious yellow dust to enable them to live without labor for the rest of life.

Almost needless to say men intent on the search for gold are not the sort that are likely to be influenced by ideals or lofty motives. A great many of these gold seekers encountered only hardship and suffering. Many of them fell ill and needed care, a great many of them had to return home disappointed and not a few of them left their bodies in Alaska. Numbers had started with scarcely enough money to reach Alaska and support themselves for a very short time. They left home with the fond delusion that they would surely find gold and be able to care for themselves. Under the circumstances it is not surprising that a great many of them fell ill and needed aid and those who fell by the wayside received very little attention and were likely to be neglected.

In the midst of this crowding mass of people, supremely forgetful of others in their mad scramble after gold, no wonder that a man who devoted himself whole-heartedly to the care of those in need attracted attention. It was not long before he came to be known by most of the inhabitants of the town. This was Father Judge, S.J., the pastor of the little church in Juneau who had succeeded in founding a hospital for the succour of the needy poor and who devoted himself to the care of the ailing and the encouragement of the down-and-outers even to the point of providing for their material needs as far as that was possible. His lack of anything like preoccupation with money proved such a contrast in the midst of that milling crowd of gold seekers that he seemed an apostle sent among them. It was not long before nearly everyone in Juneau thought of him as a personal friend and many a man who had no church affiliations and no idea of religion had his religious feelings deeply stirred because Father Judge did not preach much but did a great deal of good. He was one of those like Chaucer's Parish Priest who first did and then said.

During the epidemic of influenza in Alaska, Father Judge fairly seemed to multiply himself in order to be able to bring the consolations of religion to many poor fellows who were dying far away from home. Night and day he persisted in his ministrations, only snatching a few hours out of the twenty-four for sleep. He came to be looked upon almost as an angel of mercy. Many a poor fellow far from relatives looked his last in this world into Father Judge's eyes and had the consolation of knowing that there was one friend near him for that dread passing.

Unfortunately, as the epidemic was subsiding and most of his rush work was accomplished, Father Judge himself came down with the disease and in spite of the tenderest care on the part of the Sisters at the hospital and the solicitude of most of the inhabitants of Juneau who would have been so glad to breathe a sigh of relief at some favorable news from his bedside, Father Judge succumbed to the disease. He had gone to Alaska mainly for the sake of the hard work among the Eskimos, he was a man of well-developed muscular frame, and he would have made an ideal missionary for distant work among the natives but he was destined to find his field of labors among the gold seekers at Juneau. They learned to think as much of him as the Indians did of their black-robes. As a Jesuit he had been trained to a life of thoughtfulness for others and he had made sacrifices for that purpose though he thought that his work was to be accomplished under the adventurous circumstances that go with the dog sled and the long journeys from mission to mission in the bitter cold. He was ready to turn his hand to whatever mode of apostolate presented itself and with such success that his name has been in benediction ever since in Alaska.

When the news of Father Judge's death reached the office of the "Klondike Nugget," the daily paper in which the account of so much of Father Judge's work had appeared for ten years, the editor wrote his appreciation of him and expressed the feelings of all those who knew him:

"All Dawson mourns the death of Father Judge. There is scarcely a man in the community who has not come into personal contact with the work of this noble priest. There are good men in the world plentiful enough; but there are none here who can take up the Father's good work with the disinterestedness and unselfishness of Father Judge or who can in less than a decade win such individual trust as all felt for this physically feeble, yet charitably strong man."

"For all those to whom the magic names Forty Mile Post, Dawson City and the Klondike were realities in the 'Gold Rush' of the end of the nineteenth century, the name of Father William Judge, S.J., Alaska's missionary, will always be linked in the memories of the old-timers. They speak of him as 'Good

Father,' and such he was not alone for Catholics but for all those who were brought in intimate contact with him."

It would be easy to think that the Jesuits who volunteer for the extremely hard life involved in the missions in such regions as Alaska must be very serious-minded individuals indeed, almost inevitably profoundly puritanic in their ways, occupied almost exclusively with themselves and their personal salvation, intent on the hard things of life and without interest in the happy possibilities of human existence. To have been acquainted personally with some of them is surely to have brought home to one an utter contradiction of any such preconceived notion. To have had the privilege of knowing a man like Father Frank Barnum, S.J., who spent years on the missions in Alaska, is to appreciate the fact that missionaries are of the very salt of the earth, and that there is an abundance of the spice of life in their make-up.

Father Barnum was a member of a well-known southern family, some members of which were quite wealthy as wealth went fifty years ago. When Frank proposed to become a Jesuit there was a storm of opposition aroused in family circles because near relatives were quite sure that Frank could make something much more of his life than devoting himself to teaching and priestly ministrations. One of his uncles who thought a great deal of him left him a legacy of $100,000, a sum that meant a very great deal in those days, on the single condition that he would not become a Jesuit. Frank refused to accept the legacy on the condition set, for he thought he could find a happier, fuller life with the Jesuits than in any other way. After having taught for some years here in the East, he applied for permission to go to the missions in Alaska, and after some delay—for missionary work in hard fields is looked upon as a special privilege not to be had at once for the asking—that permission was granted.

Some of his experiences among the Eskimos as related on his

return for a visit to the East were very interesting. There was one of them particularly that demonstrated his power to see a joke even when it was on himself and that was a key to his character. He had studied medicine as a young man and therefore was able to be of no little help to the natives when for one reason or another they fell ill. They were not an ailing people as a rule. Microbes do not thrive luxuriantly in a region where the temperature during the winter, often for five or six months of the year, goes down nearly every day to from twenty to forty degrees below zero Fahrenheit. Besides, except on special occasions when food, because of the special season, was particularly abundant, they were a rather abstemious people. They seldom overate so that another great cause of illness, probably the commonest in civilization, was lacking among them.

They could be tempted, however, at certain seasons to eat more than was good for them, and then Father Barnum had to do what he could for them medicinally. A large number of wild birds live along the Alaskan coast and lay their eggs abundantly in the spring. The Eskimos used to gather these eggs though they did not eat them while they were fresh. Their custom was to put them aside, especially exposed to the sun, until they got thoroughly addled. They liked their eggs high, as so many hunters like their venison. They thought fresh eggs apparently insipid and tasteless, as a connoisseur in cheese would the very mild cream cheese which is usually set before children. When the eggs had been properly matured to their taste the Eskimos ate a good many more of them than was good for them. They quite literally ate them by the dozen, or even several dozen. Naturally they would be around the next day complaining of misery in their midst, pleading earnestly with the good missionary to give them something that would relieve the discomfort which they felt as the result of the overeating.

When Father Frank sent down to San Francisco next time for supplies for the missions, he ordered a keg of castor oil, and resolved that this would serve to teach this good flock of his a needed lesson in not indulging their appetites to excess. He felt sure that castor oil would be just about the thing for them and that they would never again overeat in the matter of eggs, particularly if they recalled that they had to take that nasty medicine after it. He had very poignant memories himself of this as an extremely efficient remedy back home among the children. After all he thought of these men and women as really children of a larger growth whom he had to care for.

When the following spring, according to tribal custom, they ate the addled eggs by the dozen to repletion and then came looking for relief and consolation from their good pastor, he ladled out the castor oil to them. He was rather surprised that they made no faces at it and made so little fuss about it. Indeed, after the first taste of it they seemed to take to it very readily. He was surprised to find how many more came for treatment than had come the preceding year. It seemed as though nearly everyone in the village wanted to have at least a taste of that new medicine. The fact of the matter was that for these denizens of the Arctic region for whom whale's blubber is a delicacy, this thick treacly medicine tasted as good as ice cream. They smacked their lips over it and evidently savored the taste of it by having it go down slowly. Any of them were willing to try it and had to be warned about the results that it would surely have. The lesson that he intended to give his flock was manifestly lost on them entirely. His effort was a failure and he was quite ready to confess his disillusionment.

The following year when he was getting his medical supplies, he ordered a drum of Glauber's salts in place of the castor oil. Those particular Eskimos do not care for salts and especially not the bitter high tasting salts such as Glauber's are. He gave them some teaspoons of this instead of the castor oil and he found that no one came back for more and no one felt the urge to go and get any of the new medicine unless he was really in need of it. They were much more careful of stuffing themselves with addled eggs after their experience with this new kind of medicine which their pastor had secured for them.

Father Barnum came to be looked upon by the Eskimos as one of their best friends. They were ready to bring all their troubles to him, and he had to map out his day's work in order to find leisure for his spiritual duties in the midst of their well-meaning but importunate demands on his time. They learned to think a great deal of their "black robe" and were ready to do anything in the world for him. He was very human himself and his humanity touched these good Arctic people, whose hearts were by no means so cold as their climate, and who learned to appreciate the great-heartedness of the missionary who was making such profound sacrifices in order to be with them. He was one of the jolliest of companions, the life of any group in which he was, ready with quips and jokes, but withal a very successful missionary in one of the hardest of missions.[1]

[1] That the Jesuits are still occupied with the most trying missions throughout the world is easy to see from the roster of Jesuit missionary efforts throughout the world. In Europe its missionaries are to be found in Albania; in Asia they are working in Armenia, Syria, Ceylon, Assam, Bengal, Bombay, Poona, Goa, Madura, Mangalore, Japan, Canton, Nanking and Southeast Tche-ly. In Africa they are in Egypt, Cape Colony, Zambesi, Rhodesia, the Belgian Congo and the islands of Madagascar, Mauritius and Reunion; in America they are working in Jamaica where such an immense majority of the population is colored, and among the Eskimos of Alaska and the Indians of Canada, South Dakota, the Rocky Mountain region, as well as Pimeria down in Arizona. They have missions in Guiana and finally in Oceanica they are toiling in the Celebes, in Flores, Java and the Philippines. In these missions nearly two thousand Jesuits are devoting their lives to missionary endeavor in direct contact with the aborigines.

CHAPTER XVI

JESUIT CHAPLAINS IN ASYLUMS AND PRISONS

THE most revealing chapter in the history of the Jesuits in the United States, the chapter that above all discloses better than any other the true inwardness of their work and the consecration of their lives, is that which tells the story of their priestly care for the paupers and prisoners in a number of our large cities. The poor who are ill unto death, though for many of them its blessed coming may be delayed for years, and who have no one to care for them so that their one harbor is that ultimate refuge of the friendless—the poorhouse; the feeble-minded and the insane in public asylums; the down-and-outs in our city institutions, all these find a father and brother in the fullest sense of those precious terms in the same "black-robe" whom the Indians long ago learned to trust so confidently and whose faithful unselfish ministrations they had not forgotten after an interval of more than two hundred years of existence as savages had passed over them.

The best example of that striking Jesuit work which recalls so definitely the intimate relations of the founder of the Order and his first companions with the hospitals and other refuges for the needy in which they spent so much time four hundred years ago, is to be seen here in New York City where for some seventy years the Jesuits have been chaplains on the islands in the East River. Here New York provides so far as abundance of fresh air is concerned an excellent situation for its paupers and dependents. On the other hand the place is crowded, many of the buildings are old, conditions are difficult, and the need of human sympathy is very great. The Jesuits have made themselves veritable guardians as well as evangelists to these poor people, who, handicapped by disease of mind or body or worn down by old age or premature degeneration of tissue, are most of them among the derelicts of mankind. Their Jesuit chaplains are a source of the deepest consolation to them and life is very different from the hopeless prospect it might be only for the ministrations of the Jesuits.

Almost needless to say there is no prestige of any kind that goes with the chaplaincy. The poor we have always with us and they are here in quantity and quality. If there is a place in the world where men devote themselves to their work with no thought of self or of worldly recognition it is in these islands. It would not be worth while to expect appreciation from those for whom they are doing so much. Gratitude, as is well known, is not a common trait among the poor, and their gratitude might be touching but it would not be very satisfying. Only a loftier than any human motive can enable men to go on with such work and find satisfaction in life, yet the holders of these positions are often among the most cheerful and light-hearted and some of them are the very life of their brother Jesuits when they are among them. Indeed one of their principal trials is the fact that they have to live apart from community life which meant much for them when they dwelt in houses of the Order.

It might readily be thought that for these poor folk, utterly ignorant as a rule, so many of whom have not the minds to make anything of life while so many others have lost whatever minds they had, almost anyone in Holy Orders would serve the beneficent purpose of bringing them the terminal consolations of religion and composing their minds and bodies for death. Some old priest, who had outlived his usefulness as a pastor or who did not feel quite equal to parochial cares or responsibilities, might be shifted over to the "islands" to say Mass and administer the sacraments to these poor creatures as they needed them. Younger priests who were not in very good health themselves might possibly be expected in the fine open-air life of the island to be able to do whatever was needed in the way of religious ministration for hospital and jail and asylum inmates. An "island" chaplaincy would seem to be—until one knows something more about it—a comparatively easy post to be filled by any clergyman not quite capable of the busier cares of parish work.

As a matter of fact, however, the men who serve as chaplains on the islands have to be as a rule in robust and vigorous health because they are likely to be called upon at any hour of the day or night and they have many more nights on the average when they are disturbed than when they are allowed to sleep through without a night call that will take them to some of the many buildings on the islands. In the city tuberculosis hospital, for instance, some ten Catholics die every week and the chaplain makes it a rule to spend some time at their bedsides just before their passing away. Ever so many of the dying pass out in the early morning hours when normally human vitality is at its lowest ebb so that the chaplain is likely to have his sleep shortened rather frequently in those early hours of the morning when sleep seems so particularly precious. The chaplains on the island, the men who are thus at the beck and call of these poor down-and-outers of humanity are well-educated cultured scholars to whom, following the rule of the Order, some fifteen years of preparation for the priesthood have been accorded by their Jesuit superiors in order that they may be properly trained for their life work. Just as with regard to the missionaries to distant and pagan countries it is not the less well-educated that fill these posts but very often some of the best men in the Order. Not a few of them before being assigned to their duties as chaplains have been recognized as teachers or preachers of distinction. Sometimes one wonders where a Jesuit of particular promise in his younger years is at work as time goes on and inquiry reveals that he is at work on the "island."

It might be expected that in these humble positions where chaplains are on duty all the time, Sunday would be the only busy day because of church services, and the priests would have time on their hands for scholarly reading and even for such writing as would enable them to publish scholarly works. Anyone at all familiar with the routine life of these chaplains, however, and the many calls that are made on their time is not likely to think that they have a store of leisure on their hands for which they have to seek extraneous occupations. As a matter of fact, even visits of friends to them on the island are, as some of us know by experience, likely to be interrupted over and over again by calls of duty and such interruptions are especially likely to come in the evenings when even slightly ailing patients often become obsessed with the fear that something may happen to them during the night or before the morning comes and send for the priest so as to be sure of his ministrations.

I have known personally probably more than a dozen of the Jesuits who have occupied chaplaincies on the islands. I have visited almost that many of them in their humble quarters as chaplains and spent some hours with them. The custom of seeing them began years ago when I was a student at Fordham. One of the good Fathers arranged for a group of collegians to go down to the islands to give religious instruction to the backward children over whom he had charge. Even a little experience soon showed us that the task seemed almost hopeless and the patience required endless. Almost needless to say we collegians soon tired of it because it was so hard to see any benefit derived from the work and so difficult to secure any results in the poor backward minds. This was one of the duties that the good chaplain had taken on himself for years. Later while teaching at Fordham I went down to visit a dear old Jesuit who had spent some twenty years on the islands. In his earlier years he had been looked upon as a scholar of high talent, deeply interested in many subjects. He made quite a collection of books that he knew he would not be able to use to any decided advantage but that he gathered in the hope that they would be of use in one of the Jesuit colleges in the time to come. He was an ardent book-lover all his life who chose to devote himself to this demanding work for the needy poor.

He was the founder of the mission on the islands and the type of man that they all were to be as the years went on, for they were all, as I remember them, kindly gentlemen who welcomed very heartily the visits that relieved something of the monotony of their duties and brought them diversion of mind in the midst of the rather drab web of existence in which they were placed.

Above all they were glad to see others interested in conditions on the islands for this might lead to amelioration of life for their charges.

I have taken meals with them on occasions and have been waited on by all sorts of bizarre individuals. Sometimes they were only sufferers from functional nervous diseases that gave them a tremor or caused them to grimace or sometimes they were the victims of tics of one kind or another that made life difficult for them among their fellows generally. Sometimes they were patients who suffered from some pathological condition that crippled them so seriously that life out in the busy world was impossible for them and yet they liked to feel that they could be useful in some way. Occasionally they were sufferers from severer ills. Once a good Jesuit Father said to me as we sat down to dinner, "When the waitress comes in do not look at her." But of course that warning only made his guest all the more anxious to have at least a peek at her and she proved to be partially lacking in nose. Some of it had disappeared in the course of cancer. That sight might have been enough to take away the appetite of some fastidious people but as a matter of fact, as the good Father had assured himself by consultation with a physician, there was not the slightest danger of contagion. It was the greatest consolation in the world for this good gentlewoman, who in her earlier years had been a school teacher, to make herself useful by waiting on the priests, and their friends. She was going to die of cancer eventually very probably and cancer of the face is very slow running so there were years of suffering ahead of her. To have the satisfaction of doing something for the father chaplain, for she was an excellent cook, made life seem ever so much more worthwhile for her under the circumstances.

This humble, faithful, self-forgetting work of the Jesuits of which no one knows anything except a few of their intimate friends, is accomplished with a cheerfulness and readiness that can come only from spiritual motives. There is not an ulterior thought of any possible kind connected with it except Christian charity. These men are following Christ and seeking out souls so as to provide for them the consolations of religion. It might possibly be thought that a special motive that prompted the work would be the feeling of loyalty to the Society of Jesus and the persuasion that the sacrifice of self was being accomplished to the ultimate glory of this wonderful association of men. Undoubtedly that is an accessory motive because these men have come to think of the Order to which they belong as in a certain sense their mother. Alone such a motive might impel men to make a noble sacrifice in a sudden emergency but scarcely for long years of humble patient sacrifice. It must not be forgotten that many of these men spend ten to twenty years or even more on the islands and so far as any mere human motive is concerned the life with its constant succession of demanding duties, many of them with natural feelings of repellence associated with them, would become intolerable. It is the supernatural motive and the spiritual vision that make life not only bearable but happy for these men. This vision of what is being done for some of the most sadly situated of all humanity enables these men to go on in the work to which they have been assigned. The assignment often did not come until they had asked more than once for the precious privilege of devoting themselves to it.

It is not as solemn, least of all gloomy, fanatics that they take up and continue the work, but as happy-hearted, cheerful, joyous companions and guides to these poor victims of circumstances and of poor human nature's weaknesses. There is no complacent pity for those they serve and no pauperization. There is the exhibition of the genuine feeling of the brotherhood of man under the Fatherhood of God that makes their ministrations all the more precious and lifts these fellow mortals up to a higher plane of appreciation of the meaning of existence. Above all there is very little or no opportunity for anything like self-seeking or for quest of prestige in these chaplaincies. There is no "humility with a hook," as the old writers of the monastic life used to term it. Outside of the Jesuits themselves only a little handful of people know about these men and their work. Their Jesuit colleagues, while they respect them highly for their self-sacrifice, have the very definite feeling that it is all in the day's work, all in a lifetime, and that these men are only doing what any of their Jesuit brothers would be quite willing to take up if they were selected for the positions.

It is all done according to the Jesuit motto, all is done in accord with the Jesuit spirit. These remnants of humanity at the tag end of existence, stricken though they may be, maimed in mind and body, have souls to save and the Jesuit chaplains are ready to help them to make out of even the terminal part of their lives all that will prepare them for another world than this. It is not philanthropy but ideal Christian charity, not human motives of any kind, but divine, that dictate it.

Anyone who thinks of Jesuits as scheming politicians intent on the advancement of their Order ought to make it a point to come in contact with them in their work in the "islands" around New York. There are many other cities besides New York throughout the country in which they are doing the same good work, but nowhere are their labors for humanity so well illustrated as in what may be seen just across the little strip of water that separates our welfare islands from Manhattan. No one ought to write about the Jesuits with any pretense of knowing anything about them who has not seen their work as it can be seen even in the course of a casual visit to these scenes of their labors for the humblest of our population.

Before the establishment of a resident chaplaincy on the islands, the Jesuit Fathers from St. Francis Xavier College in West Sixteenth Street, used to visit the various institutions in order to bring the consolations of religion to the inmates. Almost needless to say, this was a work that required deep faith and ardent zeal, for those who were the objects of their ministrations were as a rule the poorest of the poor, many of them absolutely destitute and suffering from various fatal diseases. Every now and then epidemics of disease invaded the islands and then the services of the Fathers were needed more than at any other time, and of course they knew that they ran the risk of catching these diseases. Indeed a number of them actually died from

typhus fever, epidemics of which came into New York City
every few years on board the vessels crowded with immigrants.

The other names for typhus fever are ship fever and famine
fever, because it was particularly in the crowded holds of immi-
grant vessels that the disease worked up into a serious epidemic,
and found the Irish immigrants, so often sufferers from malnu-
trition, in such poor health, with reduced resistive vitality, that
it was no wonder they died in large numbers. Deaths occurred
not only aboard the vessels but also after landing because they
were often huddled together in slum quarters so that the disease
continued its ravages and many of the poor immigrants, happy
in the thought that they were at last in the longed-for land of
opportunity found only a bed in the poorhouse from which they
went to their graves.

A series of Jesuit Fathers shortly after the middle of the
nineteenth century fell victims to these recurring epidemics.
They were devoting themselves to work among the immigrants
and the fact that their charges were suffering from disease no
matter what it might be did not deter them from their duties.
Almost needless to say, the fact that they continued to live at
St. Francis Xavier's created a certain rather serious amount of
danger for those with whom they were associated. Typhus can
be an intensely infectious disease. Over and over again when
the disease existed among prisoners in jails—and it so frequently
broke out there that one of its common names was jail fever—
when prisoners were brought into court from infected prisons,
judge and jury as well as the lawyers in the case had been known
to be stricken with the disease and many of them died in the
course of a few days. Whatever risk there was, was assumed
by their brother Jesuits who felt that the sharing of the danger
with the chaplains whose duties called them into peril was only
a risk taken in the line of duty. None of them caught the disease and manifestly the faithfully taken precautions protected
them.

The first of the Jesuit victims of typhus fever was Father John
Jaffré, S.J., a Frenchman, who had asked to be sent to America

as a missionary among the Indians, and was, for over fifteen years, located as a missionary to an Indian tribe settled near Sandwich, Ontario. When he was a man about sixty years of age his superiors thought it well to relieve him from the trials of missionary existence and assign him to duties that brought him more in contact with community life. He was transferred to New York in 1860 and not long after was appointed chaplain to Blackwell's Island. He made his first visit to the island April 8, 1861, and a month later to the day he was stricken with typhus fever and two days later died from it. Typhus fever was often thus rapidly fatal at the beginning of a severe epidemic.

This was only the beginning of a series of similar sacrifices demanded of the Jesuits. The next in the series was Father Philip Chopin, S.J., who died when he was just past forty years of age, January 16, 1864, from typhus fever caught during his ministrations as chaplain to the poor immigrants who had landed only shortly before from infected vessels. His successor in the chaplaincy—there was always another one ready to step into the position in spite of the danger involved—was Father Joseph Pancrelli, S.J., an Italian, who also was just past forty when like his predecessor he contracted a fatal form of the disease. This time the deaths were separated by almost a year. The peril to life in priestly ministrations to these patients continued but that did not dry up the fount of charity nor cause a break in the succession of candidates for the privilege of service to the poor.

There was a severe and prolonged epidemic of typhus about this time and it was only less than two months later before the next of the chaplains fell victim to the disease. This was Father George Laufhauber, S.J., who was born in 1820 in Lerchenfeld, Austria, who had become a member of the Jesuits when he was thirty-four, and died a victim of typhus February 22, 1865. This was not the last of the Jesuits to take this glorious road to the end of their careers, for some years later Father Robert Pardow, S.J., while serving as chaplain to the island was the victim very probably of the same disease, though it was not definitely recognized until subsequent developments with regard to the affection made it clear that this dread affection was sometimes active and unrecognized.[1]

One of these Jesuit chaplains whom I count it among the privileges of life to have known personally was Father Henry Duranquet, S.J. He was given the title of "apostle of the criminals" in New York City. For twenty-five years he devoted all his energies to the care of prisoners confined in the Tombs and inmates of Blackwell's, Randall's and Hart's Islands. It was difficult to understand where he got the energy to do all that he did. All during his life he had to contend with ill health. For years he suffered from an ailment that threatened the loss of one of his legs and even of his life and which always made it a severe exertion for him to walk any distance. In spite of these handicaps at a time when transportation was not the easy problem that it has since become, Father Duranquet for thirty years or more visited these prisons. Few criminals in New York were executed without his administering to them the consolations of religion. His goodness of heart, his utter disregard for himself and his constant thoughtfulness for others, his "personal holiness" as one of those who knew him best said, secured him deep influence over prisoners and he came to be greatly respected by people who had little or no sympathy with his religious faith, and some of whom, though knowing little about his Order, felt because of old traditions inherited from English ancestors, that traditions justified utter detestation of the Jesuits.

A sketch of his life is typical of that of many of the French Jesuits who came to this country for missionary labors in the seventeenth and eighteenth centuries and who were still volun-

---

[1] Dr. Thomas Addis Emmet, the well-known New York specialist in women's diseases, who in his earlier medical life was an attending physician on the islands, tells in his memoirs of the fearful virulence of typhus fever and cholera just after the middle of the nineteenth century in New York. Once when he went back to the island to make his daily visit to a barracks in which the patients were gathered, he found not only all the patients but all the nurses dead. The deaths had taken place in the course of about thirty-six hours. On another occasion Dr. Emmet himself suffered from the disease and was pronounced dead but came to while he was being ferried over from the island to Manhattan in order that he might be prepared for burial. There are many striking stories of the awful ravages of these epidemics at that time.

teering for pioneer religious work in America in the early nineteenth century, because America afforded a satisfying opportunity for self-sacrifice.

Father Duranquet was the fifth son of noble and wealthy parents in France, whose father was elected to the Chamber of Deputies in 1815 on the restoration of the Bourbons. Altogether there were six sons in the family and five of them became Jesuits. This is not the record number who entered the Order from a single family, but it gives an excellent idea of the attraction the Jesuits have for certain unselfish characters. The elder three of these gave their lives to the exhausting labors of the missions in the East. Two of them fell victims to cholera before the age of forty. The third also died young, exhausted by hardship and labor. The two younger brothers, Henry and Dominic, offered themselves for missionary labors across the Atlantic. Dominic, the youngest, lived to be fourscore as a missionary among the Indians in Manitoba. Henry, in delicate health from childhood, entered the Jesuits but had to leave the Order because of recurring attacks of illness. His patience during his ailments, his thoughtfulness for others, his utter unselfishness attracted the attention of Father General Roothaan, one of the great Generals of the Society of Jesus after its restoration. The General received him once more, and for his health's sake sent him to the equable climate of New Orleans. After the restoration of his health in that mild climate, he was selected as professor of mathematics at St. John's College, Fordham, now Fordham University. Thence he went to St. Francis Xavier's, New York City, where at the age of fifty-four he took up the work among the prisoners. For twenty-five years until he was past seventy-nine he continued his work on the islands.

He was then transferred to Woodstock College, Maryland, where the younger Jesuits of this country assembled for their studies in philosophy and theology. He became the spiritual director of this group. Jesuit superiors felt that no one could be a better guide for the consciences of these young men or a surer builder up of character, or set a finer example for the direction of their lives, than this man who had spent himself for more than twenty-five years caring for those who most needed care and direction and whose only reward for all that he had accomplished was the hope that the change of life which he had induced in his prisoner friends would be lasting. His was a typical example of the spirit that the Jesuits wanted to cultivate in young men. This is exactly the spirit that so many of those who have written about the Jesuits have failed to understand. The Jesuit idea is the cultivation of unselfishness and devotion to others. To miss the significance of that spirit in the Society is to fail utterly to comprehend the lives of the Jesuits.

Almost needless to say dear Father Duranquet had suffered from many disillusionments as to men and their ways during these years of service at the Tombs and the jails. Many a prisoner who had apparently reformed under his fatherly influence proved to be only a backslider and in spite of good resolutions and promises lapsed back into his former mode of criminality a short time after the completion of a first or sometimes a second or third term in prison. Some of them used to be fearfully ashamed of themselves and would avoid meeting him as far as possible or would try to disguise themselves. This disappointing experience had not made him a pessimist. He was ready to begin all over again the work of reform in these cases, hopefully now for good and all. No one knew better than he how often the cards of heredity and environment in early life had been hopelessly stacked against these men and how often the conditions in which they had to live and had been brought up from earliest childhood were much more to blame for their offenses than their wills or their characters. A man who has recurring disappointments of this kind for a quarter of a century and can still be an optimist with regard to fellow human beings has a wellspring of charity in his heart that cannot help but make him thoroughly respected by those who are brought intimately in contact with him.

I had the privilege, a very precious one it seems to me in memory, of knowing personally and rather intimately, the first resident chaplain of Ward's Island where so many of the indigent immigrants and especially those who were ailing in any way or suffering perhaps from the long stormy voyage, used to be sheltered a generation ago. This was Father Prachensky, a Pole, born at Prague in Bohemia to which his family had migrated after the division of Poland made life almost impossible for them in their native country. He was noted for his knowledge of languages and indeed it was his language facility that made him feel he could be of service to the polyglot population of Ward's Island. As a student he had exhibited talents of no mean order, and at the age of seventeen he was received among the Jesuits. While making his theology, a revolution broke out in Austria, and the Jesuits, as has been so often the case, were the first victims. Their property was confiscated, and they were sent into exile. The time for Father Prachensky's ordination to the priesthood was anticipated and as a priest he came to America and spent a dozen years as a missionary and teacher. He had lived in the south before the war so he became the chaplain of the Third Alabama of the Confederate forces, accompanying them in their campaigns as far as Norfolk, Va., and garnering a sheaf of memories of the war time.

His descriptions of camp life were vivid and usually very interesting. Some of the young Jesuits used to like to tempt him to reminisce and like all old soldiers he was not loath to be tempted to repeat his memories of the war. War seemed to those young men a very distant experience and not likely ever to be repeated in their time. Some of them were destined to be war chaplains in a war much worse than the Civil War, though that was one of the worst up to that time. Good Father "Prach," then, as he liked to be called, seemed a veritable maker of history. As army chaplain he had been a favorite with Catholics and Protestants alike. There were many fewer Catholics among the Southern troops than among the Northern, but he won all hearts. The sermons, usually delivered by the light of a camp fire, were listened to very attentively by men who respected him highly. They knew that their chaplain was not backward in seeking out men in the firing line when wounded and they loved him for his courageous devotion to duty, sometimes even at the risk of his life. Catholic chaplains have always made a reputation for themselves because they have been ready to share the dangers of the men. Father Prachensky was only one of many Jesuits whom soldiers during the Civil War learned to love and admire.

After the war he taught at St. John's College, now Fordham University, until his appointment as chaplain to Ward's Island (1868). He has told in some of his letters his experiences in the efforts to secure proper religious consolation for the Irish immigrants:

"I saw that permanent residence on the island was absolutely necessary for efficient work, so without asking formal leave I took it for granted. I sought and found board and lodging with a Catholic family. Once I was established there, the commissioners did not have the heart to send me away. Though the majority of them were non-Catholics they probably realized that the work among Catholics on the island demanded the constant presence of a chaplain. My next step was to find a lodging nearer to the Catholic chapel. I made application and after some explanation my request was granted." This is what some might term Jesuitical conduct. If using every proper means at his disposal for the accomplishment of a good purpose is to be called Jesuitical, then Father Prachensky's conduct deserves the adjective. He made friends with all with whom he was brought in contact and he used them all for the benefit of his poor immigrants.

Some idea of his utter devotion to his needy flock will be appreciated from further passages of this letter: "I then set about furnishing and embellishing my little chapel so that it became attractive both to inmates and visitors. Even the commissioners themselves remarked not without pride: 'This is the way the priest spends his money.'" The quarters that were secured for worship were about as unsuitable as possible but the immigrants crowded to them so that Father Prachensky could not find accommodations for them all at one Mass and had to say two. His own description of the chapel gives the best idea of it: "The chapel is in the upper story of a large frame building which is used as a nursery. Unfortunately it is difficult of access to the old and the infirm. Moreover it is extremely hot in summer and altogether too small in winter." There were seats for some five hundred but all those who wanted to come could not be accommodated. Father Prachensky asked for a new chapel then and the commissioners though thirteen in number and ten of them Protestants were so much pleased with the new spirit that Father Prachensky had introduced among the immigrants that they appropriated $35,000 and ordered the work to begin as soon as possible. No little bigotry was aroused over this and a bill was passed at Albany to suppress the Immigration Commission but the governor refused to sign it and it never became a law.

The supreme trial for him during his life on the islands was that he was so much away from his brother Jesuits and nothing brought him more pleasure than to entertain some of them and especially the younger men in his own simple way at his island home. In the summer particularly he liked to welcome the young scholastics, that is the younger Jesuits who were not yet ordained but were engaged in their studies in preparation for the priesthood, part of their experience being to teach for five years in the colleges between their three years of philosophy and four years of theology. The young men who came to see him would have a swim in the East River not far from his house— it was not then so foul as it has since become—and they would have dinner with him afterwards. He made it a gala occasion, usually picking out some special saint's day for the visit so that rules would permit extraordinary dishes at table and above all the presentation of several desserts for he knew the young men's weakness for sweets and then besides after a good swim there is a craving for carbohydrates in order to make up for some of the glycogen that has been burned up by the coolness of the water and the muscle exercise involved. Dear Father "Prach" knew of that craving and liked to supply it for his young brother religious.

Father Prachensky's successor was Father Gelinas, S.J. He began his theological studies at St. John's, Fordham, and completed them in Georgetown University where he was ordained to the priesthood in 1867. His first assignment was to the chaplaincy of Blackwell's Island and from there he was transferred to Randall's Island and from Randall's to Ward's. He spent over forty years of his priestly career on these three islands, ministering to every form of human infirmity. When his superiors sent him for a needed rest to the novitiate near Poughkeepsie he begged to be sent back to the islands in the East River that he might live or die among his beloved poor and afflicted. He lived to be some eighty-one years of age beloved by all who knew him, the dear friend and adviser of the poor and the afflicted, a man utterly forgetful of himself and eminently thoughtful of others. The younger Jesuits were very proud of his acquaintance because he was looked upon as a man who was fulfilling in hearty way the example of their founder. The chaplains of recent years, Father Rufus Duff, Father Raymond and many others—not to mention the living—were personal friends whose friendship I have always been proud of, glad to feel that here indeed were men who had something of the highest qualities of men developed in them—more interested in others than in themselves.

CHAPTER XVII

RETREATS FOR MEN—ALUMNI SODALITIES

About the beginning of the twentieth century there developed in Belgium a very modest social movement which soon attracted attention not only in most of the countries on the continent but also in England and Ireland and in the United States. This was what was called the "retreat movement" for men. It consisted essentially of the practice of business and professional men making their way once a year to some place of retirement on Friday evening and staying until Monday morning, spending the intervening time—with due intervals for meals, relaxation and sleep—in spiritual exercises. Almost needless to say these week-end retreats were not conducted too solemnly and indeed the men as a rule enjoyed them as an experience and felt that they brought an interesting diversion into their lives.

A group of forty or fifty men, sometimes more, would gather for dinner some time between five and six o'clock on Friday. They would be introduced to such among them as they did not know and about half-past six they would sit down to dinner together. After dinner the rule was to spend some time in social intercourse and cementing acquaintanceship. At eight o'clock or so, there would be a talk from the retreat master or director as regards the method and time table of the exercises of the retreat, followed by some spiritual suggestions for thought before retiring and for meditation on rising in the morning.

The rising hour was six o'clock and all the men went to Mass at seven after spending some time in meditation on the subjects that had been suggested. They then had breakfast, followed by a brief interval for personal duties of various kinds, before the regular day's round of exercises began. At three different times during the day there are conferences by the retreat master with points given for each meditation, that is thoughts for consideration for some time after the conference is over. After meals there are periods frankly called recreation when the men get together and discuss subjects of special interest among themselves these being usually connected with retreat matters. No subject is barred, not even politics, for this is too precious an opportunity for emphasis on the duties of citizens for it to be allowed to pass without profit.

The retreat activities continue during Saturday and Sunday and finish on Monday morning when the men are able to get away so as to reach their offices about the usual time on Monday morning. As a rule those participating go to Communion each of the three days but that is entirely a personal matter. Confessions are heard at convenient hours, and extra priests are at hand so that there need be no long wait.

The retreats, then, are week-ends away from business and professional occupation and away also from the distractions of family life. All sorts of men come together though occasionally by special arrangement most of the retreatants are of one profession, lawyers or doctors or dentists or bankers, so that the suggestions for meditation on one of the days at least are directed particularly to the ethics of that profession. Many men thoroughly enjoy their three days' retreat and some regret that it comes only once a year. Occasionally there are repeaters within the year, men who feel that a second dose of spirituality of this kind would be a benefit for them.

The Jesuits themselves always make an eight-day retreat every year and devote themselves much more strictly than do the men of the week-end retreats to the consideration of problems of their lives. It does not matter what a man may be doing, whether he is a missionary in distant Alaska or in the Philippines or whether he is a busy college executive or perhaps the president of a university, he makes his annual eight-day retreat. None is exempt, not even the provincials or the general of the Order, and all are expected to devote themselves to the consideration of the meaning of life and how best they can arrange their affairs so as to get most out of life. Their experience for years with retreat-making furnishes valuable material for helping others make retreats.

Usually each of the men who make the retreat has the opportunity to have a private talk with the retreat master. At this conference the retreatants discuss such questions and problems as occur in their daily lives and they are thus enabled to straighten out the ethical problems of their professions or occupations. The aim is to bring out rather by the retreatant's own thinking than by what is said to him how he should make up his mind with regard to his ethical problems. He should find out for himself by meditation rather than by sermons the ampler meaning of life and the response to the question, "What shall it profit a man if he gain the whole world and lose his own soul?" For a man may lose his soul not alone for eternity but for this world where the cult of trivialities, as Father Shealy used to insist, leads to dissipation of interest in realities. Shall a man spend life sordidly in the accumulation of materials he cannot take with him while eternity is ahead of him?

A favorite expression of Father Shealy, S.J., the founder of retreats for men in this country, was, "Only the man who thinketh not in his heart says there is no God." The men on retreat then are given the lessons and exercises in meditation that open up new vistas of thought on religious subjects. They come away feeling that they have attained a new outlook on life and a new source of thoughtfulness. Many of them had learned the significance of John Boyle O'Reilly's verses of a generation ago:

> *The Infinite always is silent:*
> *'Tis only the Finite speaks*
> *Our words are the idle wave caps..*
> *On the deep that never breaks.*
> *We may question with wand of science*
> *Explain, decide and discuss;*
> *But only in meditation*
> *The Mystery speaks to us.*

Almost needless to say an interlude of this kind in life every year is extremely valuable in lifting men's minds above the sordid practical round of everyday life for a short time at least and in giving a new outlook on or a renewed glance at the meaning of human existence.

Abroad the retreat movement for men was largely in the hands of the Jesuits so that it was not surprising that here in America the first of the organizers, the man who did more than any one else to make the retreat movement in this country a success, was Father Terence Shealy, S.J. Some of his inspiring appeals meant more than anything else in making men appreciate the value of these retreats for them. Fortunately he had a store of magical phrases which attracted men to him and his ideas were expressed with a terseness that impressed them deeply on men's minds. For instance he called a retreat, "a stocktaking in matters appertaining to man's destiny." The first retreats were given in 1909, and before the end of two years his enthusiastic followers enabled him to purchase a fine old estate on Staten Island, the mansion and outbuildings of which when refitted were made over into a very comfortable home for the retreatants during their week-end stays. Here once more Father Shealy had a phrase for it. It was, "a spiritual country club," and he named it Manresa after the little town in Spain where Ignatius found himself and his life work when, after the healing of the wound that he had received at the siege of Pampeluna and the long months of suffering that he had undergone in order to avoid the crippling that nevertheless came to him, with nothing else to do, he had occupied himself with the only books available, the lives of the saints, and was so much affected by them that he resolved to devote himself to another kind than earthly warfare.

Father Michael Earls, S.J., said in his brief biographic sketch of Father Shealy (Worcester, 1922): "From this American Iona (in Staten Island) he carried the lay apostolate to Harrisburg and Emmitsburg, to Atlantic City, Oswego, Springfield, Mass., and Hartford, as well as to Albany and Washington. Philadelphia soon emulated New York and acquired a permanent home for the retreatants out at Malvern. Morristown, N. J., did likewise and men's retreats became the order of the day. In the meantime a magnificent Father Shealy Memorial Building has been erected at Manresa, a monument of memory to him and of service for the work that was his zeal." Some idea of what he accomplished will be obtained from the fact that during the year before his death (1922) over two thousand men attended his New York retreats. The work has gone on and promises to be a permanent feature of Catholic life in this country.

A good many non-Catholics have come to these retreats and have been welcomed though there would be at most two or three of them in any retreat group. There was no proselytism and the retreat meditations and conferences were given exactly as when Catholics exclusively were making the retreat. As a matter of fact usually the presence of non-Catholics was unknown to any except the retreat master. At all times anyone who was a believer in God, even those who were not quite sure of their belief in the Deity, were welcomed to join these spiritual exercises. A good many Jews have asked to be allowed to join and have found themselves deeply stirred by the retreat conferences. The fact of the matter is that interest in the great mystery of existence is lost by people in their preoccupation with merely material and worldly affairs and it is refreshing for those thoughtfully inclined to have the chance once a year at least to devote some serious thought to the meaning of life and the universe around them. After all, we are larger in some fashion than anything we can grasp and comprehend, however imperfectly. The human mind that can measure the six hundred years of light across the Milky Way is ampler than the material universe around it. We share the bodies of the animals but our minds place us in another category entirely.

We are not here merely to work today so that we shall have money enough to buy food for tomorrow and so on till the end, but human existence has a meaning far beyond that. Man with reason must try and find that meaning and devote himself to working it out in terms of life. Those who believe there is a God cannot but feel that they are here to work out the greater honor and glory of God and the exclusive preoccupation day in and day out with merely earthly concerns is foolish to the last degree. "Life," Father Shealy once said, quoting an old Irish philosopher, "is a dangerous thing at best and very few of us get out of it alive." The great question then becomes, "after death what?" The answer to this means everything for the direction of life as it should be lived.

Father Shealy could be an extremely interesting man because of his deep knowledge of the classics, his devotion to literature, his wide scholarship and his thoughtful consideration of the problems of life. He knew the Greek and Latin fathers well and knew them, as has been so well said, not in their matter only but in their form. Chrysostom and Augustine were his favorites and they shaped his own oratory. Many a retreatant came away with "thoughts that breathe and words that burn" in his heart because a distinguished scholar had given hours to him and to his companions during their week-end retreat.

A note from one of his retreats will give an idea both of the matter and the manner of his retreat conferences. It is easy to understand how men went away with deep thoughts seething in their minds as the result of suggestions of this kind which were not merely listened to but were taken up for serious personal consideration afterwards and somehow kept coming back for more and more consideration especially just before retiring at night and when rising in the morning when the mind is freshest for the consideration of deep thoughts.

This paragraph of Father Shealy's now nearly twenty years old is so reminiscent of many of the things that are said at the present day in consideration of the commercial and financial crisis through which we are going that it will serve as a reminder that depressive things such as are said today were being said a long while ago. Father Shealy said:

"In this world of ours we have changed the horizon of the soul of man. All our perspectives and values are changed; we would find a new center of gravity for life. We are trying to find a new standard in matter, and we are bankrupt in the midst of our inventions and triumphs. We are sick at heart; we are in the midst of distress, distrust and conflict. We are submerged by overreaching competition and jobbery, by strange values and valuations. But when we turn to the Gospel we find that there is one central thought running through it all; that thought centres in the sacredness of human life. If there is one mark in the Gospel it is this individualization. The reform of the soul through Christ the Lord is the soul of all reform; and He would renew the heart and spirit of man, and through that heart and spirit renew the face of the earth. And so, the question of our time, the central question of all time, is not the political question, it is not an industrial question, it is not a social question; under whatever aspect you conceive it, it is in its last analysis an ethical question. For there is not a human act that has not an ethical value. This is the one power in which the great Reformer, the great Civilizer, the great Educator, the great Liberator, Christ the Lord, centered His vision, centered His education—the soul and heart of man."

The surprise for those who have not been in intimate touch with the retreat movement is to note the kind of men who are interested enough to take a week-end off in order to make a little retreat. Judges of the Supreme Court may be found taking their places in chapel or conference room or refectory beside bank clerks or the floorwalkers of department stores, or busy practising physicians and prominent lawyers with writers and printers. Editors, reporters, business men in all the various lines, sometimes men from the humbler tasks of life who have learned to think for themselves and who like to have material for future consideration supplied them turn up at these retreats, some of them in successive years regularly. Fifty or sixty men in a retreat will represent a cross section of modern life.

In Europe where class consciousness is more marked there is not so great a variety in the avocations of the retreatants but it is surprising how the movement has served to break down social barriers of all kinds and bring men of many different types together at moments when they are ready to think serious thoughts about life and its meaning. Employers and employees will sometimes be brought together in this way for friendly discussion quite apart from crises in the industrial world when exacerbation of feeling hinders mutual understanding. Indeed from the very beginning of the retreat movement questions relating to the social order which became so emphatic during the depression were freely discussed and the necessity for recognizing the brotherhood of man under the Fatherhood of God was made a principal topic of discussion and recognized as the only real solution of the social problems that face us.

The various exercises of the retreat movement, that is the occupations of the different hours of the day, are all founded on what are called the "Exercises of St. Ignatius," that is the method of meditation and consideration of the meaning of life which was put in definite form by St. Ignatius during the time after his serious wound at the siege of Pampeluna when his mind became occupied to the exclusion of everything else with the contemplation of the mystery of human destiny here and hereafter. These "Spiritual Exercises," as they are called, have gradually come to be looked upon as the most readily followed and stimulating system of meditation on religious mysteries that there is and they have come to be very generally employed by churchmen and religious generally in their own retreats. They do not represent rigid formulas but, on the contrary, afford a great deal of liberty to the human mind in its search for spiritual values and they carry with them without the necessity for much familiarity with them a stimulus to serious thinking better than can be secured in any other way.

If the retreats did nothing more than make men familiar with these spiritual exercises and afford them training in the use of them, that of itself would be a definite addition to the mental equipment and a very precious practical adjuvant to the employment of the mind in the consideration of serious spiritual subjects. These exercises do not require profound intelligence nor even any special training of mind. They can be adjusted to men of all kinds and it is surprising how men of many different intellectual calibers are able to find the pabulum for their own best thinking in these very simple directions and the considerations that go with them. Men come away from their first weekend retreat very often with the feeling that they have a new intellectual instrument and that they have secured a definite lesson in the use of their own minds. These retreat exercises are not sermons though they give men very interestingly and convincingly the reasons for the faith that is in them and they make them ever so much more capable of appreciating their religion and incidentally of making responses to objections that may be made against it.

ALUMNI SODALITIES

One of the features of Jesuit college life is the Sodality of the Blessed Virgin, a union of picked students whose purpose is the cultivation of piety very much in the same way as a debating society cultivates the power of debate and a dramatic society acting ability. These sodalities—we would call them fraternities —were founded in the Jesuit colleges about the end of the first fifty years after the foundation of the Jesuits. They have been solemnly recognized and highly eulogized by many popes, beginning with the great Gregory XIII (1584), after whom the Gregorian calendar is named, down to Leo XIII and his successors in the present century. The highest commendation was bestowed on the Sodality by the learned Pope Benedict XIV who was one of the great scholars of his time—the middle of the eighteenth century—and was looked upon as one of the most scholarly popes who ever occupied the papal throne. As a former pupil of the Jesuits and himself a member of the Sodality while at college he was in a favorable position to form a competent judgment and express an opinion not only with regard to their value during student days but also as a preparation for life afterwards.

The Sodalities cultivated not only the spirit of prayer but also the spirit of charity. Many of the Sodalities in these early colleges united in groups to purchase articles of food and clothing for distribution among the poor. This charity was performed not by delegating it to others and charging it to the expense of the Sodality but by the sodalists themselves who thus came to know something of poverty and destitution at first hand and who acquired a deeper sympathy for the poor as a result of their personal acquaintance with them. Besides, they visited prisons and instructed the prisoners and thus often brought new hope into the minds of men who felt that they had no further chance in the world. In many places the student members of the Sodality under proper direction went to the hospitals which was a very common practice among the Jesuits, but they also visited the squalid quarters of the city to look after the sick who were often found sadly in want in those days when so many forms of epidemic disease were rife and when it so often happened that both father and mother would be down with disease and there would be practically no one to care for the children. Schwickerath in his "Jesuit Education" says, "What the students thus began to practise in college was continued by many throughout their lives." There is an attraction to this sort of thing once it has been taken up seriously and its satisfactions experienced that readily makes it a pleasant habit to be pursued.

The Jesuits came to recognize that these unions among their students were not only beneficial to them during their student days but also would be of great service in their after life. Accordingly there came the organization of what are called Alumni Sodalities consisting of graduates of the colleges but admitting also former non-graduates. Only a little experience was necessary to demonstrate how much good could be thus accomplished so the Jesuits organized these Sodalities not only for their own students but also the students of other colleges of religious or even of secular universities. The all-important requisite for admission was that one should be a college man and a Catholic. Usually there is one of these Alumni Sodalities, sometimes containing as many as a thousand members, in each large city in this country. The principal functions of the alumni sodality are the reception of Communion four times each year. After these there are what are called Communion breakfasts, that is all those who wish to stay after Mass may have breakfast with a group of sodalists and thus renew old college acquaintances and usually there are visitors or older members of the sodality who are asked to make addresses and who sometimes have very interesting and valuable messages for brother sodalists.

When Sodality members have been visiting in neighboring

countries or when as delegates to conventions they have gone to distant, and especially foreign cities, or when they have been having special contacts with distinguished men, they are asked to stay to breakfast and talk over matters with brother sodalists. Above all is this true whenever in neighboring countries where they have visited there may have been revolutionary disturbances with any reflections on the Church. The actual condition of affairs as knowledge of them is obtained from personal observation is described and the significance of various events pointed out. Distinguished Catholics from other cities are brought to these Communion breakfasts and find an intelligent and very attentive audience.

There are smaller meetings once a month when the sodalists meet for devotional purposes mainly and when they recite the Little Office of the Blessed Virgin. They sing the hymns with which they were familiar in their student days and happy reminiscences of college life come back to them. The associations represent in certain ways almost idyllic recalls of youthful feelings and bring with them renewal of adolescent devotion.

The members of the Sodalities who as young men took up piety as one of the desirable acquisitions of college life were by no means the sort of young fellows to whom the word "pious" is usually applied. They were neither "softies" nor milksops but on the contrary were the pick of the student body. I have known the officers of the Sodality at Fordham, three in number, to be respectively president of baseball that is manager of the team, centre on the football team, and captain of the ice hockey team—they called it shinny. I have known four of them to make an unbeatable handball team. I recall that on one occasion the Prefect of Sodality, tired at the constant bickering between two members of his class who were always threatening what they would do to each other and taking it all out in growling, brought them into a private room and told them to go at it and that he would referee the fight. In ten minutes it was over and each of them had black eyes and in ten days they were good friends and continued to be so for the rest of the year. When word of the fight got to the authorities it somehow leaked out that the Prefect of the Sodality had refereed it and he was sent for to explain his part in the affair. He told why he did it and that he was sure it was for the best, so the prefect of discipline dropped the matter and nothing more was said about it.

The Alumni Sodalities often organize "academies" presided over by the bishop or archbishop or it may be the cardinal of the province in which they are situated, in which phases of faith and of the history of the Church are discussed and for which special invitations are issued that bring the women relatives of the sodalists to the meetings. Sometimes these academies are organized for the purpose of doing honor to someone who has been prominent for fifty years or more in sodality affairs. Sometimes the recipient of the honor is a newly elected prelate. The addresses made at these academies are usually thoroughly prepared and are often published either through some periodical or in book or pamphlet form. Sometimes the academies discuss mooted points of history or set forth conditions in some country where the Church is being persecuted and in general serve to keep the sodalists in touch with events that affect the Church anywhere and everywhere in the world.

Almost needless to say these organizations of men of various ages who are thus brought intimately in contact with one another represent a very valuable incentive to the renewal of piety and to the practice of the duties of religion.

These two movements, Retreats for Men and the Alumni Sodalities, are indices of the influence that the Jesuits maintain over men and particularly men of developed intelligence. Long ago women were spoken of as the devout female sex and there is no doubt at all that it is much easier to influence them in religious matters than it is the men. From the very beginning the founder of the Jesuits endeavored to direct his institute in such a way as would make the members of his Order give much more attention to men than to women. Like everything else that Ignatius had in mind this idea has worked out very well among the Jesuits in the after time and the value of his direction in this matter has become more noteworthy in the course of time. It is not easy to get men interested in religious subjects but there is no doubt at all that their interest can be aroused and very often their religious sense once aroused proves very practical and efficient in its action upon life and conduct. That is why after centuries of experience the Jesuits are found to be heart and soul with religious movements that appeal to men and this is quite as striking now after four hundred years as it was at any time during the history of the Order.

CHAPTER XVIII

AMERICAN JESUITS ON FOREIGN MISSIONS

THE men who were ready and willing to face the hardships of life among the Indians in the Rocky Mountains fifty to one hundred years ago and who took up so devotedly the missions among the Eskimos in Alaska, probably the most difficult missionary country in the world, were manifestly prepared for any other missionary tasks that might be assigned them. A Jesuit province is considered to lack a special blessing from on high on its activities if there is not a difficult mission attached to it for which ardent souls may volunteer their services and provide examples of self-forgetfulness and readiness to stand hardships that cannot but prove a source of emulation for others.

The Jesuits of the United States have been assigned difficult work, almost in the tropics, in the West Indies, especially in the British possessions; they have taken up the task of confirming the faith in the Philippines almost under the equator. They have the great Patna mission in India and they have taken in hand the establishment of the Catholic University of Japan and of a Catholic college in Bagdad, the old capital of the new kingdom of Iraq. For more than three hundred and fifty years Jesuit missionaries have come to various parts of the United States and now natives of this country are taking up the duty of repaying something at least of what had been done for Americans in the pioneer period and for immigrants in America in more recent years.

Missions composed of American Jesuits were sent to many and various parts of the world where their services were needed, where the work was hard, where conditions were trying and where only men thoughtless of themselves and ready to make sacrifices for others would be capable of going on with the work. It is surprising to read the roll of these foreign missions and to realize that every one of them represents a focus of trials for human nature that is diametrically opposed to the modern spirit of taking life as easily and above all as comfortably as possible. Comforts and conveniences, the aim of modern striving to so great an extent, must be given up entirely. These foreign missionary tasks demand character and persistence and self-forgetting devotion for others, such as make a man a hero among men. But it is not with any idea of personal prestige or exemplary exhibit of commendable traits that this work is done. I doubt whether character would bear up under the trials the missionaries are very often called upon to endure for any such selfish motive or mere bit of worldly vanity as that is.

JAMAICA

In 1894 the American Jesuits at the direction of the General of the Jesuits took over the missions in the island of Jamaica. These had been under the care of the English Jesuits as the island was under the rule of Great Britain but as the English province had to supply missioners for South Africa there were not enough men for the work to be done. Besides Jamaica is much nearer to the United States than to Great Britain. The population of Jamaica is more than seven-eighths Negro with less than 15,000 whites in a population of 850,000. The climate is rather trying for white men as a rule, there is a leper colony with more than one hundred patients to be cared for, the island is sometimes seriously disturbed by hurricanes and unfortunately also by earthquakes. The American Jesuits built a number of churches, erected a number of schools and have established the Church in Jamaica on a substantial footing. There are about 40,000 Catholics in the population with 56 churches and chapels, one secondary school, two convents for young ladies and some 25 elementary Catholic schools with 6,500 children. The leper home in Spanish Town is attended regularly by the pastor of the Spanish Town Church. The Jesuits have accomplished wonders among the colored population of Jamaica and have won many whites to the Church.

THE PHILIPPINES

Some years after the United States took over the Philippines, in accord with the Jesuit policy of having the members of the Order as far as possible citizens of the government under which they lived, Jesuits from the United States took up work in the archipelago. Six of them, all personal friends and some of them classmates of mine in the earlier years, went to Manila in 1904. They had been just good examples of American college boys when I knew them first but they proved to have the stuff of heroes in them. Father McDonough, who had been with me for several years at Fordham and who had been one of our best liked students, lively and companionable to a striking degree, always cast in comic characters in college plays, went to labor among the savage Moros and I was not surprised to hear that he very soon acquired an immense influence over them. American army officers who got to know him and his work thoroughly thought of him as a man among men in his forgetfulness of self and his intense preoccupation with his missionary work. I remember him so well, serious but whimsical, one of the best liked men in the house, and carrying that character with him wherever he went. I was not surprised to learn that the Moros came to like and trust him, everybody else did.

Father Becker, whom I had known very well when he seemed but a boy and who was the very life of his companions, became the chaplain of the Culion leper colony in the Philippines. This is the largest leper colony in the world with some six thousand leper inmates. More than a quarter of a century after Father Becker took over the position of chaplain, the Jesuits are still in charge of this beneficent work and two Jesuit Fathers and a Jesuit lay brother are there caring for the victims of the disease. While so much is heard of those who have devoted themselves to the care of lepers in other places, almost nothing is known about our own United States Jesuits out there in the Philippines doing their work so modestly that they are exemplifying marvelously the motto of à Kempis "love to be unknown"—and yet so efficiently.

After many years of experience in teaching in our American colleges Father Finnegan became the guide, director and friend of the large student population of Manila and came to be beloved of them as he was of groups of young men particularly, wherever he was located. "Dear Father Phil" he will always be for me— how could it be otherwise?—for to know him was to love him. Father Thompkins, another one of the American Jesuits in the Philippines, accomplished almost incredible labors as an apostle among the barbarous Ilocanos. What a contrast of character there was between Father Thompkins and Father McDonough, and yet what magnificent work they accomplished among the savages living almost under the equator in the Eastern hemisphere.

Another of these American Jesuits who exerted deep influence on the Filipinos, was Father John Monahan. He found that a large number of the Filipinos were gradually losing the faith in Christianity which they had obtained from the Spanish friars in the Philippines. This falling away was largely the result of contact with Americans, so many of whom were not Catholics, that the Filipinos were led to believe that there were almost no Catholics in the United States. Father Monahan organized a movement for the distribution of American Catholic literature, journals and magazines and books, especially among the teachers, but also among all those who were gradually being taught English under the new régime. As a result of his work he came to be known and loved throughout the immense territory of the Philippines and to a great many of the natives. He was a striking example of what a Jesuit can achieve. As a boy just out from Ireland he had to work for his living as a waiter and street-car conductor, he did not begin high school until he was twenty-two. He studied dentistry and practised for some years so that he did not begin his philosophical studies until he was thirty-three.

He tried to devote himself so deeply to his studies that his health broke down and he was three months in the hospital and was four times given up for death. After his ordination he asked to be sent to the Philippines and in the course of a very few years he became widely known throughout the archipelago. For a while he was one of the faculty at the Ateneo, the Jesuit college in Manila, but then became a missionary to whom the natives were deeply devoted. Because of his distribution of about a million pieces of printed matter among the Filipinos, he came to be known as the "Padre of the Press." The Philippine climate proved a serious handicap to him in his work and he died untimely but not until he had set an example which made itself felt not only among Jesuits in the Philippines but also among those back home in the United States who had known him and were sorry to hear of his death but heard at the same time of the wonderful work that he had accomplished in the Philippines.

It is of men of this kind that the Jesuits are proud and it is of them that they write biographies which hold them up for emulation. Father Monahan's life, as it was passed in Viegan, in Zamboanga where he followed the footsteps of St. Francis Xavier, and in Cagayan where he lies buried, has been written by Father Thomas Feeney, the Jesuit poet. The sketch serves to bring out the ideals that the Jesuits hold and what they are holding up as exemplary among themselves.

Almost needless to say the number of American Jesuits available for work in the Philippines was entirely too small at the outset in 1904 for the immense needs of the situation out there. The Philippines were rapidly being Americanized; courts, legislature, schools, industries, all taking up by degrees our American character. To keep the Catholic populations in the islands from being entirely secularized under the conditions, these half-dozen American Jesuits with a handful of American secular priests, never probably numbering more than a dozen, were totally inadequate. It was not for more than fifteen years later in 1921 that the American Jesuits had enough men available to be able to send the numbers needed for work in the Philippines. That year twenty priests and scholastics reached the archipelago and most of them were assigned to the Ateneo de Manila, the college which had been founded by the Spanish Jesuits centuries before. That foundation, curiously enough, was made from Mexico where the Jesuits came to have almost as many colleges in the seventeenth and eighteenth centuries as they have in the United States at the present time.

The number of American Jesuits in the Philippines has increased to nearly one hundred. Easter Sunday, 1927, the Philippine mission was formally transferred from the Spanish province of the Jesuits of Aragon in Spain to the Maryland-New York province of the United States. Geographically these American Jesuits labor in their missionary work from Manila in the great northern island of Luzon down past the leper colony of Culain in the mid-Vizean, to Mindanao and Sulu, whose southern regions are five degrees north of the equator. It is easy to understand what a trying life missionary work among savages in this climate must be and yet the Jesuits have taken it up and are maintaining it exactly in the same spirit in which, nearly four hundred years ago, the Jesuit missionaries began their work in the Orient and in the western colonies of Spain and Portugal on this continent. In spite of the many years that have passed, there are still natives just as savage in their conduct and just as barbarous in their manners as were those with whom the Jesuits were brought in contact in the first fervor of their missionary work in that earliest generation of Jesuits. Yet there is no doubt at all that the spirit of the Jesuits is just as self-forgetting and self-sacrificing as it was in those old times of long ago.

The Jesuits have charge of several highly important institutions in Manila. The observatory and weather bureau just opposite the government university of the Philippines was founded in 1865 as a branch of the Ateneo, and in 1867 Padre Faura, after whom the avenue is named on which the institution stands, was the first director. Spanish and American governments in succession declared this the National Observatory and Weather Bureau and supplied it with funds for equipment and for proper development. In 1924 the organization had one hundred and sixty-two official meteorological stations throughout the islands with seventy additional volunteer stations and a central observatory the finest in all Asia. Five Jesuit scientists—three Spanish and two American—are in charge of this important work under Father Miguel Selga, S.J., as director in chief. The official government weather reports, the official time determination, astronomical, seismological, and volcanic studies are made by this bureau. In the locating of typhoons the studies of the bureau are invaluable for Asiatic commerce and shipping, and they offer conspicuous proof to the Orient of the Catholic Church's zeal for science and humanity.

The principal work of the Jesuits in the Philippines is the Ateneo de Manila, the well-known college for lay students which is looked upon as one of the leading educational institutions in the archipelago. Its graduates are prominent in every walk of business and public life and, because of the prestige that it has secured, its present roster of over a thousand students includes the names of sons of prominent families from almost every town of any importance in the islands. Besides this the Jesuits are in charge of the College of San José for the training of secular priests. Here they have some sixty student seminarians but lack of endowment cripples the work and in some years as many as twenty applicants have to be rejected for lack of means to support them. The large majority of the students pay nothing or but a comparatively small sum for their support and education.

The Jesuits are deeply intent in carrying out the wishes of the pope that a native priesthood should be created. Gradually this purpose is being accomplished but it is made possible largely through the personal sacrifices made by the Jesuits who devote themselves so cordially to this work because it means so much for the future of the Church in the Philippines and represents the fulfilment of the formal wish of the pope to whom they owe special obedience. This policy of training a native priesthood everywhere throughout the missionary world, as far as is possible, is now being pursued, particularly in the Oriental missions, and promises enduring results for the Church. Protestant foreign missions are gradually crumbling and are meeting with great discouragement at home and abroad, while Catholic missions through the self-sacrificing efforts of the religious orders of the Church are everywhere flourishing in spite of the economic depression.

This educational and scientific work in Manila occupies about one-half of the Jesuits in the Philippines. The other half are engaged in parishes, in the cities, most of them in mission stations, in the "bush" of the islands of Mindanao and the Sulu archipelago. These comprise an area as great as that of the State of Pennsylvania. There are no railroads and few roads. Travel is very slow. This entire difficult missionary region is entrusted to the Jesuits with the exception of the small province of Surigao with a population of 100,000 administered by the Dutch Fathers of the Sacred Heart. Jesuit missionaries in the Philippines, then, are trying to care for some 400,000 Catholics as well as laboring to bring into the fold 100,000 Aglipayan schismatics and 600,000 pagans and infidels.

The efforts of the Fathers are particularly focused on the Catholic population, the fruits of the missionary work of the Spanish Jesuits and other religious orders in the Philippines for the past two hundred and fifty years. They are in charge of fifty-nine parishes and several hundred mission stations. Each priest has the impossible task of caring for ten thousand souls. The trials and hardships involved in these missionary labors are almost incredible but the Jesuits continue them with a peace and joy of heart almost impossible for people of the modern time with our cult of conveniences and comforts to understand unless they have been brought in close contact with the missionaries. These are all men of culture, most of them scholars far beyond the average of educated men in knowledge, and yet willing to give up their lives to the great purpose that has inspired them of preaching the Gospel to all the nations and then teaching by example rather than precept, for first they do and then they teach.

They are laboring for the conversion of pagans and infidels. Mindanao and Sulu are the last strongholds of Mohammedanism in the Philippines. The Holy See has designated the Maryland-New York Jesuit province, our own American Jesuits, to bring them the light of faith. Many of them live in mountain fastnesses or on tiny islands that are difficult even to reach. The Jesuits have taken up the task gladly and are accomplishing the work very successfully. The accounts of their missionary efforts as these are described in the periodical, "Jesuit Missions," correspond in many ways to the "Jesuit Relations" or so-called "Edi-

fying Letters" of the older time. The story of the hardships
through which the missionaries have to go is attracting many
young men to their novitiates. Idealism mingles with youthful
enthusiasm and men do things under its influence that seem almost impossible in colder blood. These American Jesuits in distant foreign missions under the most trying conditions have taken
up the task assigned them so whole-heartedly that it comes to be
all in the day's work. Having put their hands to the plow there
is for them no looking back, and when one falls out of the ranks
through death several are ready to step into his place, so that it
is easy to understand how much is accomplished.

Their college work brings the Jesuits in contact with the better-
to-do in the educated classes of the population. They have volunteered to take up the difficult tasks of chaplaincies of many
kinds to the poor and the needy. Besides the leper colony at
Culion with some six thousand patients they have the chaplaincy
of Cebu leper colony which houses some five hundred lepers.
Besides they are the chaplains to the huge Bilibid penitentiary in
Manila as well as the general hospital and also to St. Paul's
Hospital and to the San Lazaro Leper Hospital, to the Convent
of the Good Shepherd which houses wayward girls and to the
sailors of the American fleet.

Their principal subject of rejoicing in the midst of their work
is over the fact that the number of native Filipino Jesuits is constantly on the increase. There are now about sixty of them.
Through the generosity of an anonymous American friend it
was made possible to erect a special novitiate or house of novices
for the Filipino Jesuits at Novaliches some fifteen miles from
Manila. With all this accomplished and finely organized in
scarcely more than ten years of occupancy by the American Jesuits the promise of the future for the Church in the Philippines
is very great. The growth in numbers of native secular priests
as well as Filipino Jesuits will undoubtedly help immensely in
the solution of the many social and political problems that are
sure to come in the archipelago in the course of the next generation. The presence of these native ecclesiastics will aid in that
consolidation of the Church that follows the multiplication of

its own people among the clergy of a region or country. In China, not far away, special care has been taken for the selection of Chinese bishops for the episcopal sees of China and undoubtedly that same development will come for the Philippines.

THE AMERICAN MISSION IN INDIA

American Jesuits are at work as missionaries in Patna, the north of British India, comprising almost all of Behar and the whole of the independent kingdom of Nepal. The famous Mount Everest marks its northern boundary. Through the middle of Patna mission flows the holy river of the Hindus, Mother Ganges, and thirty miles west is the so-called Rome of the Hindus, the sacred city of Benares. Over 22,000,000 people live in the British section of Patna mission and over 5,000,000 in the independent kingdom of Nepal. Over 2,500,000 are Mohammedans and nearly 4,000,000 are aboriginals or Hindus of such low caste that they are untouchable. In all there are nearly 28,000,000 persons in the mission. Less than 10,000 of these are Catholics.

For a dozen of years Patna mission has been a diocese entrusted to the American Jesuits of the Chicago province. They began their work in 1921. Altogether there are 65 Jesuits in the mission. There are 45,000 cities, towns and villages in Patna mission so that the immense task of the missionaries can be understood. There are Patna districts with populations greater than those of such states as Indiana, Minnesota or Virginia without a single missionary or church.

To convert the aboriginals in the so-called depressed (untouchable) classes of the Hindus, the missionary must live in great hardship, traveling under blazing skies and torrential rains, eating the food of the people, dwelling in wretched mud huts, separated from those who speak his own language. Often he and his converts are subjected to petty persecutions by those who bitterly resent conversion to the Catholic faith. The Mohammedans present special difficulties and all converts are considered by the Hindus as "untouchables." The main purpose is to give the very best Catholic education to the Indian Catholics so that they may be an example to pagans and may supply priests, religious and catechists to convert their countrymen.

Since 1930 intensive work among the aboriginal Santals of the southeastern portion of the mission resulted in some three thousand becoming Catholics. An American anonymous benefactress has enabled the Jesuits to establish Khrist Rajah High School, a splendid institution, a center for operations for missionary work among the Hindus and Mohammedans of the northern portion of the mission. The American Jesuits in India feel that they are the heirs of the great Jesuit missioners of the seventeenth century who accomplished so much among the people of southern India. The spirit of the Jesuits lives on and they are accomplishing in spite of the difficulties of the climate and conditions what their brother Jesuits did in the earlier golden age of the Jesuit missions.

The United States is paying back her debt for the Faith to the older countries of the world by the establishment of American missions in various parts of the globe. Among these Jesuit missions some deserve special consideration because of their historical background. One of the latest of these is the establishment of a Jesuit college at Bagdad in the kingdom of Iraq. This is one of the newer nations in the Near East set up by the Treaty of Versailles. Great Britain was given the mandate and in the dozen of years since has gradually established the full sovereignty of Iraq. On October 6, 1932, Iraq, on the recommendation of Great Britain, was admitted to the League of Nations with full sovereign powers. After nearly seven centuries of rule by alien races the rich valley of the Tigris and Euphrates is once more inhabited by a free and independent people. The great majority of the population is Arab. They are almost wholly Mohammedan but there are a number of Christians among them and there is the opportunity for further development of Christianity. The Pope suggested that the Jesuits should establish a college in Bagdad and the General of the Jesuits asked the members of the Order in the United States to take up this task which may prove of very great promise.

A college has been established at Bagdad that will very probably grow as Jesuit colleges nearly always do. It must not be forgotten that Bagdad holds an important position between East and West and has been one of the greatest cities of the world. As late as the tenth century it was reputed to be the largest city in the world with a population of over two million. Its population today is scarcely more than one-tenth that, but it is the principal city of a country that has the advantage of not being overcrowded with inhabitants but on the contrary could support a great many more than it actually does. Professor William C. Bagley of Teachers College, Columbia University, New York, was a member of the commission appointed by the Iraqi Ministry of Education in 1931 to draw up an educational program for the country. He declared ("Current History," April 1933) the present population is estimated at about three million. "Yet the resources are such that a population of 20,000,000 or even 30,000,000 could easily be supported." He adds, "Thus Iraq is one of the few underpopulated countries of the Eastern Hemisphere and offers opportunities for settlement and development that can be equalled in few other parts of the world. " He is enthusiastic about the prospect and says that "it is well within the range of possibility that the Iraqis inspired by independence and responsible sovereignty may ultimately make their country the center of a new Arab civilization."

Meantime a group of American Jesuits who are to be added to as needs require and the resources of the province by which they are sent will permit, have taken up the task of establishing a college in the old Arab capital. This will bring Arabian civilization once more in touch with Christianity as it is represented by the oldest of the churches. If there should be peace in the world it would not be long before conciliation, as the Jesuits know how to exercise it, would help to bring about a better condition of affairs in the Near East. Mohammedanism as a faith is dying but Christianity needs to be presented from the new angle of youthful intelligence that is occupied with the thoughts of today and yet with the faith of yesterday and of all time.

CHAPTER XIX

JESUIT WAR CHAPLAINS

Ignatius Loyola, the founder of the Jesuits, followed the vocation of a soldier until he was past thirty. His military instincts remained with him even in his foundation of the Jesuits, whom he loved to call, as we have said, the Little Company of Jesus. It is doubtful, then, if anything in the subsequent history of his Order would, humanly speaking, give him so much pleasure as the utterly fearless way in which his sons have, when duty called, faced death or wounds in time of war. The Jesuits have been utterly fearless in the midst of warlike dangers, and as a result they have made ideal chaplains for army service, for they were ever ready to share the dangers of the battlefield with the men, and they won the admiration of both privates and officers for their dauntless courage.

Here in the United States, Americans were provided with the opportunity to recognize Jesuit courage and self-abnegation during the Mexican War when Fathers Ray and McElroy served with distinction and won the hearts of their soldiers because of their ardent devotion to duty and to all the interests of their soldiers.

In the Civil War Father Ouellet, S.J., who had been professor at Fordham for some years was appointed chaplain of the 69th New York regiment of militia when it was mustered into service. This was the well-known Irish regiment and it was generally understood that wherever the 69th was in the line there was to be some real fighting and their chaplain might be expected to have to fulfill his duties where bullets were thickest and where he might readily prove the victim of one. To quote a contemporary expression with regard to him, Father Ouellet "was always found

where the dying lay closest, where the danger was greatest, caring nothing for himself or his own safety, indeed endangering
his life every moment in order that his beloved soldiers might
have the consolations of religion." It was said of him that he was
worth a company of soldiers himself, so well did he inspire the
men with the idea of duty well done in the cause of country as
the best preparation for death, if death was going to come to
them.

Father Ouellet's persuasion was that patriotism was a virtue to
be exercised at whatever cost. If it involved suffering and even
death it represented sublime sacrifice for love of country only
just next in value to the love of God himself. With regard to the
justice or injustice of a cause, that was a matter for government
authorities to settle; for citizens obedience was the highest duty.
Only a few years before Tennyson, the English poet laureate,
sang of the Light Brigade and its charge at Balaklava,

> *"Theirs not to reason why,*
> *Theirs not to make reply,*
> *Theirs but to do and die."*

Father Ouellet felt that he should be ready to share the dangers
of his soldiers.

When the famous Billy Wilson's Zouaves were recruited from
among the roughs and toughs in New York, there were many
among them of the more or less criminal classes who had often
been disturbers of the peace around the Five Points and other
city quarters deservedly of unsavory reputation in those days on
the lower East Side. Some of them were the sort of people whom
we would call gangsters in our day. Their presence in the city
made the matter of policing the metropolis ever so much more
difficult than it would otherwise have been so that the movement
for recruitment amongst them was favored by all the city officials.
It was hoped that their unsocial tendencies might find an outlet
in warlike adventure and that they might thus prove a help
rather than a hindrance to war conditions in the North. Under
the circumstances it is easy to understand that discipline was a

rather difficult matter in the regiment. The chaplain chosen for them was a Jesuit, Father Nash, and the men learned to love and almost venerate him. General McMahon who knew the conditions very well declared that Father Nash who had been one of his old teachers at Fordham "did more to discipline Billy Wilson's Zouaves than all their officers put together."

Another of these Jesuit chaplains was Father Tissot, S.J., who after the war became the president of Fordham. He had been on the faculty there before the war. Like the other Jesuit chaplains he distinguished himself in the fulfilment of his duties so that he came to be known very well not only by the officers and men of his regiment but also of other regiments. By his bravery and devotion to the wounded under fire and his utter forgetfulness of self even in the midst of the most serious danger he attracted the attention of General Winfield Scott Hancock, one of the most distinguished of the Civil War generals and afterwards candidate for the presidency of the United States. General Hancock came to appreciate Father Tissot very highly for his utter devotion to the men. These three Jesuit chaplains from New York enjoyed for some years after the war, a reputation not unlike that which came to Father Duffy during the Great War. For years afterwards the soldiers of their regiments used to make it a point to come to see them because they felt so grateful for all that the good Jesuits had done for them at critical moments during the war.

During the Great War (1914-1918) there were no less than fifty chaplains to the United States troops who were Jesuits. They volunteered for the service and would have been glad to supply even more chaplains for the troops if the government had required them. Most of them were noted for their zeal and thoroughly self-forgetting devotion in their care of the soldiers. They proved to be model military chaplains. Suffering and even death meant little to them when duty called, as they have to so many of their Jesuit brothers on distant missions among savage peoples or under climatic conditions that were just as likely to be forerunners of death as the bullets of the enemy.

In France the priestly dignity did not carry with it exemption from military service, so that they were private soldiers in the ranks as well as chaplains and stretcher bearers. Altogether the number of Jesuits who served under the allied colors during the four years and four months of the World War ran up to 2,014. Altogether there were at that time less than 17,000 Jesuits in the world, so that about one in eight of the Jesuits were in war service. They were noted particularly for the number of distinctions which they earned. Of the 83 English Jesuits serving as chaplains, 5 died while in service, 2 won the Distinguished Service Order, 13 the Military Cross, 3 the Order of the British Empire, 21 were mentioned in dispatches, 2 were signalized as having performed very valuable services, and 4 received foreign decorations—a total of 45 distinctions, that is more than one out of every two Jesuits in the service was the recipient of some martial honor.

It was in France, however, that the martial spirit of the Jesuits, where there was question of life or death, was particularly noticeable. From the four French provinces of the Society, 855 Jesuits were called to the service. Of these 107 were officers, 3 commandants, 1 lieutenant commander, 13 captains, 4 naval lieutenants, 22 lieutenants, 50 second lieutenants, 1 naval ensign, and 5 officers in the health service. The Jesuits because of their education and above all their special training in mathematics made readily available material for officers and so when French officers fell in such large numbers many of the Jesuits were advanced from the ranks to the rank of commissioned officer. Altogether 165 of the French Jesuits were killed. Twenty-eight of these were chaplains, 30 higher officers, 36 sub-officers, 17 corporals, and 54 privates. "The number of distinctions won is," as Father Thomas Campbell, S.J., says in his work "The Jesuits 1534-1921," "almost incredible. The decoration of the Legion of Honor was conferred on no less than 68, the *Medaille militaire* on 48, the *Medaille des Epidémies* on 4, the *Croix de Guerre* on no less than 320." But that was not all. The Moroccon or Tunisian Medal was conferred on 3, while 595 were mentioned in dispatches and 18 foreign decorations were received. Only a little calculation is needed to show that in all 1,056 distinctions were won by the

Jesuits in the French army and navy. Something more than a distinction and a quarter were thus awarded for each of the Jesuits in the service. Is it any wonder that "Italia," the Italian newspaper which had so often uttered editorial opinions unfriendly to the Jesuits, asked the very pertinent question, "What party or group or club or lodge can claim a similar distinction?"

After reading this story of unexampled devotion to their mother country at the cost of death and wounds, one needs to have as a background the history of the treatment accorded to the Jesuits by the French government before the war. The French Jesuits performed this sublime service to their country "in spite of the fact that the government of that country had closed and confiscated every one of their churches and colleges from one end of France to the other and by so doing had exiled these loyal subjects from their native land. To add to the outrage, the Jesuits were summoned back for the defense of their country when the war began and not one of them failed to respond immediately, returning from distant missions among savages at the ends of the earth or from civilized countries that were more hospitable as a rule than their own, though in the defense of it they were now willing to offer their lives. Now when the war is over they have no home to go to."

Their founder would have been proud indeed of this military record which demonstrated so clearly that his Little Company of Jesus had exhibited some four centuries after its foundation in very striking way his own spirit of the most absolute fearlessness in time of danger, and he would have admired and commended their utter readiness to devote themselves to the care of others quite forgetful of any danger there might be for themselves in their activity. Jesuit chaplains are the best criterions of the Jesuit spirit as it was exhibited at the beginning and is manifest in our time. For those who find it hard to understand the enthusiastic devotion of the Jesuits to missions among barbarous people, even a little familiarity with the many distinctions which came to them as army chaplains and the way they won the love of their men will enable people to comprehend that profound sense of duty and their readiness to sacrifice all for principle.

In the old days when epidemics of disease were frequent and when high mortality among humanity was the rule, the Jesuits were just as careless of the danger of this dread spectre of death from epidemic disease which takes the heart out of so many as they were of death in any other form. On the battlefield it was easy for men accustomed to facing danger as they were in some of its most terrifying forms to distinguish themselves by their lofty courage and devotion to others where so many around them were sharing the danger with them. The French Jesuits who had been compelled to go into exile and who returned at the call of their native country to display on the battlefield the high courage and lofty disregard of death and danger, represent the best phase of Jesuit life for people to study who want to understand, as far as they can, the veritable spirit of the Jesuits.

APPENDIX

PIONEER JESUIT COLLEGES IN NORTH AMERICA

The first Jesuit college founded on this continent was that of St. Ildefonso established in Mexico City in 1573. This was just sixty-five years before the foundation of Harvard, and one hundred and twenty-five years before the foundation of William and Mary, the second of our colleges in the English-speaking colonies in this country. During the forty years which elapsed from the foundation of the Jesuits in Paris (1534) and the foundation of this first American college in Mexico, the Jesuits had founded a series of colleges in many of the countries of Europe and their colleges had come to be looked upon as the best educational institutions of the time not only by Catholics but also by the most thoughtful Protestants.

King Philip II of Spain to whom recent historians have been doing justice in greater measure than the English tradition of religious prejudice in all things Spanish would permit until our generation, was a close friend and great admirer of the Jesuits. He knew what they had accomplished in the East under the leadership of St. Francis Xavier for the rival kingdom of Portugal in its eastern colonies. The great Jesuit University of Coimbra in Portugal furnished brilliant teachers for colleges in the distant East founded in pursuance of a policy to provide a native priesthood. Coimbra itself became one of the great world centers of learning of the time. The Spanish king wanted to secure the prestige of the Jesuits in education for his colonies so that it is not surprising under the circumstances that the first college of the Jesuits in Mexico soon came to be famous for the thoroughness of its education, nor that it gained rapidly in numbers.

It might possibly be presumed that the Jesuit superiors would have the feeling that some of their less brilliant men would prove sufficient for the faculties of these distant colonial colleges. As we have already said, that was not the policy. Two conditions militated against it. First the Jesuits were anxious to promote the plans of their friendly patron, King Philip, and this prompted them to pick out some of their most promising men for the colony, but besides this, missionary work in distant countries was largely carried out by volunteers who offered themselves for the missions and not a few of these men were among the most intellectually developed and most valuable members of the Order both as regards character and mental attainments. No wonder, then, that we hear of the eminent success of these Jesuit colleges and the thoroughgoing satisfaction with them on the part of the king and his Spanish subjects in New Spain.

The second college of the Jesuits in America, that of San Pedro y San Paulo, was founded also in Mexico City and proceeded to reap similar golden opinions to those of its predecessor. After some years an amalgamation of these two institutions brought into existence the most important college in the city which before the end of the sixteenth century had some five hundred students in attendance. The graduates of this college were particularly proud of their Alma Mater. The education given was very thorough and quite equal to that of the Jesuit colleges in Europe at a time when the Jesuits had accorded them even by their enemies the reputation of being the best teachers in the world.

The foundation of these Jesuit colleges was accomplished everywhere according to the same formula. The first step consisted in securing the gift of a foundation represented by a house for the Jesuits themselves to live in together with accommodations for their classrooms and equipment necessary for teaching purposes as well as an endowment that would enable the Jesuits to live modestly and maintain and develop their library and equipment. When these conditions were fulfilled the house was open to students and no fees for tuition were asked.[1] This state of affairs left the Jesuits absolutely

---

[1] This custom of the Jesuits of receiving no fees for their educational work has often been misunderstood. In the constitutions of the Society it is laid down as a strict rule that "no one is to accept anything which might be considered as a compensation for any ministry, education included." The regulations on this point issued by Father Natalis (Nadal), the General of the Jesuits, emphasized this rule: "The rector cannot receive anything either for any instruction or degree or matriculation; nothing as remuneration from a teacher nor any present from a scholar. In short nothing can be received not even as alms nor on any other grounds. Should the rector hear that anyone else has accepted anything, be he a teacher or an official of the school, he must see that it is returned to the person who gave it; he must severely punish the person who received it."

This rule of gratuitous instruction was faithfully kept until the nineteenth century. At present Jesuit schools are compelled by sheer necessity to accept a tuition fee because their colleges are not endowed. A special indult from the Holy See for that purpose has been granted. In old time the liberality of princes,

free to select the students that they were to receive and those that after careful observation they would care to retain. Objectionable characters were weeded out, students with the intelligence that was not of a caliber to enable them to secure for themselves properly the benefits of higher education, were eliminated. Disturbing factors of all kinds were thus eradicated or at least very definitely mitigated.

Not a few of their most talented students taken with the personality and scholarly devotion of their teachers asked and were accorded permission to join them in their life of application to study and teaching and were received as members of the Order. Others were touched by the idea of a life of self-abnegation as missionaries always with the supreme thought of bringing pagans to the knowledge of Christ. The same motives impelled young men in Mexico to follow the example thus set them, so that the Order grew apace. They were able to found a series of colleges and before the end of the sixteenth century sent a group of Jesuits to the Philippines in order to found a college there.

A whole series of Jesuit schools were founded outside of the capital in the generation after this foundation of colleges in Mexico City. Priestley, who is the associate professor of Mexican history at the University of California, in his history of the Mexican Nation [2] gives a list of Jesuit foundations in the provinces where he says the Jesuits were conspicuous educators. They began a college in Zacatecas in 1616. Not long afterwards Jesuit colleges were founded at Valladolid (New Spain) and Patzquaro. The College of San Luis Potosi was founded in 1623. Another was established in Queretaro a few years later and others at Pueblo, Tepotzotlan and elsewhere. The college at Guadalajara was founded in 1659. At the beginning of the eighteenth century when Harvard had altogether less than a hundred students, there were some twenty-five Jesuit colleges in Mexico with an average attendance in each of them of several hundred students. Priestley says that Jesuit influence was supreme in education.

As to the character of Jesuit teaching at this time, we have abundant evidence as to its efficiency from men who were in a position to know very well what they were talking about and whose opinion is for many reasons unquestionable and their lack of any partiality beyond this. Lord Bacon in his "Advancement of Learning" went

ecclesiastics and cities furnished all that was necessary for the endowment of a college. Gradually as their circumstances improve their ideal of gratuitous education will once more become possible.

[2] "The Mexican Nation," New York, 1926.

so far as to say, "All that was best in ancient discipline hath been in some sort revived of late times by the colleges of the Jesuits." By discipline Lord Bacon was old-fashioned enough to mean both training of mind and regulation of conduct. About the time that Lord Bacon said this the "Ratio Studiorum" or "Method of Studies" of the Jesuits had been brought into form under the distinguished General of the Order, Claudius Aquaviva, and it has continued to be the guiding rule of Jesuit education ever since. This method of studies does not put Jesuit education into such fetters as would cramp their system of instruction and not permit them to give a place to the advancement of knowledge that has been made since. Theirs were schools of liberal studies and there was nothing iron-bound about their methods.

Scientific and mathematical progress was carefully evaluated for adaptation in Jesuit curriculum. Some of the best textbooks in education even in these subjects were written by Jesuits. Father Athanasius Kircher's series of scientific books written during the seventeenth century are a striking exemplification of that. Their publication began shortly after the time that Bacon made his declaration. Teachers everywhere were glad to get in touch with Kircher's work because it was so helpful for educational purposes. They resembled in this respect some of the books on astronomy written by Father Secchi, S.J., in the nineteenth century, so many of the features of which were borrowed by the writers of textbooks in astronomy.

Boyd in his "History of Western Education" published more than a dozen years ago translated Bacon's well-known compliment, "You are so good that I wish you were on our side." Boyd himself said of the Jesuits, "Concerning the excellence of the Jesuit colleges there has never been serious question. Even opponents who have no sympathy with the other activities of the Order and who mistrust the social effects of its religious work, recognize the Jesuits as masters of the art of education." Many other well-known writers who have a right to an opinion on this subject might be quoted to the same effect. Professor Paul Van Dyke of Princeton in his life of St. Ignatius Loyola, the founder of the Jesuits (New York, 1926), said that, "The colleges of the Company (that is of the Jesuits) founded on that training of humane letters and on Latin, Greek and Hebrew, were the shrines of the New Learning." In another passage he declared, "It is because the Jesuit schools were in method up to date that influential people wished to send their sons to them." The sons of the nobility and of the better classes everywhere throughout Europe were in attendance at the schools of the Jesuits. It was the cause of no little objurgation that sons of prominent Protestants and of the Protestant nobility were so often found in attendance at the Jesuit schools.

In spite of all this testimony to the efficiency of Jesuit education, the great majority of people in our time and especially those who pride themselves on the knowledge of the history of education, would be more than a little inclined to think that the education afforded by the colleges of English America, once they were established, must have been very different and surely better calculated to afford mental development to the students than that which was provided in Spanish America. Recent research in the history of education, however, has made it very clear that the curriculum in the colleges of Mexico and those of the United States differed so little from one another that the difference was quite negligible.

The curriculum of the Jesuit colleges in Mexico was dictated by the "Ratio Studiorum." They finished their classics during the first two years of college and then devoted themselves during the last two years to philosophy and mathematics. The course in philosophy was broad enough to comprehend a number of subjects of study that involve the application of principles of various kinds to human conduct personal and political.

INDEX